AMERICAN
ARCHITECTURAL BOOKS

A LIST OF BOOKS, PORTFOLIOS, AND PAMPHLETS
ON ARCHITECTURE AND RELATED SUBJECTS
PUBLISHED IN AMERICA BEFORE 1895

by

HENRY-RUSSELL HITCHCOCK

UNIVERSITY OF MINNESOTA PRESS · MINNEAPOLIS

Library of Congress Catalog Card Number: 62–11970

This book has been reissued with the assistance of a grant from
the Graham Foundation for Advanced Studies in the Fine Arts

PUBLISHED IN GREAT BRITAIN, INDIA, AND PAKISTAN BY THE OXFORD UNIVERSITY PRESS,
LONDON, BOMBAY, AND KARACHI, AND IN CANADA BY THOMAS ALLEN, LTD., TORONTO

PREFACE

This bibliography is intended to serve students of American architecture of the periods between the Revolution and the end of the nineteenth century, as well as institutions and individuals who collect American architectural books.

Before the Revolution the American Colonies imported their technical publications from England. The first architectural book published in America appeared appropriately enough in the summer of 1775. The title, however, was *The British Architect* and it was merely a Philadelphia edition of a work by the English carpenter-builder Abraham Swan. This work had first appeared in London thirty years before, and several London editions were already well known in the colonies. Of the second American architectural book, *A Collection of Designs in Architecture,* also Abraham Swan's, only the first number, dedicated to John Hancock and issued later in 1775, is known.

The British Architect is of the "Builders' Guide" type—that is to say, the graphic material consists chiefly of plates of the orders, together with other plates showing elements of detail both structural and ornamental. There are also some plates with plans and elevations of houses; and such plates were evidently intended to make up the whole of the other work. Books in which plans and designs for houses form the bulk of the graphic material may properly be called "House Pattern Books" as distinguished from Builders' Guides.

Because of their many plates of direct practical usefulness to the builders and carpenters of their time, Builders' Guides and House Pattern Books are perhaps the most interesting American architectural publications, and it is the chief purpose of this bibliography to list material in these two categories. Down into the 1830's books of the Builders' Guide type predominated, but from the mid forties on, House Pattern Books began to appear in greater quantity and soon superseded the Builders' Guides almost completely. First in the year 1857 and again in 1868, 1878, 1885, and 1889 as many as a dozen House Pattern Books appeared, although in the intervening years their numbers dropped to two or three. Thus, the output of the publishers in this field parallels rather closely the curve of building production.

In 1786 John Norman issued in Boston *The Town and Country Builder's Assistant,* a Builders' Guide compiled, presumably by Norman, from various English sources. Pirating English works and forming new works by compilation from English sources long remained the regular and unashamed practice of those who prepared and issued American architectural books. Moreover, French and German works were usually pirated from translations made and published in England. Talbot Hamlin in *Greek Revival Architecture in America,* 1944, remarks that there was hardly an American author in the first half of the nineteenth century who did not draw the greater part of his material on construction from the English technical author Peter Nicholson. Several of Nicholson's books on construction, moreover, were published in America in the first quarter of the nineteenth century and kept in print by their American publishers through two generations. Even Asher Benjamin, the first American architectural author, drew heavily from Nicholson.

Benjamin's *Country Builder's Assistant,* published in Greenfield, Massachusetts, in 1797, is in a truer sense than Swan's *British Architect* or Norman's *Town and Country Builder's Assistant,* the first American architectural book. For it includes many plates of detail of Benjamin's own invention as well as borrowed English material. Owen Biddle, like Benjamin, a native American carpenter, was the first to stress his independence of English sources in *The Young Carpenter's Assistant,* published in Philadelphia in 1805. Well down through the midcentury, however, Americans remained colonial in their dependence on English architectural sources, despite the increasing originality of actual American buildings.

Early descriptive works, such as guide books, which include views of existing buildings and information about them, may or may not be considered architectural

iii

books in the sense of having influence on the architectural production of their own day in the way Builders' Guides and House Pattern Books do. They are, however, of great importance to modern architectural historians. A large collection of such titles, organized regionally and by period and style, will be found in Frank J. Roos, Jr.'s *Writings on Early American Architecture*, 1943, which includes also general historical works touching incidentally on architecture, and magazine articles as well as separate publications. I never made a serious attempt to match Mr. Roos in this field, and in this edition I have added titles of which I learned from his list (published after the second edition of this bibliography was issued) only when I could easily find locations for them.

The increasing interest in early American building after the Civil War is reflected in many local antiquarian studies which are exhaustively listed by Mr. Roos for the use of present-day students of the Colonial period. These publications were undoubtedly important in forming the architectural taste of the late nineteenth century, and their illustrations often served, whether or not they were prepared for that purpose, as documents of Colonial style for Colonial Revival architects and builders from the 1870's on. Therefore, all such works of which I could locate copies were already included in the earlier editions of this bibliography if they were well illustrated and not purely anecdotal in character.

For magazine articles of the early period the appendix by Sarah H. J. Simpson Hamlin in Talbot Hamlin's *Greek Revival Architecture* entitled "Some articles of architural interest published in American periodicals prior to 1851" is valuable for its comments and its intelligent selection. A study of the American periodicals devoted entirely to architecture and related subjects, which began to be published in the second half of the nineteenth century, and of architectural articles in more general periodicals would also be well worth having. In this bibliography, however, magazine articles are included only when they also appeared separately or were reprinted in books.

In studying the architecture of the last fifty years a selective, rather than an exhaustive, use of contemporary literature is generally indicated. This may justify the somewhat arbitrary selection of 1895 as the terminus of this bibliography.

Most early American architectural books, whatever their prime classification, contain various kinds of material—descriptive, historical, critical, and technical. Later, as treatises in the field of the building arts and sciences grew more specialized, it is often very hard to say whether or not particular classes of books should be considered architectural publications. Many engineering works dealing with metal construction are included in this bibliography because of their particular relevance to the development of the skyscraper. Yet I have generally excluded publications of carpenters' and builders' Rules, believing that they belong rather to the economic history of the building industry. Those of the early period will, I believe, be studied in a forthcoming publication of Louise Hall. Among the publications of the generation after the Civil War, I have excluded many books concerned with matters of technical detail like stair-railing and plumbing. Even treatises on carpentry first published after the Civil War are included only if they contain plans or architectural designs or have some other special interest. The headings in the Subject Index should indicate the other general types of material that this bibliography includes. Some of the notes under particular authors, by referring to works of those authors which are not included, will indicate the irregular boundaries of the field I have attempted to cover.

Several prime bibliographical puzzles remain, such as Davis' "Rural residences" and Ritch's "American architect," which I am far from having resolved. There are also the bibliographical jungles represented by the semi-periodical publications of compilers and publishers like the Woodwards, the Bicknell-Comstocks, the Pallisers and the Shoppells which await plate-by-plate analysis from some student of the broad building currents of the period 1865–95. Finally, I will call attention to the many presumptive editions of books of different periods of which I have been unable to locate copies. I have left numbers for them in the sequential numbering of items, and I trust that anyone who knows of their actual existence will inform me. Indeed I will be most grateful for any additional information about issues, editions, titles, and authors relevant to the scope of this list for use in a possible later edition.

The earlier editions of this bibliography could not have been prepared without the generous collaboration of some sixty-five institutions and individuals to whom the mimeographed sheets were sent for checking. In preparing this edition I have been notably assisted once more by the librarians of many of the same institutions and by those of a few additional libraries. I am most grateful for the kindness of all who have supplied me with indications of new holdings and various other additions and corrections. Quite a few hitherto unrecorded editions and some new works and even new authors I owe to a check made in the spring and summer of 1945. It would be invidious to single out a few names only for more specific thanks. I should mention my friend Joseph Brewer, however, who gave me both time and technical advice in setting up the subject headings in the Index. He should have the credit for proposing the inclusion of the Index as well as for assisting notably in its preparation, although I must take the blame for the use of certain headings more familiar to students of American architecture than to librarians and for making references only to authors and not to specific works.

A few points of form might be mentioned in conclusion. Collations vary somewhat according to the amount of detail required to distinguish editions and issues, and also according to the type of information I was able to obtain. Wherever possible the full number of plates is given, in arabic numerals unbracketed, followed by the indication "pl." regardless of whether the plates are numbered or in what way, and regardless of the particular character of the material on the plates. Plans and diagrams are not specifically noted in the collations. Where they occur on text pages the general indication "illus." covers them as well as other types of illustrative material. Tables are not indicated in the collations, nor preliminary leaves except in the case of a few issues otherwise hard to differentiate. In some cases the character of new material added in later editions has been indicated in the notes, particularly for the books of the 1830's, which I have had occasion to study in some detail. The sign * indicates foreign authors. The following table provides a key to the symbols used to indicate the holders, which are for the most part those of the Union Catalog in the Library of Congress. Thanks to the Union Catalog of the Philadelphia Area, I was provided with an *embarras de richesses* in the way of Pennsylvania library holdings. I have usually given only the holdings of the larger libraries, unless works were held in that area only by smaller libraries. Individual holders are not given unless theirs are the only copies I have been able to locate.

Henry-Russell Hitchcock

PREFACE TO THE NEW PRINTING

Over the fifteen years since the earlier printed edition of this work was issued in 1946 a very considerable number of copies — in the thousands, I should estimate — of the publications listed must have been added to the many public collections already represented; and quite a few additional libraries have also begun to collect in this field. The following, I understand, have been especially acquisitive of late years: American Institute of Architects, Washington, D.C.; University of Delaware, Newark, Delaware; Bethlehem Steel Company, Bethlehem, Pennsylvania; Eleutherian Mills Historical Library, Wilmington, Delaware; University of Kansas, Lawrence, Kansas; Syracuse University, Syracuse, New York; Colonial Williamsburg, Williamsburg, Virginia; and Winterthur Museum Library, Winterthur, Delaware.

Yet to attempt a new census of holdings would be in itself a most formidable task, while incorporating in *American Architectural Books* the additional information thus obtained would probably necessitate a resetting of the whole work. This has not been feasible. But the present reprinting of the book by offset, made possible by a grant from the Graham Foundation for Advanced Studies in the Fine Arts to the University of Minnesota Press, the original publisher, will again make available the information provided in 1946, and to a far greater number of libraries, private collectors, scholars, students, and book dealers than were able to obtain the few hundred copies of the earlier edition.

Fortunately it is possible in this new Preface to provide some thirty emendations of the original list. These items are listed below according to the position (indicated by preliminary numbers) in which they are to be considered as interpolated in the original sequence. There are two new authors (Nos. 183a and 507a); three new titles (Nos. 500a, 915, and 986b); five new editions or issues (Nos. 153a, 561a, 561b, 986a, and 1137a); and a score of minor corrections of collations and imprints.

101. 59, not 61, pl.

153a. Bicknell, Amos Jackson
        Public Buildings . . . New York, Wm. T. Comstock, c1877.
           The Comstock imprint ordinarily suggests a date of 1881 or later.   H.R.H.

183a. Billings, John S   , and others.
        Hospital plans. Five essays relating to the construction, organization and management of hospitals . . . New York, William Wood & co., 1875.
           353 p. illus.   H.R.H.

257. Add: col. front.

258. Delete: In this edition the title begins: *The builder's assistant.*

334. Ampersands in publishers' names should read "and." Collation should read: 2 p. 1. 187 p. illus., 12 pl. (1 col.). There are designs for twelve, not ten, houses, one of which is illustrated in the text (p. 104) not on a plate.

335. Same correction as for No. 334.

336. Collation should be: xii, 180 p. illus., 12 pl. incl. front. (1 col.).
       There are twelve, not fifteen, house designs as in the earlier editions.

389. Has added engr. t.-p.

430. Collation should be: 2 p. 1. [3] — 14 p., 10 1., 9, [4], 13, 2 p., 1 1., 67 pl.

459. The publisher of the H.R.H. copy is G. P. Putnam, not D. Appleton & company.

500a. Garnsey, George O
        Beautiful houses and how to build them . . . Designs for model modern buildings. Chicago, The Illustrated Publishing co., 1886.
           [48] p., tables, diagrs., illus., incl. 18 "designs"

507a. Gillmore, Q   A
        Report on the compressive strength, specific gravity, and ratio of absorption of
        the building stones in the U.S. . . . New York, D. Van Nostrand, 1876.
            37 p., 32 tables, diagrs., 2 pl.   H.R.H.

561a. and 561b. There were additional issues of the 7th ed. in 1871 and 1872.
                                                                        NNC-A; R.W.D.

915. Technically a new title; this and Nos. 916–918 are not the same work as No. 914
       (unfortunately the *wording* of the title is all but identical).

973. Collation should be: 3 pts., illus., 10 pl., as three, not two, parts of Vol. I were issued.

986. Collation should be: 243 p. illus.

986a. Reed, Samuel Burrage
        House plans for everybody . . . New York, Orange Judd company, 1891. H.R.H.

1130. The collation of the H.R.H. copy is: T.-p., 62 l., 61 pl., nine more plates than in
        the only other copy located, that at CU.

1137. Collation should be: 618 p. illus., 29 pl.

1137a. Scott, Frank J
        The art of beautifying suburban home grounds of small extent . . . plans for
        residences and their grounds . . . New York, American book exchange, 1881.
            618 p. illus., 29 pl.   H.R.H.
        With the original 1870 copyright.

1192. "S.," not "G.," is the publisher's middle initial.

1200. Collation should be: 355 p. illus., 53 pl. (2 col.). The color plates are advertisements
        of tiles and stained glass.

1201. Same correction as for No. 1200. Despite the new 1866 copyright the plates are
        identical.

1262a. Todd, Sereno Edwards
        Todd's Country houses and how to save money . . . Philadelphia, Bradley &
        company, 1871.
            656 p. illus., 13 pl., incl. front.   H.R.H.

1275. In the H.R.H. copy the imprint is New York, London, D. Appleton & co.

1365. In note "Continental" should be "Centennial."

1370. Publisher's name should be C., not Charles, Scribner.

1404. In title: "the country," not "this country."
        Collation should be: 2 p. l., 1 (i.e., 50) p., 2 l., 157 p. illus.
        The same corrections apply to Nos. 1405–1407.

1442. Woollett's name should have two l's. The date should not be bracketed.

    In October 1955 the American Association of Architectural Bibliographers issued on
mimeographed sheets *A Chronological Listing of the Items in* American Architectural
Books *by Henry-Russell Hitchcock,* prepared by Professor William H. Jordy's students
at Brown University. Although it had only a rather limited circulation this extremely
useful collateral tool cannot be included here since that would require an additional
ten or more pages. Much of its special value to scholars as regards the earlier periods may,
however, be provided in simplified form merely by listing in sequence the succession
of authors — rather than works — from 1775 through 1860: (1775–1800) Swan, J. Norman,
Pain, Benjamin; (1800–1810) Langley, W. Norman, Biddle, Johnson, Latrobe; (1810–
1820) Pope, Haviland, Nicholson; (1820–1830) Town, Bulfinch, Sganzin, Lafever; (1830–
1840) Brunton, Eliot, Shaw, Fay, Howe, Memes, Alcott, Mills, Gallier, Dunlap, Hills,
Van Osdel, Hopkins, S. H. Long, Davis, Tredgold, Walker, Ellet, Gilman; (1840–1850)

Hall, Strickland, Young, Barnard, Downing, Lossing, Tower, Willard, Hatfield, Lang, J. J. Smith, Wyman, Arnot, Ritch, Wightwick, Brown, Elliott, Fowler, Hatfield, Thomas, Tuthill, Kelt, Knapen, R. C. Long, Minifie, Owen, Ranlett, Reynolds, Ruskin; (1850–1860) Sidney, Smeaton, Spooner, Williamson, Wills, Cupper, Greenough, Haupt, Leuchars, Ludlow, Meikleham, Overman, Allen, Hosking, Sloan, O. P. Smith, Upjohn, Bullock, Congregational Churches, Field, Gould, W. Smith, Tuckerman, C. H. Smith, Barrett, Brewer, Bullock, Carstensen, Fairbairn, Johnson, Burrowes, Dwyer, Wheeler, Baker, Bowler, Cleaveland, Dwight, Heck, Moseley, Reid, Thomson, Hart, A Plea, Vaux, Worthen, Bell, Chamberlain, French, Hammond, Reminiscences, Silloway, Dexter, Jacques, Johonnot, Wilson, King, Norton, Turner.

In concluding this Preface a few words may be repeated from that of the 1946 edition: I will be most grateful for any additional information about issues, editions, titles, and authors relevant to the scope of this list for use in a possible later edition.

Henry-Russell Hitchcock

Northampton, Mass.
November 1961

KEY TO SYMBOLS FOR HOLDERS

CSmH	Huntington Library, San Marino, Cal.
CtHWatk	Watkinson Library, Hartford, Conn.
CtMW	Wesleyan University, Middletown, Conn.
CtNlC	Connecticut College, New London, Conn.
CtY	Yale University, New Haven, Conn.
CtY-F	Yale School of Fine Arts
CU	University of California, Berkeley, Cal.
DAU	American University, Washington, D. C.
DDA	U.S. Department of Agriculture, Washington, D. C.
DE	U.S. Office of Education, Washington, D. C.
DLC	Library of Congress, Washington, D. C.
DSG	U.S. Surgeon General's Library, Washington, D. C.
H.R.H.	Henry-Russell Hitchcock, Middletown, Conn.
I	Illinois State Library, Springfield, Ill.
IaAS	Iowa State College, Ames, Iowa
IaU	University of Iowa, Iowa City, Iowa
ICA-B	Burnham Library, Art Institute, Chicago, Ill.
ICA-R	Ryerson Library, Art Institute, Chicago, Ill.
ICHi	Chicago Historical Society, Chicago, Ill.
ICJ	John Crerar Library, Chicago, Ill.
ICN	Newberry Library, Chicago, Ill.
ICU	University of Chicago, Chicago, Ill.
InI	Indianapolis Public Library, Indianapolis, Ind.
IU	University of Illinois, Urbana, Ill.
J.P.C.	John Phillips Coolidge
LNT	Tulane University, New Orleans, La.
M	Massachusetts State Library, Boston, Mass.
MB	Boston Public Library, Boston, Mass.
MBAt	Boston Athenaeum, Boston, Mass.
MBHo	Boston Horticultural Society, Boston, Mass.
MCE	Episcopal Theological School, Cambridge, Mass.
Md	Maryland State Library, Annapolis, Md.
MdBE	Enoch Pratt Free Library, Baltimore, Md.
MdBM	Maryland Institute, Baltimore, Md.
MdBP	Peabody Institute, Baltimore, Md.
Me	Maine State Library, Augusta, Me.
MeB	Bowdoin College, Brunswick, Me.
MH	Harvard University, Cambridge, Mass.
MH-A	Arnold Arboretum, Harvard University
MHi	Massachusetts Historical Society, Boston, Mass.
MiD	Detroit Public Library, Detroit, Mich.
MiGr	Grand Rapids Public Library, Grand Rapids, Mich.

MiH	School of Mines, Houghton, Mich.
MiOC	Olivet College, Olivet, Mich.
MIU	University of Michigan, Ann Arbor, Mich.
MLy	Lynn Public Library, Lynn, Mass.
MnM	Minneapolis Public Library, Minneapolis, Minn.
MnU	University of Minnesota, Minneapolis, Minn.
MoS	St. Louis Public Library, St. Louis, Mo.
MPly	Russell Library, Plymouth, Mass.
MSaE	Essex Institute, Salem, Mass.
MSaP	Peabody Institute, Salem, Mass.
MU	Massachusetts State University, Amherst, Mass.
MW	Worcester Public Library, Worcester, Mass.
MWA	American Antiquarian Society, Worcester, Mass.
MWelC	Wellesley College, Wellesley, Mass.
NB	Brooklyn Public Library, Brooklyn, N. Y.
NBu	Buffalo Public Library, Buffalo, N. Y.
NcD	Duke University, Durham, N. C.
Nh	New Hampshire State Library, Concord, N. H.
NHi	New York Historical Society, New York, N. Y.
NIC	Cornell University, Ithaca, N. Y.
NjHi	New Jersey Historical Society, Newark, N. J.
NjP	Princeton University, Princeton, N. J.
NjR	Rutgers University, New Brunswick, N. J.
NN	New York Public Library, New York, N. Y.
NNC	Columbia University, New York, N. Y.
NNC-A	Avery Library, Columbia University
NNCoCi	College of the City of New York, New York, N. Y.
NNCoo	Cooper Union, New York, N. Y.
NNE	New York Engineering Society, New York, N. Y.
NNGS	Grolier Society, New York, N. Y.
NNHo	New York Horticultural Society, New York, N. Y.
NNMM	Metropolitan Museum of Art, New York, N. Y.
NNMMo	The Museum of Modern Art, New York, N. Y.
NNSo	New York Society Library, New York, N. Y.
NNUW	Washington Square College, New York University, New York, N. Y.
NPV	Vassar College, Poughkeepsie, N. Y.
NRU	University of Rochester, Rochester, N. Y.
NWM	U. S. Military Academy, West Point, N. Y.
OCi	Cincinnati Public Library, Cincinnati, Ohio
OClMA	Museum of Fine Arts, Cleveland, Ohio
OClWHi	Western Reserve Historical Society, Cleveland, Ohio
OO	Oberlin College, Oberlin, Ohio
OU	Ohio State University, Columbus, Ohio
PBa	Academy of the New Church, Bryn Athyn, Pa.
PBm	Bryn Mawr College, Bryn Mawr, Pa.
PCH	American Baptist Historical Society, Chester, Pa.
PChhC	Chestnut Hill College, Chestnut Hill, Pa.
PHatU	Union Library, Hatboro, Pa.
PHC	Haverford College, Haverford, Pa.

PHi	Pennsylvania Historical Society, Philadelphia, Pa.
PNt	Newtown Library Company, Newtown, Pa.
PP	Free Library, Philadelphia, Pa.
PPA	Athenaeum of Philadelphia, Philadelphia, Pa.
PPAmP	American Philosophical Society, Philadelphia, Pa.
PPAp	Philadelphia Apprentices Library, Philadelphia, Pa.
PPBAss	Philadelphia Bar Association, Philadelphia, Pa.
PPCC	Carpenter's Company, Philadelphia, Pa.
PPCP	College of Physicians, Philadelphia, Pa.
PPD	Drexel Institute, Philadelphia, Pa.
PPE	Board of Education, Philadelphia, Pa.
PPFr	Friends Free Library, Germantown, Pa.
PPFrankl	Franklin Institute, Philadelphia, Pa.
PPGi	Girard College, Philadelphia, Pa.
PPHo	Philadelphia Horticultural Society, Philadelphia, Pa.
PPI	Illman Training School, Philadelphia, Pa.
PPL	Library Company, Philadelphia, Pa.
PPM	Mercantile Library, Philadelphia, Pa.
PPPM	Philadelphia Museum of Art, Philadelphia, Pa.
PPPrHi	Presbyterian Historical Society, Philadelphia, Pa.
PPTU	Temple University, Philadelphia, Pa.
PPWa	Wagner Free Institute of Science, Philadelphia, Pa.
PSC	Swarthmore College, Swarthmore, Pa.
PSt	Pennsylvania State College, State College, Pa.
PU	University of Pennsylvania, Philadelphia, Pa.
PU-ETS	Towne Scientific School, University of Pennsylvania
PU-F	Furness Memorial Library, University of Pennsylvania
PU-FA	Fine Arts Library, University of Pennsylvania
PU-Penn	University of Pennsylvania: School of Education
PVC	Villanova College, Villanova, Pa.
RIBA	Royal Institute of British Architects, London, England
RP	Providence Public Library, Providence, R. I.
RPAt	Providence Athenaeum, Providence, R. I.
RPB	Brown University, Providence, R. I.
RPD	Rhode Island School of Design, Providence, R. I.
RPJCB	John Carter Brown Library, Providence, R. I.
ScC	Charleston Library Association, Charleston, S. C.
Vi	Virginia State Library, Richmond, Va.
ViU	University of Virginia, Charlottesville, Va.
WaU	University of Washington, Seattle, Wash.
WHi	Wisconsin Historical Society, Madison, Wis.

AMERICAN ARCHITECTURAL BOOKS

1. Abernathey, R   James
    Practical hints on mill building . . . Moline, Ill., The author, 1880.
        298 p. incl. front., illus., pl.   NNC-A

2. Adams, Herbert Baxter
    Thomas Jefferson and the university of Virginia . . . Washington, D. C.,
    Government printing office, 1888.
        308 p. illus.   NNC-A

3. *Adams, William Henry Davenport, 1828–1891
    Temples, tombs and monuments of ancient Greece and Rome . . . Boston,
    D. Lothrop and co., Dover, N. H., G. T. Day and co., 1871.
        307 p. incl. front., illus., pl.   MBAt,OCi

4. ── ──── Boston, D. Lothrop; Dover, N. H., G. T. Day & Co., 1872.
        307 p. incl. front., illus., plates   DLC
    The Nelson editions of this work, with imprint London, New York, etc.,
    are not properly to be considered American imprints. The same is true of
    Adams' *Triumphs of ancient and modern architecture* and *Lighthouses and
    lightships*, published by Nelson, and of his other works, which are guide-
    books rather than works on architecture, in any case.

5. Alcott, William Andrus, 1798–1859
    Essay on the construction of schoolhouses, to which was awarded the prize
    offered by the American institute of instruction August 1831 . . . with an
    appendix. Boston, Hilliard, Gray, Little and Wilkins, and Richardson, Lord
    and Holbrook, 1832.
        66 p. incl. 2 plans   CsmH,CtHWatk,CtY,DLC,ICJ,IU,MB,MBAt,
                                    MH,MnU,MSaE,MWA,MoS,NHi,NN,NNC-A
    The middle name is given as Alexander by the DLC, but the form used
    here is that given in the *Dictionary of American Biography*.

6. Aldrich, William Sleeper, 1863–
    Notes on building construction and architecture . . . [Philadelphia] W. S.
    Aldrich, c1889.
        40, 24 numb. l. 7 pl.   DLC,OU,PPFrankl
    At head of title: Philadelphia Manual Training school.
    The 24 leaves at the end have separate caption title.

7. Allen and Ginter, *firm*
    General government and state capitol buildings of the United States. Rich-
    mond, Va., Allen and Ginter, c1890.
        13 p. illus.   NcD,OCi

8. Allen, Frank P.
    Artistic dwellings . . . from $700.00 upwards . . . Grand Rapids, Mich.,
    F. P. Allen, c1891.
        104 p. illus., pl.   DLC

9. ── ──── [2d ed.] Grand Rapids, Mich., F. P. Allen, c1892.
        119 p. illus.   DLC,NN

11. ── ──── [4th ed.] Grand Rapids, Mich., F. P. Allen, c1893.
        123 p. illus.   DLC,MB,OCl
    The information in the titles of the c1892 and c1893 editions varies slightly.
    There were many later editions from 1895 on. The presumptive [3d ed.] has
    not been located. Item No. 10 would apply to that edition when found.

1

12. Allen, Fred Hovey, 1845–1926
          The great cathedrals of the world . . . Boston, Haskell and Post [ᶜ1886]–88.
          2 v. 130 pl.   CSmH,CtY,ICA-B,IU,MB,MBAt,MH,MnU,MoS,MWA,
                                            NN,NNC-A,NNMM,OCi,OO,PHC,PP,Vi
          Issued in 26 parts. V. 2 has imprint: Boston and New York, Haskell and
          Post company. Description from NNC-A. The DLC does not agree with
          this description, giving instead two entries: Boston, Haskell & Post [ᶜ1887–
          88] 2v; and Boston, Haskell & Post ᶜ1888. Others' descriptions also vary
          slightly in dates given. It is therefore possible that the total 26 parts were
          grouped somewhat differently in slightly varying issues. For instance
          MWA gives Pts I–VI [ᶜ1886], Pts VII–XXII [ᶜ1887] and Pts XXII–XXVI
          ᶜ1888.

13. Allen, Lewis Falley, 1800–1890
          Rural architecture: Being a complete description of farmhouses, cottages and
          outbuildings . . . New York, C. M. Saxton, 1852.
          384 p. illus., 20 pl., incl. front.   CU,CtY,ICA-B,IU,MB,MH,
                                            MiOC,MSaE,NNMM,OCl,PP,Vi

14. —— —— New York, C. M. Saxton, 1853.
          378 p. illus., 20 pl., incl. front.   NN,OU

15. —— —— New York, C. M. Saxton, 1854.
          378 p. illus., 20 pl., incl. front.   NN
          Offered for sale by Fowlers and Wells for $1.25 in 1855.

16. —— —— New York, C. M. Saxton & company, 1856.
          378 p. illus., 20 pl., incl. front.   MB,OO,PP,PPFrankl,PPM

17. —— —— New York, C. M. Saxton, Barker & co., 1860.
          378 p. illus., 20 pl., incl. front.   NB,NPV

18. —— —— New York, A. O. Moore, 1863.
          378 p. illus., 20 pl., incl. front.   MBHo,NNC-A

19. —— —— New York, A. O. Moore, n.d.
          378 p. illus., 20 pl., incl. front.   DLC,MB,MH,MiD,NN,OU
          This is identical with the 1863 edition and may possibly precede it in date.

20. —— —— New York, Orange Judd company, 1865.
          378 p. illus., 20 pl., incl. front.   NN
          Still with original 1852 copyright.

21. The American architect and building news
          The cathedral of St. John, the Divine, New York city. A portion of the
          designs submitted in the first competition. Boston, the American architect
          and building news, 1891.
          1 p. l. [57] pl.   OU
          Designs by Huss and Buck, and by Heins & LaFarge were also published
          separately.

22. Americanus, *pseud*.
          Description of design and drawings for the proposed Centennial buildings, to
          be erected in Fairmount Park . . . Philadelphia, King & Baird, printers, 1873.
          11 p.   PHi
          Compare another pamphlet with identical title by Samuel Sloan.

23. Architecture. Part I. Ancient architecture.
          See Howe, Hezekiah, 1775–1839.

24. The architect's and builders' reference book . . . Chicago, The Mercantile publish-
          ing co., ᶜ1889.
          117 p. pl.   DLC,ICJ

25. The architects' directory and specification index . . . [1st ed.]. New York, William
    T. Comstock, ᶜ1894.

                                                                                    DLC

    Armengaud, Jacques Eugène, 1810–1891
        See Johnson, William, *translator*

26. Arnold, Charles Dudley
        Studies in architecture at home and abroad. New York, The Photogravure
        co., 1881.
            1 p. l. 20 pl.   NNC-A

27. —— —— Troy, N. Y., Nims and Knight, 1888.
            1 p. l. 20 pl.   MdBE,NHi,OClMA

28. —— —— New York, The Photo-gravure co., ᶜ1888.
            1 p. l. 20 pl.   DLC,OCl
        Arnold was one of the official photographers of the 1893 Chicago World's
        Fair, responsible with H. D. Higginbotham for *Official views of the
        World's Columbian exposition,* ᶜ*1893.*

29. Arnot, David Henry
        Animadversions on the proceedings of the regents of the Smithsonian insti-
        tution in the choice of an architect for their edifice at Washington . . . New
        York, 1847.
            15 p.   DLC,RIBA

30. —— Gothic architecture applied to modern residence . . . New York, D. Appleton
        & co., 1849.
            6 pts.   MSaE
        Issued in parts. Prospectus on back page of No. I is dated: New York,
        Oct. 1848. No title page, but original paper cover gives equivalent in-
        formation.

31. —— —— New York, D. Appleton; Philadelphia, George S. Appleton, 1850.
            41 p. illus., 39 pl. incl. 3 col.   IU,InI,NNC-A
        Additional colored title page with short title and date ᶜ1850.   True title
        continues ". . . : containing designs of all the important parts of a private
        dwelling, exhibited in elaborate perspective drawings: together with large
        and copious details . . ." The back of this title page carries the original
        1849 copyright.

32. —— —— New York, D. Appleton & company, Philadelphia, George S. Apple-
        ton, 1851.
            41 p. illus., 39 pl., incl. 3 col.   DLC,MB,MWA,NNMM,OCi,PPM
        With the same additional colored title page.

    Artistic country seats
        See Sheldon, George William

33. Artistic houses; being a series of interior views of a number of the most beautiful
        and celebrated homes in the United States, with a description of the art treas-
        ures contained therein . . . New York, printed for the subscribers by D. Ap-
        pleton and company, 1883–84.
            2 v. in 4. 200 photographic pl.   CtY,DLC,ICA-B,MB,MH,NjP,NN,
                                                            NNC-A,NNMM,NHi,PP,PU
        Edition limited to 500 copies.
        ICA-B and NNC-A copies have 203 plates; NNMM copy has 204 plates.

34. Atwood, Daniel Topping, 1836–
        Atwood's Rules of proportion; compiled and original; and adapted to modern
        practice . . . Vol. I. [New York] The author, 1867.
            71 p. 5 pl.   DLC,NN

Atwood, Daniel Topping
35. Atwood's Rules of proportion . . . 2d ed. New York, Bicknell & Comstock, 1879.
    67 p. 13 pl.   DLC,IU,MnU,PPM
    With title: *Atwood's Revised rules of proportion* . . .

36. —— —— 3d ed. New York, William T. Comstock, 1892.
    91 p. incl. 13 pl.   DLC,ICJ,IU,MB,NNC-A,OU,PP
    With the 1879 title.

37. —— Atwood's country and suburban houses. Illustrated with about 150 engrav-
    ings . . . New York, Orange Judd & company, [1871].
    287 p. incl. front., illus.   DLC,ICJ,IU,MB,MBAt,MBHo,
                                                                    MH,NN,OCl

38. —— —— New York, Orange Judd & company, 1883.
    287 p. incl. front., illus.
                                                    NNC-A

39. —— —— New York, Orange Judd & company, 1885.
    287 p. incl. front., illus.
                                                    NjR
    The Judd address is given as 245 Broadway. NjR also has a variant issue
    identical with this except that the "&" is omitted from the publisher's firm
    name and the address is given as 751 Broadway.

40. —— Atwood's modern American homesteads . . . New York, A. J. Bicknell & co.,
    1876.
    6 p. 26 l. 46 pl.   DLC,MB,MH,NNC-A,NNMM,OU,PP

Audsley, George Ashdown, 1838–1925
See Audsley, William James

41. Audsley, William James, 1833–
    Outlines of ornament . . . New York, Scribner and Welford, 1882.
    14 p. 59 pl.   CtY,DLC,ICA-B,MiD,NjP,NNCoo,PP
    George Ashdown Audsley was joint author. First appeared London, 1881.

42. —— Popular dictionary of architecture and the allied arts . . . (3d ed.) New
    York, G. P. Putnam's sons; London, Sampson, Low, Marston, Searle & Riv-
    ington, 1881–82.
    3 v.   CSmH,CtHWatk,CtMW,CtY,DLC,ICA-B,MSaE,MWA,
                                 MdBE,MoS,NN,NNC-A,NNCoo,NNMM,OCi,PP
    George Ashdown Audsley was joint author. Vols. 1–3 cover A-But only.
    No more was published. Vol. 1 only gives (3d ed.). Vol. 1 was first pub-
    lished Liverpool, 1878. There are also undated London editions of Vols. 2
    and 3. Audsley settled in America; otherwise this would not be consid-
    ered here as an American edition.

Austin, Henry, 1804–1891
See Hills, Chester

43. B   , W
    New York and Brooklyn churches . . . Nelson and Phillips, 1874.
    128 p. illus.   NHi,NNCoCi,PPPrHi
    A descriptive and historical rather than an architectural work.

44. Babcock, Charles, 1829–1913
    Elementary architecture . . . New York, D. Appleton & co., 1876–[77].
    Nos. 1–9   CU,CtY,DLC
    Krüsi's Industrial drawing course.
    Babcock published a book on *Vaults* in 1884, too technical for inclusion in
    this list.

45. —— —— New York, D. Appleton & co., n.d.
    [57] p. incl. 54 pl.
                                                    RPB
    At head of title: Krüsi's Industrial drawing course.
    With original 1876 copyright.

4

46. Bacon, Leonard, 1802–1881
> The genesis of the New England churches . . . New York, Harper & brothers, 1874.
>> 485 p. incl. front., illus., 7 pl., 2 port., 2 maps   DLC, MnU

47. Baker, Z.
> The cottage builder's manual . . . Worcester, Z. Baker & co., 1856.
>> 176 p. front., illus., 2 pl.   ICA-B,MH,MW,MWA,NN,NNC-A,NHi,PPM

48. —— —— Boston, Higgins, Bradley & Dayton, 1857.
>> 208 p. front., illus., 2 pl.   ICA-B,MH
> With title: *Modern house builder from the log cabin and cottage to the mansion.*

49. —— —— Boston, Higgins, Bradley and Dayton, n.d.
>> 208 p. front., illus.   H.R.H.
> With same title and 1857 copyright as 1857 edition.

50. *Barba, Joseph
> The use of steel for constructive purposes . . . New York, D. Van Nostrand, 1875.
>> 101 p. illus.   CU,DLC,DP,ICJ,MB,MH,NjP, NN,NNC,PP
> Translated from the French; with a preface by Alex. L. Holley.
> First appeared Paris, 1874.

51. —— —— New York, D. Van Nostrand, 1891.
>> 110 p. illus.   PSt,RPB

52. Barber & company
> New model dwellings and how best to build them. Containing a great variety of designs, plans and interior views of modern dwellings . . . rev. ed. Knoxville, Barber & company, n.d.
>> 120 p.   OO
> Very probably later than 1895. No other edition has been located.

53. Barnard, Henry, 1811–1900
> Armsmear: the home, the arm and the armory of Samuel Colt. A memorial . . . New York [Alvord, printer] 1866.
>> 399 p. front., illus., pl.   CU,CtWatk,CtMW,CtY,DLC, MB,MH,NN,OCl,PHi

54. —— Practical illustrations of the principles of school architecture . . . Hartford, 1850.
>> 175 p. illus.   NN
> ". . . selections with some modifications from a larger work on school architecture." First published in: *National convention of friends of public education.* Appendix. Philadelphia, 1850.

55. —— —— Hartford, Press of Case, Tiffany and co., 1851.
>> 175 p. illus.   CU,CtWatk,CtY,DE,MB,MH,MSaE,MWA,NN,NcD

56. —— Report on school architecture and plans for graded schools by the commissioner of education. Washington, Government printing office, 1870.
>> 2 p. l. pp. [517]–647. [1] illus.   ICN,MWA
> Cover title; a second title page reads: School architecture. Part II. Plans for graded schools. Preliminary report.

57. —— —— Washington, Government printing office, 1871.
>> 2 p. l. pp. [517]–647. [1] illus.   DE
> Cover title; at head of title: U.S. Bureau of education.

Barnard, Henry

58. School architecture; or, Contributions to the improvement of school houses in the
    United States . . . New York, A. S. Barnes & co., Cincinnati, H. W. Derby
    & co., 1848.
       365 p. incl. front., illus.   CtMW,MB,NNC-A,NPV,PU
       Material first prepared in 1838 and partially presented in *Schoolhouses* and
       School-house architecture, below, as well as in the 1846 and 1847 edi-
       tions of Chester Hills' *The builder's guide,* q.v.

59. —— —— 2d ed. New York, A. S. Barnes & co., Cincinnati, H. W. Derby &
    co., 1848.
       383 p. incl. front., illus.   CU,CtY,ICJ,ICN,MB,MSaE,MiD,
                                                       MiOC,NN,NNC-A,NHi,RPB

60. —— —— 2d ed. New York, A. S. Barnes & co., Cincinnati, H. W. Derby & co.,
    1849.
       381 p. incl. front., illus.   MnU

61. —— —— 3d ed. New York, A. S. Barnes & co., Cincinnati, H. W. Derby & co.,
    1849.
       383 p. incl. front., illus.   DLC,ICA-B,IU,M,MB,MH,MSaE,
                                            MWA,MoS,NNC,NHi,NjR,PPA,RIBA

62. —— —— 4th ed. New York, A. S. Barnes & co., Cincinnati, H. W. Derby &
    co., 1850.
       425 p. incl. front., illus.   DLC,IU,MWA,MiU,MoS,WaU

63. —— —— 5th ed. New York. Charles B. Norton, 1854.
       464 p. incl. front., illus.   MB,MH,MoS,NPV,OCi,PP
       Offered for sale by Fowlers and Wells for $2.00 in 1855.

64. —— —— 6th ed. Cincinnati, H. W. Derby & co., New York, J. C. Derby,
    Boston, Phillips, Sampson and co., 1854.
       464 p. incl. front., illus.   OCl,OU

65. —— —— 6th ed. H. W. Derby and co., New York, J. C. Derby, Boston,
    Phillips, Sampson and co., 1855.
       464 p. incl. front., illus.   DE,DLC,MH

66. —— —— 6th ed. New York, A. S. Barnes & Burr, 1860.
       464 p. incl. front., illus.   CU,MB,MnM,PPFrankl

67. —— School houses . . . Providence, 1884.
       72 p.   CtHWatk,DSG,MH,MSaE,NNUW
       Cover title.

68. —— School-house architecture . . . Hartford, printed by Case, Tiffany & Burn-
    ham, 1842.
       xii, 48 p. illus.   DLC,CtHWatk,MB,MH,MWA,NcD,NN,MWA,RIBA
       Woodcut on title page and paper cover.
       A document appended to the Annual report of the Board of commission-
       ers of common schools of Connecticut.
       Includes woodcuts of plans, elevations, and perspectives of schools in vari-
       ous New England towns and cities.

69. —— —— n.p., n.d.
       48 p.   MSaE
       Cover title; perhaps an incomplete copy of the item above rather than a
       separate issue.
       See also Hills, Chester

70. Barnes, Alfred C.
    The New York and Brooklyn suspension bridge . . . New York. J. H. Fisher, c1883.
    32 p. illus.   PP

71. Barrett, George
    The poor man's home, and rich man's palace. Or, The application of the gravel wall cement to the purposes of building . . . Cincinnati, Appelgate & co., 1854.
    60 p. incl. front.   DLC,MoS,NjR,NN

72. —— —— Cincinnati, Appelgate & co., 1856.
    60 p.   MoS

73. Bascom, John, 1827–1911
    Aesthetics; or, The Science of beauty . . . Boston, Crosby & Nichols, 1862.
    256 p.   CtMW,MH,MiOC,NN,PPL
    Two lectures on architecture, pp. 182–215.

74. —— —— Boston, Crosby and Ainsworth, 1867.
    256 p.   IaU,NN

75. —— —— corr. and enl. ed. New York and Chicago, Woolworth, Ainsworth & co., 1872.
    268 p.   DLC,IU,NN,PP
    With a new 1871 copyright.

76. —— —— New York, and Chicago, Woolworth, Ainsworth & co., 1874.
    268 p.   CtMW,DLC,MH,NPV

77. —— —— New York, Potter, Ainsworth & co., n.d.
    268 p.   MB
    With the 1871 copyright.

78. —— —— new ed. rev. and enl. New York, G. P. Putman's sons, n.d.
    340 p.   OU
    With the 1871 copyright.

79. —— —— new ed. enl. New York, G. P. Putman & co., 1881.
    340 p.   MB,MnU,NNC

80. —— —— new ed. enl. New York, G. P. Putman & co., 1886.
    340 p.   MnM,PPAp

81. —— —— new ed. enl. New York, G. P. Putman & co., 1893.
    340 p.   PPD

82. Bates, Robert Charles
    The elementary principles of architecture and building . . . Boston, G. H. Ellis, 1892.
    147 p.   DLC,ICA-B,NNC-A,OCi
    From the preface: "Substantially the author's lectures before his classes at Claflin university at Orangeburg, S. C., during the winter of 1891–92."

83. Bauman, Frederick
    The art of preparing foundations for all kinds of buildings, with particular illustration of the "method of isolated piers" as followed in Chicago . . . Chicago, J. M. Wing & co., 1873.
    38 p. incl. 19 illus.   ICA-B,ICHi
    This early description of an important step in the prehistory of the skyscraper was afterwards incorporated in the various editions of George Townsend Powell's *Foundations and foundation walls,* q.v.

7

Bauman, Frederick
84. Thoughts on style, a lecture prepared for delivery before the American institute of
architects at their meeting in Chicago 1892. [Chicago? 1892?].
11 p.   ICN

85. *Baxter, Lucy E   (Barnes), 1837–1902, Leader Scott, *pseud.*
The renaissance of art in Italy . . . New York, Scribner and Welford, 1883.
384 p. front., illus., pl.   CU,ICA-R,MH,MnM,MPly,MoS,NjP,
                                                          NNC,OCl,PPM

86. ——— ——— Boston, Estes and Lauriat, 1888.
384 p. front., illus., pl.   MdBE
Mrs. Baxter's other works are even less relevant than this.

87. Bell, William E
Carpentry made easy; or, The science and art of framing on a new and
improved system. With specific instructions for building balloon frames,
barn frames, mill frames, warehouses, church spires, etc. Comprising also
a system of bridge building . . . Philadelphia, J. Challen & son, 1858.
134 p. illus., 38 pl.   CtY,DLC,IU,MB,MoS,OCi
Bell is described as "architect and practical builder." Early reference to
balloon frame construction.

88. —— ——— Philadelphia, J. Challen & son, 1859.
134 p. illus., 38 pl.   MH,NN,NNC-A,PPFrankl

89. —— ——— Philadelphia, Howard Challen, 1868.
134 p. illus., 38 pl.   ICA-B,PPCC

90. —— ——— 2d ed. enl. and imp. Philadelphia, Howard Challen, 1875.
152 p. illus., 44 pl.   DLC,ICJ,PPFr
This edition carries a new 1875 copyright.

91. —— ——— 2d ed. enl. and imp. Philadelphia, Ferguson bros. & co., 1887.
152 p. illus., 44 pl.   NN

92. —— ——— 2d ed. enl. and imp. Philadelphia, Ferguson bros. & co., 1888.
152 p. illus., 44 pl.   MoS

93. —— ——— 2d ed. enl. and imp. Philadelphia, Ferguson bros. & co., 1889.
152 p. illus., 44 pl.   NNCoo,PPFrankl

94. —— ——— 2d ed. enl. and imp. Philadelphia, Ferguson bros. & co., 1891.
152 p. illus., 44 pl.   MB

95. —— ——— 2d ed. enl. and imp. Philadelphia, Ferguson bros. & co., 1894.
152 p. illus., 44 pl.   MnU,PP
There was an issue as late as 1900, still with the 1875 copyright.

96. Bender, Charles Balthazar
Principles of economy in the design of metallic bridges . . . New York, John
Wiley and sons, 1885.
195 p. 12 fold. pl.   DLC,ICJ,IU,MB,MH,MiH,MnM,NjP,NN,NNC,PP

97. —— ——— [2d ed.] New York, John Wiley and sons, 1891.
195 p. 12 fold. pl.   MnU

98. Bender, Charles E.
Practical treatise on the properties of continuous bridges . . . New York, D.
Van Nostrand, 1876.
150 p. diagrs.   DLC,ICJ,MB,MH,MiH,MnU,MWA,NN,OCi
Van Nostrand's Science series, no. 26

Bender, Horace, *pseud.*
See Greenough, Horatio, 1805–1852

99. Benjamin, Asher, 1773–1845

The American builder's companion; or, A new system of architecture particularly adapted to the present style of building in the United States of America . . . Boston, Etheridge and Bliss, 1806.

70 p. 44 pl.   CSmH,CtHWatk,DLC,MB,MH,MWA,
                                          NHi,NNMM,NWM,PHi,PPLR

Daniel Raynerd is given as joint author. The nationalistic phrasing of the title imitates, and indeed outbids, that of Owen Biddle's *Young carpenter's assistant* of the previous year. This was Benjamin's second work, following a year after the latest issue of *The country builder's assistant.*

100. ——— ——— 2d ed. corr. and enl. Charlestown, printed by Samuel Etheridge, Jnr., 1811.

104 p. 59 pl.   IU,MB,MBAt,MH,MWA,NcD,NNC-A,
                                                NHi,OCi

The words: "new" and "in the United States of America" are omitted, and the title continues: "Treating on practical geometry. The origin of building. Of the five orders of architecture. Of their particular parts and embellishments, and of their application. Also very fully of stairs. On churches, court houses, &c. On sashes, sash frames, shutters, doors, cornices, base and surbase mouldings, architraves, &c. &c."

Sixteen of the plates of the 1st edition were dropped and twenty-nine new plates were added.

From the preface: "Note. It may perhaps be asked, why Mr. Raynerd's name, which appeared in the first edition, does not appear in this; I answer, he sold all his right and title to the work soon after its first publication. The plates in this edition, which were drawn and explained by him, have his name affixed to them."

101. ——— ——— 3d ed. corr. and enl. Boston, R. P. & Co. Williams, 1816.

104 p. 61 pl.   DLC,MH,MWA,NHi,NN,NNGS,NWM,OU,RPJCB

102. ——— ——— 4th ed. corr. and enl. Boston, R. P. & C. Williams, 1820.

104 p. 61 pl.   DLC,MH,MSaE,MWA,NHi,NjHi,NN,PU

"With a plan and elevations of a church" on added plates K and L, between plates 58 and 59.

103. ——— ——— 5th ed. corr. and enl. Boston, R. P. & C. Williams, 1826.

106 p. 63 pl.   MWA,NHi

"With two additional plates on handrails for circular stairs." These are plates H and I between plates 50 and 51.

104. ——— ——— 6th ed. corr. and enl. Boston, R. P. & Co. Williams, 1827.

114 p. 68 pl.   ICA-B,IU,MH,MWA,NHi,NN,NNC-A, OO,PP

The title mentions "70 (*sic*) copper plate engravings." This is the first edition of a work by Benjamin to offer "Grecian architecture." Added plates A, B, C, DE, and FG between plates 25 and 26 illustrate the Greek Doric of the Parthenon, the Greek Ionic of the Temple on the Ilissus, and a comparison of the Greek and Roman Doric.

——— The architect; or, Complete builder's guide.
See The builder's guide

——— The architect; or, Practical house carpenter.
See The practical house carpenter

——— The builder's assistant.
See The country builder's assistant

——— The builder's guide and the architect or practical house carpenter.
See The practical house carpenter

Benjamin, Asher

105. The builder's guide, illustrated by sixty-six engravings, which exhibit the orders of architecture. Designed for the use of builders, particularly of carpenters and joiners . . . Boston, Perkins & Marvin, Philadelphia, Henry Perkins, 1839.
83 p. 66 pl.   MH,NHi,OO
The sixth of Benjamin's works in chronological order. It consists for the most part of the Greek orders and "Grecian" exterior and interior detail. Plates 49 and 50 showing stair construction are identical with plates 49 and 50 in Benjamin's *Practice of architecture*, 1833. Plate XLVIII shows "Grecian" shop fronts, and plate LVIII and LIX an Ionic church.

106. —— —— Boston, Benjamin B. Mussey, 1843.
83 p. 66 pl.   NHi
The title reads: *The builder's guide; or, Complete system of architecture*, with the further addition of "and other elements of the art" after "the orders of architecture." Despite its confusingly similar title, *The builder's guide and the architect and practical house carpenter*, 1840, is not an issue of this work but of *The practical house carpenter*.

107. —— —— Boston, Benjamin B. Mussey, 1845.
83 p. 66 pl.   NNC-A
With title *The architect; or, Complete builder's guide* . . .

108. —— —— Boston, Benjamin B. Mussey and company, 1850.
83 p. 66 pl.   ICA-B,MBAt,MiD
With the 1843 title. This is the first posthumous issue of this work, as the preceding probably came out before Benjamin's death in that year.

109. —— —— Boston, Benjamin B. Mussey and company, 1854.
83 p. 66 pl.   MdBP

110. —— —— Boston, Bazin and Ellsworth, n.d.
83 p. 66 pl.   MB,MH,NN
This still carries the original 1838 copyright and the 1843 title. The form of the firm name: Bazin and Ellsworth, determines that this issue appeared in the years 1858–62 and is therefore the latest Benjamin item.

111. —— The country builder's assistant: containing a collection of new designs of carpentry and architecture . . . Greenfield, printed by Thomas Dickman, 1797.
[2], [30] p. 30 pl.   MWA,OO,RPJCB
This is the earliest original American work on architecture, as John Norman's *Town and country builder's assistant*, 1786, was a compilation of English material; and other earlier American imprints were local editions of English authors. Benjamin, however, still leans heavily and frankly on English sources: Chambers for the orders and Nicholson for construction details.

112. —— —— Boston, printed by Spotswood and Etheridge, 1798.
36 p. 37 pl. (2 fold.)   CSmH,CtY,DLC(imp.),ICA-B,ICJ,MH,MHi,
                                               MWA,NHi,NNC-A,NNSo,PPL-R,RPJCB
The title reads: *The country builder's assistant, fully explaining, the best methods for striking regular and quirked mouldings: for drawing and working the Tuscan, Doric, Ionic and Corinthian orders* . . . and mentions a "Plan elevation & section of a meeting-house with pulpit at large" also "Plans and elevations of [3] houses." The complete imprint ". . . for the Author, sold by him, and by Alexander Thomas, Worcester," sometimes leads to the mistaken impression that this is a Worcester and not a Boston publication.

10

Benjamin, Asher

113. The country builder's assistant . . . 3d ed. Greenfield, Mass., printed by Thomas Dickman, 1800.
    34 p. front., 37 pl. (2 fold.)   MWA,NHi,PP
    In this edition the title begins: *The builder's assistant* . . .

114. —— —— Greenfield, Mass., printed by John Denio, 1805.
    36 p. front., 37 pl. (2 fold.)   MWA,NHi,NN,NNC-A(imp.),
                                                          NNMM,PP

115. —— Elements of architecture, containing the Tuscan, Doric, Ionic and Corinthian orders, with all their details and embellishments. Also the theory and practice of carpentry, exhibiting thirty-six experiments made in various ways on European timber by European artists; and on the strength of iron, steel, copper, brass, tin, lead, stone, bricks, cement, &c. &c. with practical rules for their application . . . Boston, Benjamin B. Mussey, 1843.
    viii 232 p. 28 pl.   DLC,ICA-B,IU,MB,MBAt,MdBP,MH,
                                                  NNC-A,NHi
    This was the seventh and last of Benjamin's works to appear.

116. —— —— 2d ed. Boston, Benjamin B. Mussey, 1849.
    232 p. 28 pl.   NHi,PPFrankl
    The only posthumous appearance of one of Benjamin's least popular works.

117. —— The practical house carpenter. Being a complete developement of the Grecian orders of architecture . . . containing one example of the Tuscan order, three examples of the Doric order, three examples of the Ionic order, one example of the Corinthian order, and one example of the Composite order . . . to which are added a series of designs for porticos, frontispieces, doors, . . . Boston, R. P. & C. Williams and Annin & Smith, 1830.
    119 p. 64 pl.   CSmH,CtY,DLC,ICA-B,MBAt,MH(imp.),
                             MSaE,MWA,NNC-A,NNE,PPFrankl
    Benjamin's fourth and most popular work. Some order plates are still Roman and based on chambers.

118. —— —— 2d ed. Boston, S. Walker, Baltimore, D. Sullivan, Philadelphia, J. Moorhead, 1830.
    119 p. 64 pl.   NHi,PPM

119. —— —— 3d ed. Boston, The proprietors, 1832.
    119 p. 64 pl.   MH,MWA,NHi,RP
    The word: "containing" is omitted from the title.

120. —— —— 4th ed. Boston, The proprietors, New York, J. P. Peaslea, 1835.
    119 p. 64 pl.   NjP,NNC-A
    The preface, otherwise unchanged, concludes: "Three editions of this work, each containing a thousand copies, having been sold, the author is encouraged to publish a fourth . . ."

122. —— —— 6th ed. Boston, Benjamin B. Mussey, Philadelphia, Thomas Cowperthwait & co., New York, Collins, Keese & co., 1839.
    119 p. 64 pl.   MnM,NcD
    With a new 1839 copyright and title: *The architect; or, Practical house carpenter* . . .
    The preface of the 4th ed. is retained as in all the later issues. No copies of the presumptive 5th ed. have been located.

123. —— —— Boston, Benjamin B. Mussey, 1841.
    119 p. 64 pl.   MSaE
    The title of this edition with a new 1841 copyright begins: *The builder's guide and the architect or practical house carpenter.* It should not be confused with *The builder's guide,* of which no issue appeared in this year.

Benjamin, Asher

124. The practical house carpenter . . . Boston, Benjamin B. Mussey, 1841.
    119 p. 64 pl.   MdBP,OO
    With the title of the 6th ed., which is retained in all the later issues.

125. —— —— Boston, L. Coffin, 1843.
    119 p. 64 pl.   MH,NHi,OCl
    The wording of the later phrases of the title of this issue ". . . illustrated
    by sixty-four engravings, which exhibit the orders of architecture and
    other elements of the art: designed for the use of carpenters and builders,"
    is bewilderingly similar to that of the 1843 issue of *The builder's guide.*

126. —— —— Boston, L. Coffin, 1844.
    119 p. 64 pl.   MiD,NN,NHi

127. —— —— Boston, Benjamin B. Mussey, 1845.
    119 p. 64 pl.   IU,NHi

128. —— —— Boston, Benjamin B. Mussey, 1848.
    119 p. 64 pl.   NHi,PPL
    The first posthumous issue, with a new 1847 copyright.

129. —— —— Boston, Benjamin B. Mussey & co., 1850.
    119 p. 64 pl.   CtMW,MB,MH,MnU,NHi

130. —— —— Boston, Benjamin B. Mussey & co., 1851.
    119 p. 64 pl.   DLC,ICA-B

131. —— —— Boston, Benjamin B. Mussey & co., 1853.
    119 p. 64 pl.   MWA,MoS,NB

132. —— —— Boston, Benjamin B. Mussey & co., 1854.
    119 p. 64 pl.   PPM

133. —— —— Boston, Sanborn, Carter and Bazin, Portland, Sanborn and Carter,
    1856.
    119 p. 64 pl.   MH

134. —— —— Boston, Sanborn, Carter, Bazin and co., n.d.
    119 p. 63 pl.   MdBP
    This still carries the 1847 copyright. The form of the firm name: San-
    born, Carter, Bazin and co., makes all but certain that the date of issue
    was 1857.

135. —— Practice of architecture. Containing the five orders of architecture and
    an additional column and entablature, with all their elements and details
    explained and illustrated. For the use of carpenters and practical men . . .
    Boston, The author, and Carter, Hendie & co., New York, Collins and co.,
    1833.
    116 p. 60 pl.   DLC,MBAt,MWA,NHi,NNC-A,NNCoo
    Greek orders and exterior and interior trim, plans, elevations, and details
    of a Doric church on plates 51–56.

136. —— —— 2d ed. Boston, The author, and Carter, Hendie, co., New York,
    Collins & co. and Bliss & Wadsworth, 1835.
    116 p. 60 pl.   CSmH,MB,MiU,NN (imp.)

137. —— —— 3d ed. Boston, Benjamin B. Mussey, Philadelphia, Desilver, Thomas
    & co., 1836.
    116 p. 61 pl.   IU,PU
    "With alterations and improvements," and a new 1836 copyright. An
    added plate A between plates 44 and 45 shows "Four additional designs
    for base mouldings."

Benjamin, Asher

138. Practice of architecture . . . 4th ed. Boston, Benjamin B. Mussey, 1839.
116 p. 61 pl.   ICA-B

139. —— —— 4th ed. Boston, Perkins and Marvin, Philadelphia, H. Perkins, 1840.
96 p. 61 pl.   DLC,NHi

140. —— —— 5th ed. Boston, John P. Hill, Philadelphia, Thomas Cowperthwait
& co., New York, Pratt, Woodford & co., Collins, brother & co., and Huntington & Savage, Baltimore, Cushing & brother, 1847.
96 p. 61 pl.   NN
The first posthumous issue. The NN copy contains two plates 57.

142. —— —— 7th ed. Boston, Benjamin B. Mussey & co., 1851.
92 p. 61 pl.   DLC
With a new copyright of 1851. Plate A is between plates 43 and 44. No
copies of the presumptive 6th edition have been located.

143. —— The rudiments of architecture; being a treatise on practical geometry, on
Grecian and Roman mouldings: showing the best method of drawing their
curves, with remarks on the effects of both. Also on the origin of building,
on the five orders of architecture, on their general and particular parts and
embellishments; with examples for cornices, base and surbase mouldings, architraves, and stairs . . . Boston, printed for the author by Munroe and Francis, 1814.
96 p. 32 pl. (1 fold.)   ICA-B,MB,MBAt,MH,MWA,NjP,
NHi,NN,NNC-A
Benjamin's third work in chronological order.
Includes two designs for doorways.

144. —— —— 2d ed. enl. Boston, R. P. & C. Williams, 1820.
96 p. 35 pl. (2 fold.)   IU,MBAt,MH,MWA,NHi,
NNC-A,PP,PU-F,RPJCB
"With a plan and elevations of a church" on the three added plates.

145. Berg, Walter Gilman, 1858-1908
Buildings and structures of American railroads . . . New York, John Wiley
& sons, inc., 1893.
500 p. illus.   CU,DLC,ICJ,MB,MdBE,MnU,NN,
NNC,OCl,OU,PP

146. Bergh, Louis de Coppet
Safe building. A treatise giving in the simplest forms possible the practical and theoretical rules and formulae used in the construction of buildings . . . Volume one. Boston, Ticknor and company, 1889.
271 p. illus., pl., 25 tables (part fold.)   DLC,IU,MB,MH,MdBE,
NNC,PPFrankl
Bergh's name is sometimes given as Berg.

147. —— —— 2d ed. rev. Boston, Ticknor and company, 1890.
271 p. illus., pl., 25 tables (part fold.)   ICA-B,IU,MB,MH,PP

148. —— —— 3d ed. Boston, Ticknor and company, 1892.
271 p. illus., pl., 25 tables (part fold.)   MdBE

149. —— —— 4th ed. Boston, Ticknor and company, 1892.
271 p. illus., pl., 25 tables (part fold.)   PPD,RIBA
There may have been a later issue of the 4th edition in 1894.

150. —— Safe building . . . Volume two. Boston, Ticknor and company, 1892.
279 p. illus., pl., 18 tables (part fold.)   DLC,ICA-B,IU,MH,MdBE,PP
The DLC entry for Safe building only gives: Boston, Ticknor and company, 1889-92, 2 v., equivalent to items 146 & 150 here.

151. Bicknell, Amos Jackson
Bicknell's Cottage & villa architecture, containing sixty-six plates of wood-en and brick buildings with details . . . New York, A. J. Bicknell & co., 1878.
26 p. front., 66 pl.   DLC,MB,NNC-A,PP,PPL
This is a new edition of the first 66 plates of Bicknell's *Wooden and brick buildings*, 1875. The next four titles include the rest of that ma-terial, originally issued as a single work in 2 volumes with 160 plates in all, now reissued as five separate works, but with the original plate numbers.

152. —— —— New York, William T. Comstock, 1881.
28 p. front., 66 pl.   DLC

153. —— Bicknell's Public buildings, Containing twenty-one plates (90 to 108 and 133 and 135) wooden and brick buildings, with details. Showing libraries, town hall, masonic hall, hotels . . . Designs and details to scale. New York, A. J. Bicknell & co., 1878.
6 l. 22 pl. (1 fold.)   DLC,ICJ,MnU,NNC-A,PPM

154. —— Bicknell's School house and church architecture. Containing twenty-three plates (109 to 132) wooden and brick buildings with details . . . Designs and details to scale. New York, A. J. Bicknell & co., 1878.
3 l. 24 pl.   DLC,MWA,PP

155. —— Bicknell's Stables, out buildings, fences and miscellaneous details. Con-taining twenty-four plates (136–160) wooden and brick buildings with de-tails . . . Also, summer houses, sea side cottages . . . New York, A. J. Bick-nell & co., 1878.
6 l. 25 pl. (1 fold.)   DLC,PP

156. —— —— New York, Bicknell & Comstock, n. d.
6 l. 25 pl. (1 fold.)   ICJ,MWA
With the 1877 copyright. The Bicknell & Comstock imprint suggests a date of issue of 1879 or 1880, the only years in which this firm name was used.

157. —— Bicknell's Street, store & bank fronts, containing twenty-two plates (67 to 89) wooden and brick buildings, with details. Showing thirty-four designs for street fronts for dwellings, stores, and banks including several plates of details. Designs and details to scale. New York, A. J. Bicknell & co., 1878.
4 l. front., 23 pl.   DLC,ICJ,MH

158. —— —— New York, William T. Comstock, n. d.
4 l. front., 23 pl.   OO
With the 1877 copyright. The Comstock imprint suggests a date of 1881 or later.

159. —— Bicknell's Village builder. Elevations and plans for cottages, villas, sub-urban residences, farm houses . . . also exterior and interior details for public and private buildings, with approved forms of contracts and specifications . . . Troy, N. Y. and Springfield, Ill., A. J. Bicknell, 1870.
[44] p. front., 54 pl.   DLC,IU,MB,MWA,NN,NNC-A,
                                                             NNMM,PP
Bicknell's earliest work.

160. —— —— rev. ed. New York, A. J. Bicknell & co., 1872.
[44] p. front., 55 (i.e., 56) pl.   DLC,ICA-B,ICJ,OCl
"With three additional plates and a variety of details." The *Supplement to Bicknell's Village builder*, q.v., is usually bound with this edition with half-title: Bicknell's Village builder and Supplement; but not apparently in the DLC copy.

Bicknell, Amos Jackson

161. Bicknell's Village builder . . . rev. ed. New York, A. J. Bicknell & co., 1874.
     [42] p. front., 55 (i.e., 56) pl.   MBHo,MiD
     The *Supplement* is often bound with this issue with the half-title as in
     the edition above.

163. —— —— 5th ed. New York, A. J. Bicknell & co., 1878.
     [57] p. front., 76 pl. (1 col.)   DLC,ICJ
     Half-title: Bicknell's Village builder and Supplement. Supplement has
     separate t.-p. This edition regularly incorporates the *Supplement*, q.v.,
     as is not the case with all copies of the 1872 and 1874 editions. It is not
     clear whether there was a [4th] edition.

164. —— Detail, cottage and constructive architecture . . . showing a great variety
     of designs for cornices, brackets, windows, window caps, doors, piazzas . . .
     New York, A. J. Bicknell & co., [1873].
     2 p. l. front., 75 pl.   CtY,DLC,MB,MnM,NNC-A,
                            NNMM,OU,PPM

165. —— —— New York, William T. Comstock, 1873.
     2 p. l. front., 75 pl.   CtHWatk,DLC,IU,MB,MWA,
                                MiD,NN,PPSt
     With the 1873 copyright. The Comstock imprint ordinarily suggests a
     date of 1881 or later.

170. —— —— 7th ed. New York, William T. Comstock, c. 1886.
     2 p. l. front., 75 pl.   NNC-A
     No copies of the four presumptive issues between those of 1873 and this
     have been located. This edition is frequently listed under Comstock rather
     than Bicknell as it does not carry Bicknell's name at all.

171. —— Specimen book of one hundred architectural designs, showing plans, ele-
     vations and views of suburban houses, villas, seaside and camp-ground cot-
     tages, homesteads, churches and public buildings, also several original designs
     for modern styles of mantels and furniture, prepared especially for this
     work . . . New York, A. J. Bicknell & co., 1878.
     80 p. incl. advert., front., illus.   ICA-B,MB

172. —— —— New York, A. J. Bicknell & co., 1879.
     80 p. incl. advert., front., illus.   CtY

173. —— —— New York, Bicknell & Comstock, 1880.
     80 p. incl. advert., front., illus.   IU

174. —— Supplement to Bicknell's Village builder, containing eighteen modern de-
     signs for country and suburban houses of moderate cost with elevations,
     plans, sections, and a variety of details, all drawn to scale, also, a full set
     of specifications, with approved form of contract, and estimates of cost.
     New York, A. J. Bicknell & co. [c1871].
     2 p. l. [7] p. 20 pl.   CtY,DLC,MB,MH,MiD,MiU,NHi,
                            NNCoo,OCl
     Usually bound with the 1872 and 1874 editions of *Bicknell's Village builder*
     with half title: Bicknell's Village builder and Supplement. It is collated
     by the DLC as incorporated with the 1878 edition but is apparently no
     less regularly incorporated with most copies of the 1872 and 1874 editions.

175. —— Wooden and brick buildings, with details, published under the direction
     of A. J. Bicknell, containing one hundred and sixty plates, plans, elevations,
     views, sections and details of villas, cottages, farm houses, country seats,
     street fronts for dwellings . . . New York, A. J. Bicknell & co., 1875.
     2 v. fronts., 160 pl. (2 double)   CtHWatk (v. 2 only), CtY (v. 2 only),
                           DLC,ICA-B,ICJ,IU,M,MBAt,MH,
                           MWA,MdBP,MiD,NN,OU,PP,PPD

Bicknell, Amos Jackson

Bicknell's Cottage & *villa architecture*: *Bicknell's Public buildings*: *Bicknell's School house and church architecture; Bicknell's Stables and out buildings;* and *Bicknell's Street, store and bank fronts,* constitute together an 1878 edition of this work, the total of their numbered plates equaling the original 160 and carrying the same plate numbers.

176. Biddle, Owen, 1774–1806
The young carpenter's assistant, or A system of architecture, adapted to the style of building in the United States . . . Philadelphia, printed and sold by Benjamin Johnson, 1805.

64 p. 44 pl. (2 fold.)   MH (imp.),MWA,NHi,NNCo,NNMM,PP,
PPCC,PPL,Vi

The last two pages give "Subscribers' names." Biddle is described on the title page as "House carpenter and teacher of architectural drawing." A native-born American, like Benjamin, Biddle emphasizes in his title that his book is especially suited for American use, and that there is by this time "a style of building in the United States" distinguishable from that of England. Benjamin imitated this title the next year in that of the first edition of the *American builder's companion.*

177. —— —— Philadelphia, Johnson and Warner, 1810.

61 p. 44 pl. (2 fold.)   ICA-B (imp.),MB,MWA,NHi,PPPM

The subscribers' names are omitted. This was "sold at [Johnson and Warner's] bookstores in Philadelphia; Richmond, Virginia, and Lexington, Kentucky," but it is hardly to be considered a southern imprint. The first posthumous issue.

178. —— —— Philadelphia, Johnson and Warner, 1815.

61 p. 44 pl. (2 fold.)   CtY,NNC-A,NHi

". . . sold at [Johnson and Warner's] bookstores in Philadelphia, and Richmond, Virginia."

179. —— —— Philadelphia, Benjamin Warner, 1817.

61 p. 44 pl. (2 fold.)   NNSo,NHi

". . . sold at [Warner's] bookstores in Philadelphia, and Richmond, Virginia."

180. —— —— Philadelphia, McCarty and Davis, 1833.

52 p. 64 pl. (2 fold.)   NHi,PPCC

With a new 1833 copyright and title: *An improved and enlarged edition of Biddle's Young carpenter's assistant,* being a complete system of architecture for carpenters, joiners, and workmen in general, adapted to the style of building in the United States. Revised and corrected, with several additional articles and forty-eight new designs, chiefly of full size working drawings of modern finish, in detail. Particularly adapted for country use by John Haviland, architect. With a new preface by Haviland, dated 1833. Plates 15–20, 25–28, 31, 32, and 53–60 are by Haviland. In addition to "modern finish" they illustrate a church, a prison, a house, and a bank.

181. —— —— Philadelphia, McCarty and Davis, 1837.

52 p. 64 pl. (2 fold.)   NNC-A

182. —— —— Philadelphia, M. Polock, 1854.

52 p. 64 pl. (2 fold.)   MoS

183. —— —— Philadelphia, M. Polock, 1858.

52 p. 64 pl. (2 fold.)   MH

With the 1837 title and the 1833 copyright. Like Benjamin's books, this work of a rival remained in circulation down into the fifties.

184. Binion, Samuel Augustus, 1824–1914
    Ancient Egypt or Mizraim . . . profusely illustrated with fine engravings
    and colored plates by the best artists from the work of L'expédition de
    l'Egypte . . . New York, Henry G. Allen and company [1887].
    4 pts. in 2 v. pl.   DLC,ICA-R,MB,MoS,NN,NNC-A,
                                          NNMM,OCi,OO,PP,PU
    "Edition de luxe" limited to 800 copies. There is a variant issue pub-
    lished by the American Polytechnic company (limited) Buffalo, N. Y.,
    with the same copyright. This was also an "edition de luxe" but limited
    to 2000 instead of 800 copies. DLC and NN have both issues, but it is
    not entirely clear which the other holders have; some, indeed, may have
    one volume of one issue and the second of the other.

185. Birkmire, William Harvey, 1860–
    Architectural iron and steel, and its application in the construction of build-
    ings . . . with specification of iron-work. And selected papers in relation to
    ironwork, from a revision of the present law before the legislature, affecting
    the public interests in the city of New York . . . New York, John Wiley and
    sons, 1891.
        201 p. illus., tables   CtY,DLC,IU,InI,MnM,PPFrankl

186. —— —— 2d ed. New York, John Wiley and sons, 1892.
        201 p. illus., tables   DLC,MB,MnU,NN

187. —— —— 3d ed. New York, John Wiley and sons, 1894.
        201 p. illus., tables   ICA-B,ICJ,MH
    There were later issues of the 3d ed.

188. —— Compound rivetted girders, as applied in the construction of buildings . . .
    New York, John Wiley & sons, 1893.
        117 p. illus., tables, diagrs.   CU,CtTY,DLC,IU,MB,MH,MoS,OU

189. —— Skeleton construction in buildings. With numerous practical illustrations of
    high buildings . . . New York, John Wiley & sons, 1893.
        187 p. illus., tables, diagrs.   DLC,IU,MB,MH,MoS,MWA,NN,
                                          NNMM,PP,RIBA

190. —— —— 2d ed. New York, John Wiley & sons, 1894.
        237 p. illus., tables, diagrs.   DLC,ICJ,MnU,OU,PP

191. *Blenkarn, John
    Practical specifications of works executed in architecture, civil and me-
    chanical engineering and in road making and sewering . . . Philadelphia, Henry
    Carey Baird, 1868.
        416 p. 15 pl.   MH,OCl
    The original 1865 Spon edition is omitted as not properly an American
    imprint.

192. Bloor, Alfred Janson, 1828–1917
    The architectural and other art societies of Europe . . . New York [Ameri-
    can institute of architects] Committee on library and publications, 1869.
        62 p. illus.   DLC,MB,MH,MSaE,MWA,NN,
                                          NNC-A,PPFrankl,RIBA

193. —— Report of A. J. Bloor, delegate of the New York chapter of the American
    institute of architects to the twenty-fifth annual convention of the insti-
    tute, held in Boston, October 28, 29, 30, 1891. New York, Press of Isaac
    Blanchard, 1891.

                                          NN

—— —— New York, 1893.
        39 p.   NNC-A
    Title refers to twenty-sixth annual convention held in Chicago, October
    20, 1892.

194. Board of church erection
Church plans of the board of church erection. New York, Board of Church Erection, 1882.
55 p. illus. MSaE

Bogardus, James
See Thomson, John W.

195. Boston. Architectural association
Sketch book of the Architectural association of Boston . . . [Boston?] 1883.
2 p. 35 pl. ICA-B,MH,PP
300 copies printed of the first issue.

196. Boston architectural club
Catalogue of the first annual exhibition of the Boston architectural club. Boston, 1890.
51, 50 p. 48 pl. MB,MH,MWA,NN,NNC-A

197. —— —— [Boston] 1890.
1 p. 30 pl. ICA-B,MnU
500 copies printed; 1891 copyright.

198. —— —— Boston, 1891.
39 p. 51 p. of pl. MB,MH,NNC-A

199. Boston. City Council
Digest of statutes and ordinances relating to the inspection and construction of buildings in the city of Boston. Boston, 1887.
75 p. MWA,OO

200. —— Re-dedication of the Old State house, Boston, July 11, 1882. 6th ed.
Boston, Rodswell and Churchill, city printers, 1893.
236 p. front., illus., pl. ICA-B

201. Boston. Committee on public buildings.
The City hall, Boston. Corner stone laid, Monday, December 22, 1862. Dedicated, Monday, September 17, 1865. Boston, Printed by authority of the City council, 1866.
vii, 130 p. front., pl. (part fold.) NNC-A

202. Boston Public library
Catalogue of books relating to architecture, construction and decoration . . . Boston, The Trustees, 1894.
150 p. DLC,MB,MH,MnU,NN,OO, PP,RIBA
At head of title: Subject catalogue no. 10.

203. Boston Society of Architects
Constitution and by-laws of the Boston society of architects with a list of the officers and members of the society and other matters of interest to its members, March, 1887. Boston, Alfred Mudge and son, 1887.
MH

204. —— First architectural exhibition under the auspices of the Boston society of architects. Boston, Art club gallery, 1886.
31 p. illus. MH

205. Bowen, James H
. . . Report on buildings, building materials, and methods of building . . . Washington, Government Printing Office, 1869.
96 p. illus. DLC,MB,MH,MiU,MnU,MWA, NN,NNC,PP

18

Bowen, James H
> At head of title: Paris universal exposition, 1867; Reports of the United
> States Commissioners. In: *U.S. Commission to the Paris exposition, 1867.*
> *Reports of the U. S. Commissioners.* Washington [1868–70.] v. 4 [pt. 2].

206. Bowler, George
> Chapel and church architecture, with designs for parsonages . . . Boston,
> John P. Jewett and company; Cleveland, Ohio, Jewett, Proctor and Worth-
> ington; New York, Sheldon, Blakeman & co., 1856.
>> 15 p. 17 l. 41. 6 pl.   DLC,ICA-B,ICJ,MB,MH,MoS,
>>   MWA,NjP,NN,OO,PPFrankl
> Added lithographic title page in colors.

207. Boyd, Ellen Wright, 1883–
> English cathedrals: their architecture, symbolism and history . . . New York,
> Thomas Whittaker, 1884.
>> 63 p. front., illus.   CtY,DLC,MH,MiD,OCl,PP,PPL

209. —— ——— 3d ed. rev. New York, Thomas Whittaker, 1888.
>> 68 p. front., illus.   MB,NN,RPD
> No copy of the presumptive 2d ed. has been located.

210. —— ——— 4th ed. New York, Thomas Whittaker, 1892.
>> 68 p. front., illus.   NPV

211. Bremer, Fredrika
> The homes of the new world . . . New York, Harper & bros., 1853, 1854.
>> 2 v.   MH

212. Bridges, Lyman
> Report on the buildings of the exhibition and on the railroad structures . . .
> Washington, Government Printing Office, 1876.
>> 34 p. pl.   DLC,MB,MH,MWA,MiU,
>>   MnU,NN,NNC,OO
> At head of title: Vienna international exhibition, 1873.
> *In*: *U. S. Commission to the Vienna exhibition, 1873. Reports, 1875–76.*
> v. 4 Aa

Bridport, Hugh
> *See* Haviland, John

213. Brown, Glenn, 1854–
> Healthy foundations for houses . . . New York, D. Van Nostrand, 1885.
>> 143 p. illus.   DLC,ICJ,IU,MB,MH,MiH,
>>   NN,NNC,PP,PPFrankl,RIBA
> Reprinted from *The sanitary engineer.*

214. Brown, William, of Lowell
> The carpenter's assistant; containing a succinct account of Egyptian, Gre-
> cian, and Roman architecture; also, a description of the Tuscan, Doric, Ionic,
> Corinthian and composite orders; together with specifications, practical rules
> and tables for carpenters, and a glossary of architectural terms. Illustrated
> with upwards of fifty plates, embracing plans, elevations, details, &c. for
> dwelling-houses . . . Worcester, Edward Livermore, Boston, Benjamin B.
> Mussey & co., Phillips & Simpson, New York, Pratt, Woodford & co., A. S.
> Barnes & co., Lowell, D. Bixby & co., 1848.
>> 140 p. front., illus., 53 pl.   MW,NNC-A,NHi

215. —— ——— 2d ed. Worcester, Edward Livermore [etc.], 1848.
>> 140 p. front., illus., 53 pl.   MdBP,NNC-A,NHi,OO

Brown, William, of Lowell
217. The carpenter's assistant . . . 4th ed. Worcester, Edward Livermore [etc.], 1851.
   140 p. front., illus., 53 pl.   ICA-B,MH,MWA
   "revised, improved and enlarged, with additions on rural architecture; embracing plans, elevations, grounds, &c., &c., of cottages, villas, and farm buildings; including new and valuable designs for church edifices. By Lewis E. Joy, architect."
   Thomas Cowperthwait & co., Philadelphia, and George H. Derby & co., Buffalo, take the place of D. Bixby & co., Lowell, among the publishers. With a new copyright.
   No copies of the presumptive 3d edition have been located.

218. —— —— 20th thousand. Boston, Edward Livermore, 1853.
   148 p. front., illus., 75 pl.   H.R.H.

219. —— —— Boston, Edward Livermore, 1854.
   148 p. front., illus., 75 pl.   CSmH,MSaE

220. —— —— 20th thousand. New York, Livermore & Rudd, 1856.
   148 p. front., illus., 73 pl.   MH

221. Brunner, Arnold William, 1857–1925
   Cottages; or, Hints on economical building, containing twenty-four plates of medium and low cost houses, contributed by different New York architects. Together with descriptive letterpress, giving practical suggestions for cottage building . . . New York, William T. Comstock, 1884.
   54 p. front., 23 pl.   CtMW,DLC,ICJ,MB,MH,NjP,
              NNC-A,NNCoo,OCi,OCl,PP,PPFrankl,RIBA
   "To which is added a chapter on the water supply, drainage, sewerage, heating and ventilation, and other sanitary questions relating to country houses. By William Paul Gerhard, C. E."
   Gerhard wrote books on similar technical topics, which are not included in this list.

225. —— —— 5th ed. New York, William T. Comstock, 1890.
   54 p. front., 23 pl.   CU,MdBE,MnM,NN,PP
   No copies of the presumptive 2d, 3d, and 4th editions have been located.

226. —— Interior decoration . . . New York, Wm. T. Comstock, 1887.
   65 p. front., illus., 15 pl.   DLC,IU,InI,MB,MH,MnM,MWA,
              MoS,NNC,PPL-R
   Thomas Tryon was joint author of this work, probably the first to bear a popular twentieth-century title.

227. —— —— 2d ed. New York, William T. Comstock, 1891.
   65 p. front., illus., 15 pl.   NN,NNC-A

228. *Brunton, Robert
   A compendium of mechanics; or, Textbook for engineers . . . New York, G. & C. & H. Carvill, 1830.
   228 p. 5 pl.   DLC,MB,MH,MnU,NN,NWM,PPM
   "Edited from the 4th London edition by J. Renwick."
   First appeared Glasgow, 1824.

229. Bryan, A   J
   Architectural proportion . . . A new system of proportion showing the relation between an order of architecture and a building of any kind . . . San Francisco, A. L. Bancroft & co., 1880.
   3 p. l. 5–33 numb. l. incl. 10 pl.   CU,DLC,MnM,NN,NNC-A,PSt

230. Buck, C   C
Buck's designs in architecture showing a variety of designs, together with a
large amount of miscellaneous matter . . . Brooklyn, N. Y., The author, n. d.
　　71 p. illus.　　　　　　　　　　　　　　MB,NNC-A,NNCoo,PPl
　　Probably issued in the eighties.

231. —— Album of mantels in wood, stone, slate & brick . . . original designs . . .
New York, J. O'Kane, 1883.
　　2 p. l. 60 pl.　　　　　　　　　　　　　DLC,NNC-A,NNMM

Buck, John Henry
See Description of drawings for . . . Saint John the divine

Bucknall, Benjamin
See Viollet-le-Duc, Eugene Emmanuel

232. Bulfinch, Charles, 1763–1844[1]
. . . Bulfinch on penitentiaries . . . Washington, printed by Gales & Seaton,
1827.
　　8 p.　　　　　　　　　　　　　　　　　DLC,MH,MWA,PP
　　[U. S.] 19th Congress 2d session. House Report. 98.

233. —— . . . Memorial of Charles Bulfinch on the subject of the house of repre-
sentatives . . . Washington, 1830.
　　11 p.　　　　　　　　　　　　　　　　　DLC,MWA,PP
　　[U. S.] 21st Congress 1st session. House Report. 123.
　　Usually entered under: U. S. Architect of the capitol.

234. —— [Statement of Charles Bulfinch on the construction and the physical and
moral effects of penitentiary prisons of the Auburn type] Washington, D.
Green, printer, 1829.
　　8 p.　　　　　　　　　　　　　　　　　DLC,NN
　　No title page. The text begins: "The subscriber . . . requests permission
　　. . . to present . . . a concise statement . . ." Very probably a new edi-
　　tion of *Bulfinch on penitentiaries* above.
　　Prison discipline pamphlets. v. 6. no. 7.

235. Bullock, John
The American cottage builder: a series of designs, plans, and specifications
from $200 to $20,000. For homes for the people . . . New York, Stringer
and Townsend, 1854.
　　326 p. front., illus., 21 pl.　　　　CtHWatk,DLC(imp.),ICJ,IU,MB,
　　　　　　　　　　　　　　MH,MWA,MoS,NN,NNC-A,NNMM, NPV,NWM,PP,PPL
　　Offered for sale by Fowlers and Wells for $1.75 in 1855.

236. —— —— new ed. rev. New York, Stringer & Townsend, 1854.
　　326 p. front., illus., 21 pl.　　　　　　　NHi

237. —— —— Philadelphia, Henry Carey Baird, 1868.
　　326 p. front., illus., 21 pl.　　　　　　　ICJ,NN

238. —— —— Philadelphia, Henry Carey Baird, 1873.
　　326 p. front., illus., 21 pl.　　　　　　　CU,WaU

239. —— The history and rudiments of architecture . . . New York, Stringer & Town-
send, 1853.
　　264, xiii p. illus.　　　　　　　　　　　CtY,DLC,ICJ,IU,MB,
　　　　　　　　　　　　　　　　　　　　　MWA,NN,NNC-A,PPM
　　"Edited by John Bullock." Contents: I. The orders, by W. H. Leeds; II.
　　Styles of various countries, by T. Bury; III. Design in architecture—
　　its principles, by E. L. Garbett; IV. Glossary of architectural terms, by
　　John Bullock. From the preface: "We have dealt freely with our au-
　　thors," in attempting to "americanize" the borrowed English material.
　　Offered by the publishers for 75 cents in 1854.

Bullock, John

240. The rudiments of the art of building represented in five sections. For the use of architects, builders, draughtsmen, machinists, engineers, and mechanics . . . New York, Stringer & Townsend, 1853.

    180 p. illus.   MiU,MoS,NN,OCi
    The contents: The general principles of construction; Materials used in building; Specifications and drawings, were taken from the writings of Edward Dobson, but doubtless "americanized" by Bullock as editor. Sometimes listed under Dobson.
    Offered by the publishers for 75 cents in 1854.

241. —— The rudiments of architecture and building, for the use of architects, builders, draughtsmen, machinists, engineers and mechanics . . . new ed. rev. New York, Stringer & Townsend, 1855.

    468 p. front., illus., 10 pl.   MB,MSaE,MdBP,NB,NHi,NPV,PPFrankl
    A new edition of the two preceding works containing I, II, III, and IV (here called V) from *The history and rudiments of architecture;* a new IV: Grecian monumental remains, taken from the *Art Journal*, and VI: The rudiments of the art of building.

242. —— —— [rev. ed.] Philadelphia, Henry Carey Baird, 1865.

    468, 24 p. front., illus., 10 pl.   IU,MH,MSaE,MWA, OCl,PP

243. —— —— [rev. ed.] Philadelphia, Henry Carey Baird, 1866.

    468 p. front., illus., 10 pl.   MnU, MoS,NNC-A

244. —— —— [rev. ed.] Philadelphia, H. C. Baird & co., 1888.

    468 p. front., illus., 10 pl.   MiH,OCl

245. Bunce, Oliver, 1828–1890

My house: an ideal . . . New York, Charles Scribner's sons, 1884.

    108 p.   ICJ,MB,MH,MSaE,NN,PPM
    Bunce also edited descriptive literature in the seventies and eighties not relevant here.

246. *Burn, Robert Scott

Model designs for mansions, villas, cottage residences, park entrances and lodges . . . New York, Virtue, Emmins, and Roberts, n. d.

    [8], 7–46, 18, [3]–24 p. illus., 179 pl. (1 fold.)   NNC-A,NHi
    First appeared London, 1853–61. This edition presumably followed shortly. Other works by Burn on *Building construction* of the seventies are not American imprints, and even this was printed abroad, though issued in New York.

247. Burnham, Daniel Hudson, 1846–1912

World's Columbian exposition. The book of the builders . . . Chicago, Columbian Memorial publication society, 1894–

    pts. illus., col. pl.   DLC,ICA-R,ICJ
    Francis Davis Millet was joint author. Publication of the parts extended beyond 1894. This is perhaps the best of the dozen or more publications on the architecture of the Chicago World's Fair of 1893 and the only one here listed. Most of the others exist in Chicago libraries. Perhaps *Official views of the World's Columbian Exposition*, C. D. Arnold, F. D. Higginbotham, Official photographers, Chicago, World's Columbian Exposition, 1893, also deserves specific mention.

248. Burr, William Hubert, 1851–1934

A course on the stresses in bridge and roof trusses, arched ribs and suspension bridges. New York, John Wiley & sons, 1880.

    344 p. 12 fold. pl.   DLC,IU,MB,MH,MoS,NNC,NjP
    Editions 2 through 9 before 1895.

Burr, William Hubert
249. The elasticity and resistance of the materials of engineering. New York, John Wiley & sons, 1883.
    753 p. diagrs.   DLC,IU,MnU,NNC,OO,PP
    Editions 2, 3, and 4 before 1895.

250. Burrowes, Thomas Henry, 1805–1871, *editor*
    . . . Pennsylvania school architecture . . . Harrisburg, printed by A. B. Hamilton, 1855.
    276 p. col. front., illus.   CtY,ICA-B,IU,MB,MBAt,
                                        MH,MnU,NN,NNC-A,PP
    At head of title: Pennsylvania Dept. of Public instruction. ". . . directions and plans for grading, locating, constructing, heating, ventilating and furnishing common school houses." Considering the publication date it is rather curious that the copyright is 1856.

251. Butler, William Frederick
    Ventilation of buildings . . . New York, D. Van Nostrand, 1873.
    77 p.   DLC,MB,MH,PPM,NN,NNC
    London edition the same year.

252. ——— ——— New York, D. Van Nostrand, 1885.
    147 p.   DLC,MWA,PPFrankl
    "Reëdited and enlarged by James L. Greenleaf."

253. Campin, Francis
    On the construction of iron roofs . . . New York, D. Van Nostrand, 1868.
    38 p. 8 pl.   CtY,IU,MH,MnU,NN,NNC,
                                        NNCoo,OU,PPFrankl
    First appeared London, 1866. Campin also wrote a *Practical treatise on mechanical engineering*, 1864.

254. Carpenter, James H.
    The complete house builder containing fifty plans and specifications of dwellings, barns, churches, public buildings . . . Chicago, Donohue, Henneberry & Co. [ᶜ1890].
    62, [116] p. illus.   DLC,NN

255. —— Hints on building . . . Hartford, Press of the Case, Lockwood & Brainard company, 1883.
    50 p.   CtHWatk,DLC,NN

256. Carrère and Hastings, *architects*
    Florida, the American Riviera, St. Augustine the winter Newport, Ponce de Leon, the Alcazar, the Casa Monica. New York, Gilliss brothers & Turnure, the Art age press, 1887.
    46 p. 11 pl. (incl. 3 fold.)   NNMM
    Advertising matter on 10 pages at rear.

257. Carstensen, Georg Johann Bernhard, 1812–1857
    The New York Crystal palace . . . New York, Riker, Thorne & co., 1854.
    76 p. 6 pl.   DLC,MBAt,MH,MnU,NN,NNC-A,
                                        NNCoo,NHi,NNMM,PP
    Charles Gildemeister was joint author.
    Among the other publications about this first American exposition, the most interesting is *The crystallotype*, New York, George P. Putnam's sons, 1855, the first American book to be illustrated with inserted photographs made from negatives. This was a second edition of Benjamin Silliman and C. R. Goodrich, *The world of science, art, and industry* . . . New York, G. P. Putnam and co., London, Sampson, Low, Son & co., 1854, which was illustrated by woodcuts only.

258. Chamberlain, Nathan Henry, 1830–1901
    A paper on New-England architecture, read before the New-England historic
    genealogical society, September 4, 1858 . . . Boston, Crosby, Nichols and
    company, 1858.
    In this edition the title begins: *The builder's assistant* . . .
    30 p.   CtY,DLC,ICA-B,IU,MB,MBAt,
                                             MH,MSaE,MWA,NN,NNC-A
    Chamberlain's *The autobiography of a New England farmhouse*, 1865, is a
    work of fiction rather than an architectural book, indeed the 1888 edition
    has the subtitle "a romance of the Cape Cod lands." This pamphlet of
    Chamberlain's is probably the first separate publication on colonial archi-
    tecture.

  Chamberlain, George Howard, 1868–
  See Dehli, Arne

259. Chandler, Francis Ward, 1844–1926
    Construction details . . . Boston, The Heliotype printing co. [1892].
    1 p. l. 25 pl.   CU,DLC,IU,MB,MH,MnU,NN,
                                             NNC-A,OCl,PP,PPFrankl,RIBA

260. Chandler, Joseph Everett
    The colonial architecture of Maryland, Pennsylvania and Virginia . . . Boston,
    Bates, Kimball & Guild, 1892.
    3 p. l. 50 pl.   DLC,ICA-B,IU,MB,MBAt,MH,
                                             MnM,NN,PPM,Vi
    There were later issues after 1895.

  Chapels and churches
  See Comstock, William Thompkins

261. Chase, C. Thurston
    A manual on schoolhouses and cottages for the people of the south . . .
    Washington, Government printing office, 1868.
    83 p. illus.   CtY,DLC,MBAt,MSaE,MWA,MiOC,
                                             MoS,NN,NNC,OU,PPFrankl
    Chase was also the author of magazine articles on similar topics.

262. Chicago architectural sketch club
    Catalogue of the annual exhibition . . . Chicago, Art Institute, May, 1894.
    Cover title, [57] p.   ICA-B,NN,NNC-A

263. —— Sketches . . . [Chicago, Press of Henry O. Shepard company, c1892]
    Cover title, 1 p. l. 33 pl.   ICA-B,NN

  Child, A   C
  See National architects' union

264. Childs, George William, 1829–1894
    The Public Ledger building, Philadelphia: with an account of the proceed-
    ings connected with its opening June 20, 1867. Philadelphia, George W.
    Childs, 1868.
    186 p. front., illus., 1 pl.   MB,NN,PPL

265. —— —— Philadelphia, George W. Childs, 1868.
    205 p. front., illus., 1 pl.   NN
    With a biography of the author.

266. Cincinnati architectural club
    Selections from the national exhibition of architectural drawings and sketches
    held at Cincinnati, November, 1889 . . . [Cincinnati architectural club,
    1869].
    48 pl.   MoS,NNC-A,OCi

Cincinnati architectural club
267. Selection of drawings and sketches . . . Cincinnati [Cincinnati architectural club, 1892–93].
    25 pl.   OCi

268. Civis, *pseud.*
The office of the supervising architect, what it was, what it is, and what it ought to be . . . New York, 1869.
    8 p.   NN

269. Clark, Alfred C.
The architect, decorator and furnisher. A publication for those who build, containing elaborate and plain designs of building, with description and cost of construction. Chicago, Cowdrey, Clark & co., 1884.
    [76] p. illus.   DLC
Advertising matter interspersed.

270. Clark, Theodore Minot, 1845–1909
Architect, owner and builder before the law . . . New York and London, Macmillan & co., 1894.
    387 p.   CU,DLC,MB,MH,NN,NNC-A,
                                            NNMM,NcD,OCl,PP,RIBA

271. —— . . . Rural school architecture . . . Washington, Government printing office, 1880.
    pp. 237–342 illus., 55 pl.   CSmH,CU,CtY,DLC,MB,MBAt,MH,
                                            MnU,MoS,NN,OCl,OU,PP,PU
At head of title: U. S. Bureau of education circulars of information, 1880, no. 4.
Clark was also the author of a popular work on *Building Superintendence,* Boston, Ticknor & co., 1883; of which there were many later editions through the 12th, 1894.

272. Cleaveland, Henry William
Village and farm cottages. The requirements of American village homes considered and suggested; with designs for such houses of moderate cost . . . New York, D. Appleton & company, 1856.
    xii, 189 p. illus., 23 pl., incl. front.   CU,DLC,ICA-B,ICJ,IU,MB,
                                     MBAt,MBHo,MH,MnU,MSaE,MWA,MdBP,
                                     NcD,NN,NNC-A,NHi,NPV,OCi,OCl,PP,PPL
Added engraved title page.
William Backus and Samuel D. Backus were joint authors.

273. —— —— New York, D. Appleton and company, 1864.
    xii, 189 p. illus., 23 pl., incl. front.   CtY,DP,MB,MSaE,MoS,PU
Also has the added engraved title page, dated 1856, of the original issue.

274. —— —— New York, D. Appleton and company, 1866.
    xii, 189 p. illus., 23 pl., incl. front.   .DP,MB
With the same added engraved title page as the two earlier issues.

275. —— —— New York, D. Appleton and company, 1869.
    xii, 189 p. illus., 23 pl., incl. front.   .MSaE,MnM,Vi

276. Cleveland educational bureau
. . . House materials with hints about homes. Cleveland, Cleveland educational bureau, 1882.
    pp. [79]–111   NN,OO
At head of title: Cleveland educational bureau. Books for the people . . . Series 2, no. 3.

Cobb, Albert Winslow
See Stevens, John Calvin

277. Colburn, Zerah
      American iron bridges . . . New York, D. Van Nostrand, 1867.
         15 p. 1 pl.   IU,OCi
         Reprinted from *Minutes of proceedings,* Institution of civil engineers, London, Session of 1862–63.
         Bound in the same cover: Historical sketch of the great suspension bridge, connecting Covington and Cincinnati . . . compiled from official sources, to which is added correct and interesting descriptions of the Niagara suspension bridge and the proposed New York and Brooklyn bridge, Cincinnati, T. J. Smith & co., 31 p.

278. Comstock, William Thompkins,   , *comp.*
      American cottages consisting of forty-four large quarto plates, containing original designs of medium and low cost cottages, seaside and country houses. Also a club-house, pavilion, school house, and a small seaside chapel together with a form of specification for cottages. All in the latest prevailing styles, from the drawings of a number of prominent architects, thus securing a great variety of plans and diversity of treatment and offering the largest opportunity for selection. New York, William T. Comstock, ᶜ1883.
         2 p. l. front., 43 pl.   CtY,DLC,MB,MH,MoS,NjP,OCl,PP
         [2] p. of a *Specification for a low-priced frame cottage* by Wm. B. Tuthill are inserted between plates xxxi and xxxii.

      —— —— Architectural studies.
      See Wright, Frank Ayes
         Separately held volumes and parts of this work are particularly likely to be entered under Comstock.

      —— —— Detail, cottages and constructive architecture.
      See Bicknell, Amos J.
         The 1886 edition of this work is particularly likely to be entered under Comstock as it does not carry Bicknell's name at all.

279. —— Modern architectural designs and details containing eighty finely lithographed plates, showing new and original designs in the Queen Anne, Eastlake, Elizabethan, and other modernized styles, giving perspective views, floor and framing plans, elevations, sections and a great variety of miscellaneous exterior and interior details of dwellings of moderate cost. Also, a number of designs of low-priced cottages in the various popular styles, adapted to the requirements of seaside and summer resorts, and suburban and country places. Also, several for modern store and office fronts, counters, shelvings, etc., etc., comprising original drawings by a number of prominent architects of different localities, prepared expressly for this work. All elevations, plans and details to scale. New York, William T. Comstock [ᶜ1881].
         4 p. l. 80 pl.   DLC,IU,MB,MiGr,MnM,NjP,NNC-A,
                                            NNCoo,NNMM,OCi,OU,PP,PPM
      Published in four parts.

280. —— Selected details of interior and exterior finish for architects, carpenters and builders . . . New York, William T. Comstock, 1890.
         2 p. l. 32 pl.   DLC,ICJ,InI,MB

281. Conant, William Cowper
      . . . The Brooklyn bridge. A history of the bridge. By W. C. Conant. (Reprinted from Harper's magazine for May, 1883.) The bridge as a monument. By Montgomery Schuyler. (Reprinted from Harper's weekly, May 27, 1883.) Together with an account of the opening exercises, May 24, 1883. New York, Harper & brothers, n.d.
         36 p. incl. illus., 8 pl.   DLC,MB,NHi,NjP,PPM
         At head of title: Harper's Franklin square library, Number 321.
         Presumably issued shortly after the 1883 opening of the bridge.

282. Congregational churches in the U.S. General convention.
A book of plans for churches and parsonages . . . comprising designs by Upjohn, Renwick,Wheeler, Downing . . . New York, Daniel Burgess & co., 1853.
58 p. illus., 45 pl. (part col.)   MSaE,MH,MWA,NN,NNC-A,NNMM
At head of title: General congregational convention. *Upjohn's Rural architecture*, 1852, had the same sponsorship.

283. —— —— New York, Daniel Burgess & co., 1854.
58 p. illus., 45 pl. (part col.)   NNC,OO

284. Conway, Moncure Daniel, 1832–1917
Travels in South Kensington, with notes on decorative art and architecture in England . . . New York, Harper & brothers, 1882.
234 p. incl. front., illus., 3 pl.   CtMW,DLC,ICA-R,MH,MWA,
                          MnM,MoS,NNC-A,NNMM,OCi,PP,PPL,Vi
London edition the same year.

285. Cook, Clarence
What shall we do with our walls? New York, Warren, Fuller & co., 1881.
35 p. 5 pl.   NNMM
Cook's *The house beautiful*, New York, Scribner, Armstrong and co., 1878, is concerned with furniture.

Cooperative building plan association
See Shoppell, Robert W.

286. Corfield, William Henry, 1843–1903
Dwelling houses, their sanitary construction . . . New York, D. Van Nostrand, 1880.
156 p.   ICJ,MB,MH,MdBP,MiH,MnU,NN,
                        NNC-A,OCl,OU,PPFrankl,ViU

287. Corner, James M
. . . Examples of domestic colonial architecture in New England . . . Boston, Boston architectural club, 1891.
3 p. l. 50 pl.   CtMW,CtY,DLC,MB,MBAt,MSaE,MoS,NN,
                              NNMM,OO,PPL
Eric Ellis Soderholtz was joint compiler and photographer.

289. —— —— 3d ed. Boston, Boston architectural club, 1892.
3 p. l. 50 pl.   NN,NNC-A
No copies of the presumptive 2d edition have been located.

290. —— . . . Examples of domestic colonial architecture in Maryland and Virginia . . . Boston, Boston architectural club, 1892.
3 p. l. 50 pl.   CtMW,CtY,DLC,ICA-B,MBAt,MSaE,NN,
                            NNC-A,NNMM
Eric Ellis Soderholtz was joint compiler and photographer.

291. —— —— 2d ed. Boston, The authors, 1892.
3 p. l. 51 pl.   CtHWatk,MdBE,NHi,NN,NNC-A
Soderholtz, together with Edward Andrew Crane, bought out a further volume in this series: *Examples of colonial architecture in Charleston, S. C. and Savannah, Ga.*, New York, Hessling & Spielmeyer, 1895. These works, together with Joseph Everett Chandler's, above, provided apparently the first photographic documentation of colonial architecture in book form.

292. *Corroyer, Edouard Jules, 1837?–1904
    Gothic architecture . . . New York, The Macmillan co., 1893.
        388 p. illus.   CtY,ICA-B,InI,MH,MnM,NNC-A,OCi,OCl,PPFrankl
        Translated by Florence Simonds.
        First appeared Paris, 1891. There was a London edition also in 1893, of
        which this American edition, printed in Edinburgh, is actually a part.

293. Croff, Gilbert Bostwick
    Model suburban architecture, embodying designs for dwellings of moderate
    cost, varying from $1400 to $5000 . . . New York, Roby & O'Neil, lithr.,
    c1870.
        3 p. l. 37 pl.   DLC,MWA

294. —— Original designs for front entrance doors, embracing a choice and elegant
    variety of front entrance doors, both double and single, of original concep-
    tion, of every grade, from the plain door for the cottage to the elegant and
    costly door for the mansion or villa, together with eighteen designs of interior
    architraves, also several designs of irregular interior, ornamental architraves
    and exterior entrance finish, canopies, &c. all of modern design . . . Saratoga
    Springs, N. Y. Lithg, engg & printg company, c1871.
        3 p. l. 22 pl.   CtHWatk,DLC,NN

295. —— Progressive American architecture, presenting in illustration an extensive
    collection of original studies for dwellings, bank, school and office build-
    ings, costing from one thousand to one hundred thousand dollars, also de-
    tails of every feature, exterior and interior . . . New York, Orange Judd
    company, c1875.
        2 p. l. 97 pl. (1 col.)   DLC,MB,MnU,NN,NNC-A,OCl,PPFrankl

296. Cummings, Marcus Fayette, 1836–
    Architecture. Designs for street fronts, suburban houses, and cottages, in-
    cluding details for both exterior and interior . . . comprising in all 382 de-
    signs and 714 illustrations . . . Troy, N.Y., Young & Benson, 1865.
        [50] p. 52 pl.   DLC,MB,MH,NNC-A,NHi,OCi
        Charles Crosby Miller, an architect in Toledo, Ohio, was joint author.
        Cummings was an architect in Troy.

297. —— —— 2d ed. Troy, N. Y., W. H. Young 1866.
        [50] p. 52 pl.   CU,CtHWatk,DLC,NN,NNMM,PPCC

298. —— —— 2d ed. Troy, N. Y., The authors, A. J. Bicknell, general agent, n.d.
        [50] p. 52 pl.   H.R.H.

299. —— —— 3d ed. Troy, N. Y., The authors, A. J. Bicknell, general agent, 1867.
        [50] p. 52 pl.   MSaE

300. —— —— 4th ed. Troy, N.Y., and Springfield, Ill., A. J. Bicknell & co., 1868.
        [50] p. 52 pl.   OO

303. —— —— 7th ed. Troy, N.Y., A. J. Bicknell & co., 1870.
        [50] p. 52 pl.   MnM,NjP
        No locations of the presumptive 5th and 6th editions have been reported.

304. —— —— 8th ed. New York, A. J. Bicknell & co., 1872.
        [50] p. 52 pl.   ICA-B,IU,NN

305. —— Cummings' Architectural details, containing 387 designs and 967 illustra-
    tions of the various parts needed in the construction of buildings, public and
    private, both for the city and country. Also plans and elevations of houses,
    stores, cottages, and other buildings . . . New York, Orange Judd & co.,
    1873.
        [60] p. 56 pl.   DLC,MB,MWA,NN,OU,PPFrankl

28

Cummings, Marcus Fayette
>Probably effectively a new edition of the item above with title changed, added plates, and the omission of Miller's name as joint author.
>There seem to have been later editions through a 5th in 1876, but no locations have been reported.

306. —— Modern American architecture. Designs and plans for villas, farm-houses, cottages, city residences, churches, school-houses, &c, &c. Containing fifty-five original plates giving in detail plans and illustrations suited to all parts of the country . . . Troy, N.Y., The authors, A. J. Bicknell, general agent, 1868.
>[38] p. front., 54 pl. CSmH,IU,MB,MWA,NNC-A,NNMM,OO
>Charles Crosby Miller was joint author.

306. —— —— Toledo, O. S. Bailey & co., 1868.
>[38] p. front., 54 pl. DLC,ICJ,MB,MWA

307. —— —— New York, A. J. Bicknell & co., n.d.
>[32] p. front., 54 pl. ICJ,MWA,NN
>With the same 1867 copyright as the issues above, but probably later than 1871 when Bicknell began to publish in New York.

308. Cutter, Manly N.
>The New York building plan co.'s illustrated catalogue of examples of buildings; their exterior and interior . . . [Boston, Rand, Avery company] ᶜ1887.
>[80] p. illus. DLC

309. —— Two years work in an architect's office, New York, A. L. Chatterton & co., 1894.
>204, [6] p. NHi

310. Cupper, R   A
>The universal stair-builder . . . New York, 1851.
>29 pl. MH

311. Cyclopedia of architectural illustrations . . . Boston, Ticknor and co., 1892?.
>10 v. 1000 pl. CtY,CtMW,ICA-B
>The undated 5 v. issue of this *Cyclopedia* is of 1895 or later, as is clear from the address, 211 Tremont Street, of Ticknor and co., the publishers.

312. Dabb, A   N
>Practical plans for district school houses, for the . . . guidance of school boards and officers . . . Philadelphia, J. A. Bancroft & co., ᶜ1874.
>16 p. illus. DLC

313. Davis, Alexander Jackson, 1803–1892
>Rural residences, etc., consisting of designs, original and selected, for cottages, farmhouses, villas, and village churches: with brief explanations, estimates, and a specification of materials, construction, etc. By Alexander Jackson Davis, Esq., and other architects. Published under the superintendence of several gentlemen, with a view to the improvement of American country architecture. New York: to be had of the architect, at the New York university, and of the booksellers generally, throughout the United States, 1837.
>(?) pts. CtY,MBAt,MdBP,MnU,NN,NNC-A,NHi(3 copies)
>It is doubtful if this work was ever completely issued.
>The collations of the holders do not agree.
>The MdBP collation is 19 unnumbered leaves, printed on one side only, including 7 lithographic plates. Front cover identical with title page; back cover: Published periodically. Each part contains four designs.
>The NN collation is 3 numbers (parts?) 8 p. 5 t.p. 30 designs.
>The MBAt copy is bound in a volume with hand-lettered title page: *Architectural scraps, etchings* (sic) & *drawings by Alex. J. Davis, N. Y.*

Davis, Alexander Jackson
There are 35 numbered leaves of which the title page as given above is No. 15, followed by four unnumbered leaves. Most of the plates are lithographs, not etchings, labeled Stodart & Currier's Lith. 137 Broadway, New York; but 18 to 30 are by Bufford. This is evidently a scrapbook, prepared by Davis, including presumably all that was issued by *Rural residences,* with additional related drawings.

The CtY copy and the three NHi copies have colored lithographs in the first part. One NHi copy has six additional plates at the end, as well as the four colored plates in the first part and the five plates in the second part, and also 16 pp. of "Specifications of the materials and works required for building a dwelling house."

The NNC-A copy is similar to the MBAt copy and has many additional plates.

,The NNMM possesses many, if not all, of the plates in their collection of Davis material, some untouched, many colored and otherwise changed by Davis' hand, but they are loose and not bound.

Davis, Noah Knowles, 1830–
See Nicholson, Peter

314. De Forest, Lockwood, 1850–
Indian architecture and ornament . . . Boston, Geo. H. Polley & co. [c1887].
3 p. l. 50 pl.   DLC,ICA-B,MB,MH,MnM,NNC-A.NNMM,PP

315. —— Indian domestic architecture . . . Boston, Heliotype printing co. [c1885].
3 p. l. 25 pl.   DLC,ICA-B,IU,MdBM,MH,MnM,MnU,MoS,
NN,NNC-A,NNMM,OO,PP

316. Dehli, Arne, 1857–
Norman monuments of Palermo and environs . . . Boston, Ticknor and company; London, B. T. Batsford; Liepsig (sic), Karl W. Hiersermann, [c1892].
30 p. 72 pl.   CtHWatk,DLC,ICA-B,MH,MiU,NjP,NN,NNC-A,RIBA
George Howard Chamberlain was joint author.

317. —— Selections of Byzantine ornament . . . New York, William Helburn, c1890.
2 v. in 1, 100 pl.   IU,MB,MnU,NN,NNC-A,NNMM,OU,PP

318. Derby, Nelson L
. . . Report on architecture and the materials of construction . . . Washington, Government printing office, 1875.
31 p.   DLC,MB, MH,MnU,MWA,MdBP,NNC-A,OO,PP
At head of title: Vienna international exhibition, 1873.
In: U. S. Commission to the Vienna exhibition, 1873. Reports, 1875–76, v. 4B.

319. Description of drawings for proposed cathedral of Saint John the divine. Submitted by George Martin Huss, John Henry Buck, associated architects. New York, March, 1891.
8 l. 1 pl.   NHi
Cover title

320. Dexter, Henry Martyn, 1821–1900
Meeting houses considered historically and suggestively . . . Boston, J. E. Tilton & co., 1859.
29 p. illus.   NNC-A,MB

321. Directory of architects . . . Springfield, Mass., Clark W. Bryan & Co., 1887.
141 p.   NNC-A

322. —— Springfield, Mass., Clark W. Bryan & Co., 1890.
188 p. illus.   ICJ
"Issued annually"; but no other issues have been reported.

323. Disosway, Gabriel Poillon, 1799–1868
The earliest churches of New York and its vicinity . . . New York, J. G.
Gregory, 1865.
416 p. front., 10 pl.   CtHWatk,CtMW,CtY,MBAt,MB,MWA,
NN,NNC,NHi,OCl,PPL.

*Dobson, Edward
See Bullock, John

Donald, R.
See Lefèvre, André Paul Emile, 1834-1904

Downing, Andrew Jackson, 1815–1852
Additional notes and hints to persons about building in this country.
See Wightwick, George
This is a part title in George Wightwick's *Hints to young architects.*

325. —— The architecture of country houses; including designs for cottages, farm
houses and villas, with remarks on interiors, furniture and the best modes
of warming and ventilating . . . New York, D. Appleton & co.; Philadelphia, G. S. Appleton, 1850.
484 p. illus., 36 pl.   CU,CtHWatk,DLC,IU,MH,MSaE,MWA,
NNC-A,NNCoo,NNMM,NHi,NPV,PP,PPL,ViU

326. —— —— New York, D. Appleton & co., 1851.
484 p. illus., 36 pl.   ICA-B,MH,MSaE,MiGr,MnU,OCi,OO

327. —— —— New York, D. Appleton & co., 1852.
484 p. illus., 36 pl.   CU,DLC,MH,NHi

328. —— —— New York, D. Appleton & co., 1853.
484 p. illus., 36 pl.   CtY,DLC,MSaE,MWA,NjP,NN

329. —— —— 13th thousand, New York, D. Appleton & co., 1854.
484 p. illus., 36 pl.   MBAt,MSaE,NN,NHi,PPCC
Offered for sale by Fowlers and Wells for $4.00 in 1855.

330. —— —— New York, D. Appleton & co., 1856.
484 p. illus., 36 pl.   CtHWatk,MB,OU

331. —— —— 16th thousand, New York, D. Appleton & co., 1861.
484 p. illus., 36 pl.   DLC,MB,MdBP,NN,NPV

332. —— —— 16th thousand, New York, D. Appleton & co., 1865.
484 p. illus., 36 pl.   IU,MH

333. —— —— New York, D. Appleton & co., 1866.
484 p. illus., 36 pl.   DLC,NNC-A

334. —— Cottage residences; or, A series of designs for rural cottages and cottage
villas. And their gardens and grounds. Adapted to North America . . . New
York & London, Wiley & Putnam, 1842.
187 p. illus., 11 pl., incl. front. (1 col.)   CU,CtY,DSG,ICA-B,MB,
MBAt,MSaE,MWA,NN,NNMM,NNMMo,NHi,PPL,RIBA
Designs for ten houses.

335. —— —— 2d ed. New York and London, Wiley & Putnam, 1844.
187 p. illus., 11 pl., incl. front. (1 col.)   DLC,ICA-B,IU,MB,MH,
MBHo,MSaE,MWA,NN,NNCoo,NPV,OCi,OO,PPHo,Vi

336. —— —— 3d ed. New York and London, Wiley and Putnam, 1847.
180 p. illus., 15 pl., incl. front. (1 col.)   CU,MSaE,MWA,MeB,NN,
NNC,NHi,PP
Fifteen house designs, one of which is illustrated in the text, not on a plate.

Downing, Andrew Jackson

337. Cottage residences . . . 4th ed. rev. and improved. New York, John Wiley, 1852.
215 p. illus., 15 pl., incl. front. (1 col.)   DLC(imp.),IU,MH,NPV,
NN,NNC,NNCoo,NHi

338. —— —— 4th ed. rev. and improved. New York, John Wiley, 1853.
215 p. illus., 15 pl., incl. front. (1 col.)   I,MiU,MWA,MnU,NjR,
NN,NWM,OO,OU,PP
Offered for sale by Fowlers and Wells for $2.00 in 1855.

339. —— —— 4th ed. rev. and improved. New York, Wiley & Halsted, 1856.
215 p. illus., 15 pl., incl. front. (1 col.)   CU,MB,MH,MiU

340. —— —— 4th ed. rev. and improved. New York, John Wiley, 1860
215 p. illus., 15 pl., incl. front. (1 col.)   MB,MdBP,NPV

341. —— —— 4th ed. rev. and improved. New York, John Wiley, 1863.
215 p. illus., 15 pl., incl. front. (1 col.)   MB,MoS

342. —— —— 4th ed. rev. and improved. New York, John Wiley, 1865.
215 p. illus., 15 pl., incl. front. (1 col.)   MH

343. —— —— 4th ed. rev. and improved. New York, John Wiley & Son, 1866.
215 p. illus., 15 pl., incl. front. (1 col.)   DLC,PP

344. —— —— 4th ed. rev. and improved. New York, John Wiley & Son, 1868.
215 p. illus., 15 pl., incl. front. (1 col.)   CtHWatk,CtMW(imp.),
IU,MH,MWA

345. —— —— new ed. New York, John Wiley & Son, 1873.
261 p. illus., 29 pl., incl. front. (1 col.)   DLC,MB,MBAt,NN,PPL
This edition is "edited by George E. Harney, with additional horticultural
material by Henry Winthrop Sargent and Charles Downing."

346. —— —— [new ed.] New York, John Wiley & Sons, 1887.
261 p. illus., 29 pl., incl. front. (1 col.)

—— [Hints to persons about building in the country]
See Wightwick, George
This title is properly the 3d Amer. ed. of George Wightwick's *Hints to
young architects* with title arranged to capitalize Downing's popularity.

347. —— Rural essays . . . New York. G. P. Putnam & co., 1853.
557 p. front., illus., 8 pl.   CtHWatk,CtMW,DLC,ICJ,MB,MH,MdBP,
MWA,MnU,NNC,NPV,NWM,NN,NHi,OO,PP,PPL-R,Vi
"edited with a memoir of the author by George William Curtis and a letter
to his friends by Frederika Bremer." A collection of Downing's editorials
from his periodical, the *Horticulturist*, 1846–1852.

348. —— —— New York, Leavitt & Allen, 1854.
557 p. front., illus., 8 pl.   DLC,IU,MBAt,NN,OU

349. —— —— New York, G. P. Putnam & co., 1856.
557 p. front., illus., 8 pl.   IU,NjR

350. —— —— New York, Leavitt & Allen, 1857.
557 p. front., illus., 8 pl.   CU,CtY,MB,MBHo,MnU,NjP,NPV

351. —— —— New York, Leavitt & Allen, 1860.
557 p. front., illus., 8 pl.   CU

352. —— —— New York, Leavitt & Allen, ℗1869.
557 p. front., illus., 8 pl.   NNC-A,NNCoo,OCl

Downing, Andrew Jackson
353. Rural essays . . . New York, R. Worthington, 1881.
    557 p. front., illus., 8 pl.   CtY,ICN,MH

354. —— A treatise on the theory and practice of landscape gardening adapted to
    North America; . . . With remarks on rural architecture . . . New York &
    London, Wiley & Putnam; Boston, C. C. Little & co., 1841.
    451 p. front., illus.   CU,CtY,DLC,ICJ,IU,MBAt,MH-A,
                                        MWA,NN,NNMM,NHi,PP,PPL
    The chapter "Landscape or rural architecture" occupies pp. 296–347.

355. —— ———— 2d ed. enl. rev. and newly ill. New York & London, Wiley and Put-
    nam, 1844.
    497 p. illus., 16 pl., incl. front.   CU,CtHWatk,CtMW,DLC,DSG,MB,
                                        MBAt,MH,MWA,Nh,NN,NNHort,NHi,NPV,PPL
    The chapter "Landscape or rural architecture" occupies pp. 339–387.

357. —— ———— 4th ed. enl. rev. and newly ill. New York, George P. Putnam; Lon-
    don, Longman, Brown, Green and Longmans, 1849.
    532 p. illus., 19 pl., incl. front.   CtY,DDA,MH-A,MWA,NN,
                                        NNC-A,NNHo,NHi,OU,PP,RIBA
    This edition carries a new copyright of 1849 and a new preface dated
    Jan. 1849. No copies of the presumptive 3d ed. have been located.
    The chapter ' Landscape or rural architecture" occupies pp. 368–417.

358. —— ———— 4th ed. enl. rev. and newly ill. New York, George P. Putnam; Lon-
    don, Longman, Brown, Green and Longmans, 1850.
    532 p. illus., 19 pl., incl. front.   MH

359. —— ———— 4th ed. enl. rev. and newly ill. New York, George P. Putnam;
    London, Longman, Brown, Green & Longmans, 1852.
    532 p. illus., 19 pl., incl. front.   ICA-B(imp.),MH,NN

360. —— ———— 5th ed. enl. and newly ill. New York, G. P. Putnam & co., 1853.
    532 p. illus., 18 pl., incl. front.   CtY,DLC(imp.),MH-A,MiOC

361. —— ———— 5th ed. enl. and newly ill. New York, Riker, Thorne & co., 1854.
    532 p. illus., 18 pl., incl. front.   MWA,NN

362. —— ———— 5th ed. enl. and newly ill. New York, C. M. Saxton, 1855.
    532 p. illus., 18 pl., incl. front.   InI,MH,NNHo,OU,PPHo,NjR

363. —— ———— 5th ed. enl. and newly ill. New York, C. M. Saxton, 1856.
    532 p. illus., 18 pl., incl. front.   ICJ,IU,MB

364. —— ———— 5th ed. enl. and newly ill. New York, C. M. Saxton and company,
    1857.
    532 p. illus., 18 pl., incl. front.   MH,MoS

365. —— ———— 6th ed. New York, A. O. Moore & co., 1859.
    576 p. front., illus., 33 pl.   CU,CtY,IU,MH-A,MdBP,NjP,NN,
                                        NNHo,NNMM,NPV,OCl,ViU
    "With a supplement . . . by Henry Winthrop Sargent." This edition car-
    ries a new copyright of 1859. The chapter 'Landscape or rural archi-
    tecture" occupies pp. 318–361.

366. —— ———— 6th ed. New York, C. M. Saxton, Barker; San Francisco, H. H.
    Bancroft & co., 1860.
    576 p. front., illus., 33 pl.   DLC,NNCoo
    With the Supplement.

367. —— ———— 7th ed. New York, Orange Judd, 1865.
    576 p. front., illus., 34 pl.   CtMW,CtY,DLC,ICJ,IU,MH-A,
                                        MnM,MoS,NN,NNC-A
    With the Supplement.

Downing, Andrew Jackson

368. A treatise on the theory and practice of landscape gardening . . . 8th ed. New York, Orange Judd & company, n. d.
      576 p. front., illus., 34 pl.   CU,IU,MnU,NN,NNC,NPV, OU,PPC,Vi
      With the Supplement. This still carries the 1859 copyright.

369. ——— ——— new ed. New York, Orange Judd company [c1875].
      592 p. front., illus., 34 pl.   DLC,MH,NNMM
      With the Supplement and a second Supplement.

370. ——— ——— new ed. New York, Orange Judd co., [1879].
      592 p. front., illus., 34 pl.   MB
      With the two Supplements.

371. Drake, Samuel Adams, 1833–1905
      Historic fields and mansions of Middlesex . . . Boston, James R. Osgood and company, 1874.
      442 p. illus., pl.   CtHWatk,CtY,DLC,IU,InI,MB,MBAt,MH, MHi,MWA,NjN,NjP,NN,NNC-A,NHi,OCl,OU,PPL
      This is possibly no more to be considered an architectural work than Drake's *Nooks and corners of the New England coast*, 1876, *Old Boston taverns and tavern clubs*, 1886, *Old landmarks and historic personages of Boston*, 1873, 1874, 1875, 1876, 1883, but such works undoubtedly prepared the way for the somewhat more documentary publications on colonial architecture in the next decades, such as *Our colonial homes*, below.

372. ——— Boston, Roberts brothers, 1876.
      442 p. illus., pl.   DLC,NjP
      With title: *Old landmarks and historic fields of Middlesex.*

373. ——— Our colonial homes . . . Boston, Lee and Shepard, 1894.
      211 p. front., illus.   CU,CtMW,CtY,DLC,IU,InI,MB, MBAt,MH,MSaE, MWA,MnU,NN,NNC-A,NNMM,NHi,OCL,PP

374. Dubois, Augustus Jay, 1849–1914
      The strains in framed structures with numerous applications to cranes, bridge, roof, and suspension trusses, braced arches, roof and draw spans, continuous girders, etc. . . . New York, John Wiley & sons, 1883.
      390 p. 28 pl. (part fold.)   CtHWatk,I,ICJ,IU,MB,MnU,NNC, NjP,OU,PPFrankl

375. ——— ——— 2d ed. New York, John Wiley and sons, 1884.
      390 p. 28 pl. (part fold.)   MH,NcD,NN,NNC,MoS,OU

376. ——— The strains in framed structures with numerous practical applications to cranes, bridge, roof, and suspension trusses, braced arches, pivot and draw spans, continuous girders, etc . . . New York, John Wiley & sons, 1883.
      390 p. 28 pl. (part fold.)   CtHWatk,DLC,I,ICJ,IU,MB,NjP, OU,PPFrankl

377. ——— ——— 2d ed. New York, John Wiley and sons, 1884.
      390 p. 28 pl. (part fold.)   MH,NN,MoS,OU

378. ——— ——— 3d ed. New York, John Wiley and sons, 1886.
      511 p. 28 pl. (part fold.)   MiH

379. ——— ——— 4th ed. New York, John Wiley and sons, 1888.
      511 p. 28 pl. (part fold.)   NN,OU,PPFrankl

380. ——— ——— 5th ed. rev. and enl. New York, John Wiley and sons, 1890.
      530 p. 28 pl. (part fold.)   DLC,IU,MH
      With a new 1890 copyright.

Dubois, Augustus Jay
381. The strains in framed structures . . . 6th ed. New York, John Wiley and sons,
1890.
530 p. 28 pl. (part fold.)   NNC,OU

382. —— —— 7th ed. New York, John Wiley and sons, 1891.
540 p. 28 pl. (part fold.)   CU,PP

383. —— —— 8th ed. New York, John Wiley and sons, 1892.
540 p. 28 pl. (part fold.)   IU,MnM,NNC,PP,ViU

384. —— —— 9th ed. New York, John Wiley and sons, 1892.
540 p. 28 pl. (part fold.)   CU,CtHWatk,DLC,NNC

385. —— —— 9th ed. New York, John Wiley and sons, 1893.
540 p. 28 pl. (part fold.)   MnU,NcD
The frequent editions of this work, paralleling the early growth of the
skyscraper, contrast with several much less popular works of a similar
order that appeared in the seventies, such as Dubois, *Elements of graphical
statics and their application to framed structures*, 1875.

386. Dunlap, William, 1766–1839
A history of the rise and progress of the arts of design in the United States
. . . New York, G. P. Scott and co., printers, 1834.
2 v.   CtHWatk,CtMW,DLC,MB,MBAt,MH,MWA,MdBP,MnM,MnU,
MoS,NcD,NjP,NHi,NN,NNC-A,NNMM,NWM,NNCoo,OU,PP,RIBA

387. Dwight, Mary Ann, 1806–1858
Introduction to the study of art . . . New York, D. Appleton & co., 1856.
278 p.   DLC,MB,MH,MnU,NN,NNC,NNMM,NPV,NWM,PP

388. Dwyer, Charles P
The economic cottage builder; or, Cottages for men of small means. Adapted
to every locality, with instructions for choosing the most economical materials afforded by the neighborhood . . . Illustrated with tinted designs on
stone . . . Buffalo, Wanzer, McKim and co.; New York, J. C. Derby; Boston,
Phillips, Sampson and co.; Philadelphia, J. B. Lippincott and co.; Cincinnati,
Moore, Wilstach, Keyes and co.; Detroit, Kerr, Morley & co., 1855.
127 p. 23 pl.   DLC,MSaE,MoS,NBu,NNC-A

389. —— —— Buffalo, Wanzer, McKim & co. [etc.], 1856.
127 p. 23 pl.   DLC,ICA-B,ICJ,MH,MnU,NNMM,OO,PP,PPFrankl

390. —— The economy of church, parsonage and school house architecture adapted to
small societies and rural districts . . . Buffalo, Phinney & co., 1856.
95 p. 40 pl.   CtHWatk,CtY,NBu,MH,NNC-A,NNMM,PPL

391. —— The immigrant builder; or, Practical hints to handymen. Showing clearly
how to plan and construct dwellings in the bush, on the prairie, or elsewhere,
cheaply and well, with wood, earth, or gravel . . . Philadelphia, Claxton,
Remsen & Haffelfinger, 1872.
145 p. incl. front., illus.   DLC,MB,NN,NNCoo,OCi,PPL

400. —— —— 10th ed. Philadelphia, Claxton, Remsen & Haffelfinger, 1878.
145 p. incl. front., illus.   MB,MnU
The absence of locations for editions 2 to 9 is curious.

401. —— —— 10th ed. New York, Hurst & co. [c1884].
145 p. illus.   H.R.H.
Binding inscribed "Arlington Edition."

402. *Eassie, William, 1832–1888
    Healthy houses . . . New York, D. Appleton & co., 1872.
        228 p.   CU,IU,MB,MBAt,MH,MnM,MnU,NN,NNC,OCi,OU,PPL,Vi
    First appeared London, 1872.

403. —— —— New York, D. Appleton & co., 1876.
        224 p.   NN
    2d London edition also in 1876.
    Eassie wrote other similar books, not particularly relevant here.

404. An easy method of working by the plain and sliding rules. Collected from vari-
    ous authors and designed for the use of architects . . . Lansingburgh: Printed
    by Sylvester Tiffany, and sold at his office . . . 1793.
        24 p. fold. table   NHi,RPJCB

405. *Eastlake, Charles Locke, 1836–1906
    Hints on household taste in furniture, upholstery and other details . . .
    edited, with notes, by Charles C. Perkins . . . 1st American from the rev.
    London. ed. Boston, James R. Osgood and company, 1872.
        300 p. illus., 34 pl.   CtY,DLC,ICJ, IU,MB,MBAt,MH,MHi,NN,
                                         NNCoo,NNMM,OClMA,PP,PPPM
    First appeared London, 1868.

406. —— —— 2d. Amer. from the latest English ed. Boston, James R. Osgood
    and company, 1874.
        304 p. illus., 36 pl.   MH,MoS,OCl

408. —— —— 4th Amer. from the latest English ed. Boston, James R. Osgood
    and company, 1876.
        304 p. illus., 36 pl.   CtY,MB,MH,NN,PPFrankl,RPB
    No copy of the presumptive 3d. Amer. ed. has been located.

409. —— —— 5th Amer. from the latest English ed. Boston, James R. Osgood
    and company, 1877.
        304 p. illus., 36 pl.   DLC,MiU,MnU,NjP,NN,PP,PPFrankl

410. —— —— 6th Amer. from the latest English ed. Boston, James R. Osgood
    and company, 1878.
        304 p. illus., 36 pl.   CtY,ICA-B

411. —— —— 6th Amer. from the latest English ed. Boston, Houghton, Mifflin
    & co., 1881.
        304 p. illus., 36 pl.   PPM

412. —— —— 7th Amer. from the latest English ed. Boston, Houghton, Mifflin
    & co., 1883.
        304 p. illus., 36 pl.   MH,NHi

413. *Edis, Robert William, 1839–1927
    Decoration & furniture of town houses . . . New York, Scribner and Wel-
    ford, 1881.
        292 p. front., illus., 28 pl.   CtHWatk,MB,MH,MoS,NNC-A,OCi,PP
    First London edition the same year.

414. Eidlitz, Leopold, 1823–1908
    The nature and function of art, more especially of architecture . . . New
    York, A. C. Armstrong & son, [etc.] 1881.
        493 p.   DLC,MB,BMAt,MoS,NN,NNC-A,OCi,OCl,PPL
    First London edition the same year.

415. Eliot, William Havard, 1796–1831
A description of the Tremont House with architectural illustrations . . .
Boston, Gray & Bowen, 1830.
36 p. 31 pl., incl. front. (1 col.)   DLC,ICJ,MH,NHi,NIC,
NNC-A,NNMM
Plate I is engraved; the rest are lithographed. The author's name is supplied.

416. Ellet, Charles, 1810–1862
A popular notice of suspension bridges, with a brief description of the wire
bridge across the Schuylkill, at Fairmount . . . Philadelphia, John C. Clark,
printer, 1843.
18 p. front.   DLC

417. —— A popular notice of wire suspension bridges . . . Richmond, P. D. Bernard,
1839.
22 p.   DLC

418. —— Report and plan for a wire suspension bridge, proposed to be constructed
across the Mississippi river at Saint Louis . . . Philadelphia, William Stavely & co., printers, 1840.
58 p. 3 fold. pl.   DLC

419. —— Report on a railway suspension bridge across the Connecticut at Middle-
town . . . with a proposal for its construction . . . Philadelphia, John C. Clark,
printer, 1848.
62 p. front., illus.   CtHWatk

420. —— Report on a suspension bridge across the Potomac, for rail road and common travel . . . Philadelphia, John C. Clark, printer, 1852.
36 p. 4 pl. (1 fold.)   DLC,MH

421. —— —— 2d ed. Philadelphia, John C. Clark, printer, 1854.
36 p. fold. front., 3 pl.   DLC,MH

422. —— The Wheeling bridge [Philadelphia, 1852].
6 p.   DLC,MH

423. Elliott, Charles Wyllys, 1817–1883
The book of American interiors prepared . . . from existing houses . . . Boston,
James R. Osgood and company, 1876.
135 p. front., illus., 21 pl.   CtHWatk,CtY,DLC,InI,IU,MB,MBAt,MH,
MU,MWA,MdBE,MdBP,MoS,NN,NNC,NNC-A,
NNCoo,NHi,NNMM,OO,PPL

424. —— Cottages and cottage life . . . plans for country houses . . . Cincinnati, H. W.
Derby & co., New York, A. S. Barnes co., 1848.
226 p. front., 16 pl.   DA,DLC,MH,MdBP,NNC-A,NNMM,NHi

425. Ellis, Theodore Gunville, 1829–1883
Description of the iron bridge over the Connecticut river on the Hartford
and New Haven rail road, with a brief history of iron bridges . . . Hartford,
Published by Brown & Gross, 1866.
35 p. fold. pl.   DLC,MH,PP

426. Ellwanger, George Herman, 1843–1906
The story of my house . . . New York, D. Appleton and company, 1890.
286 p. illus.   MoS,OCl

427. —— —— New York, D. Appleton and company, 1891.
286 p. illus.   CSmH,DLC,MB,MWA,MiGr,NN

428. —— —— 2d ed. New York, D. Appleton and company, 1891.
286 p. illus.   CtY,ICN,MH,NN,PP

Ellwanger, George Herman
429. The story of my house . . . 3d ed. New York, D. Appleton and company, 1893.
    286 p. illus.   NPV,PPD
    There was a 4th ed. in 1896.

430. Eveleth, Samuel F.
    Schoolhouse architecture. Illustrated with seventeen designs in various styles with full descriptive drawings in plan, elevation and detail . . . New York, Geo. E. Woodward [c1870].
    2 p. l. [3]–14, 101, 9, [4], 13, 2, [4] p. 67 pl.   CtHWatk,DLC,IU,
                                        MB,MoS,NN,OCl,OO,PU

431. Everts, William Wallace, 1814–1890
    The house of God: or Claims of public worship . . . with designs and estimates for church buildings. New York, American tract society, 1872.
    132 p. illus.   DLC

432. Examples of architecture. Cottages and interiors by various architects. Selected from the Sketch Book. Boston, 1880.
    t.p., 70 pl.   H.R.H.

433. Examples of architecture, Street fronts, furniture, etc. by various architects. Selected from the Sketch Book. Boston, 1880.
    t.p., 50 pl.   H.R.H.

434. Examples of architecture. Views of public buildings, schoolhouses, town halls, hospitals, libraries, and asylums, by various architects. Selected from the Sketch Book. Boston, 1880.
    t.p., 75 pl.   H.R.H.
    The three items above contain most of the plates issued in the periodicals, *Architectural sketch book,* and *New York sketch book,* during the seventies.

Examples of modern architecture, ecclesiastical and domestic.
    See Scott, Sir George Gilbert, 1811–1878, and others.

435. *Fairbairn, Sir William, 1789–1874
    On the application of cast and wrought iron to building purposes . . . New York, John Wiley, 1854.
    184 p. illus.   CU,DLC,IU,MoS,NN,OU,Vi
    First London edition the same year.

436. *Falke, Jacob von, 1825–1897
    Art in the house. Historical, critical, and aesthetical studies on the decoration and furnishing of the dwelling . . . Authorized Amer. ed. trans. from the 3d. German ed. Edited with notes by Charles C. Perkins . . . Boston, L. Prang and company, 1879.
    356 p. illus., 60 pl., incl. front.   CSmH,DLC,InI,ICA-R,IU,MB,MBAt,
                                MH,MoS,NN,NNC,NNC-A,NNMM,NPV,OCi,PP
    Added lithographic title page with date 1878.

437. *Fallet, Celine, 1829–
    Les princes de l'art: architectes, sculpteurs, peinteurs, et graveurs . . . Boston, S. R. Urbino, 1870.
    324 p.   DLC,ICA-B,NjP,NN
    No copyright date. First published Rouen, 1855.

438. —— —— 2d ed. Boston, S. R. Urbino, New York, Leypoldt & Holt, F. W. Christern, 1870.
    334 p.   CtMW,MH,PP
    With an 1869 copyright.

*Fallet, Celine
439. Les princes de l'art . . . 2d ed. New York, Henry Holt and company, n. d.
    334 p.   MH,NN
    With the same 1869 copyright as the issue above.

439. —— —— . . . The princes of art: architects, painters, sculptors and engravers
    . . . Boston, Lee & Shepard, 1870 [c1870].
    340 p. front., 2 pl.   DLC,NN
    At head of title: The old masters.
    "Translated from the French by Mrs. S. R. Urbino."

440. —— —— Boston, Lee & Shepard, 1883.
    340 p. front., 2 pl.   NN
    With the 1870 copyright of the issue above.

442. Farrar, Charles Samuel, 1826–
    History of sculpture, painting and architecture . . . [2d ed.] Chicago, Town-
    send Mac Coun, 1881.
    142 p.   DLC,InI,MBAt
    No earlier edition has been located.

443. —— —— New York, Townsend Mac Coun, 1884.
    134 p. illus.   MiOC,NPV
    The phrase "Art topics" precedes the title.

444. —— —— New York, Townsend MacCoun, 1885.
    134 p. illus.   NNC-A

445. —— —— [2d ed.] New York, Townsend MacCoun, 1885.
    134 p. illus. '   NNC-A,OU,PP

446. —— —— 3d ed. Chicago, Farrar & co., 1890.
    196 p. illus.   MB,MBAt,MH,PPD
    There was a 5th ed. in 1896 and hence probably a 4th before 1895 which
    has not been located.

448. *Farrar, Frederick William, 1831–1903, and others.
    The cathedrals of England . . . New York, Thomas Whittaker, 1893.
    351 p. front., illus.   OO

449. —— —— New York, Thomas Whittaker, 1894.
    351 p. front., illus.   PP

450. —— —— New York, Thomas Whittaker, n.d.
    351 p. front., illus.   MoS,Vi
    Almost certainly of 1895 or later.

451. Fay, Theodore Sedgwick
    Views in New York and its environs. New York, Peabody and co., 1831.
    58 p. illus.   NNC-A
    Includes many drawings of architectural monuments by A. J. Davis and
    J. H. Dakin of the Town and Davis office.

452. Ferree, James Barr, 1862–1924
    Architectural education for America. Reprinted from the Engineering maga-
    zine for April and May, 1894. New York, 1894.
    15 p.   NNC-A,PP,PU,RIBA
    At head of title: "For private distribution only."
    Ferree was editor; A. Rotch and others contributed.

453. —— Christian thought in architecture . . . New York, Privately printed, 1892.
    32 p. 2 pl.   CtHWatk,NN,NNC-A,NNMM,NHi,OCi,PP,RIBA
    Also appeared in *American society for church history papers*, 1892.

39

Ferree, James Barr

454. Chronology of the cathedral churches of France . . . New York [Record and guide press] 1894.
36 p.   MBAt,MH,NNC-A,NNMM,PP,PU,RIBA

455. —— Comparative architecture . . . New York, Reprinted from the Journal of the [American] Institute [of architects] 1892.
15 p.   CtY,DLC,MH,NN,NNC-A,PU,RIBA

456. —— The high building and its art . . . New York, Reprinted from Scribner's magazine, March, 1894.
pp. 297–318, 16 illus.   NNC-A,RIBA

457. —— Primitive architecture . . . New York, 1890.
2 pts. in 1   NNC-A,PU
Cover title; two articles stapled together: "Sociological influences," extracted from the *American naturalist*, Jan. 1889, pp. 25–32; "Climatic influences," from the *American anthropologist*, April, 1890, pp.147–158. Ferree's paper, "The study of domestic mediaeval architecture," although read before the Archaeological institute of America in 1894, is as a publication dated 1895.

458. Field, M
City architecture; or, Designs for dwelling houses, stores, hotels . . . New York, George P. Putnam, 1853.
75 p. illus., 20 pl.   MB,MWA,NjP,NNC-A,NNMM,NHi,PP

459. —— —— New York [etc.] D. Appleton & company, 1854.
75 p. illus., 20 pl.   DLC,MH,MdBP,NN,PPM

460. Rural architecture; designs for villas, cottages, etc., in the Italian, Gothic, Elizabethan, old English, and Swiss styles, with descriptions, and an essay on rural architecture and landscape gardening, including a critique on Ruskin's new theoretical principles of design . . . New York, Miller & company, 1857.
135 p. illus., 20 pl., incl. front.   DLC,ICA-B,IU,MB,MWA,MoS,PPL

461. Foote, Henry Wilder, 1838–1889
Annals of King's Chapel from the Puritan age of New England to the present day . . . Boston, Little, Brown and company, 1882–1896.
3 v. front., illus., plates   DLC

462. Forrester, Allen E   , *comp.*
The city hall, Baltimore. History of construction and dedication. Baltimore, The mayor and city council, 1877.
141 p. 11 pl.   MdBP

463. Fort, George Franklin, 1809–1892
A critical inquiry into the conditions of the conventual builders and their relations to the secular guilds in the middle ages . . . New York, J. W. Bouton, 1884.
45 p.   MB,MH,NNC-A,NHi,OCi,OU,PPM
Cover title reads: Mediaeval builders.

464. —— Historical treatise on early builder's marks . . . Philadelphia, McCalla & Stavely, 1885.
158 p. illus., 9 pl.   ICJ,MB,MBAt,NNC-A,OCi,OU,PPM
Fort's other works are more concerned with Freemasonry.

465. Fowler, Orson Squire, 1809–1887
A home for all; or, The gravel wall and octagon mode of building . . . New York, Fowlers and Wells, 1848.
96 p. illus., 4 pl. (1 fold.)   PU

Fowler, Orson Squire

466. A home for all . . . New York, Fowlers and Wells, 1849.
     96 p. illus., 4 pl. (1 fold.)   MSaE

467. —— —— New York, Fowlers and Wells, 1850.
     96 p. illus., 4 pl. (1 fold.)   MiU

468. —— —— New York, Fowlers and Wells, 1851.
     96 p. illus., 4 pl. (1 fold.)   MH,PPM

469. —— —— Stereotyped ed. rev. and enl. New York, Fowlers and Wells, 1854.
     192 p. illus., 3 pl. on 2 l.   CU,DLC(imp.),ICA-B,ICJ,IU,MBAt,
                             MH,MWA,MoS,NN,NNC-A,NNMM,NHi,OO,PP,PPM,ViU
     With a new 1853 copyright.
     Offered for sale by Fowlers and Wells for eighty-seven cents in 1855.

470. —— —— Stereotyped ed. rev. and enl. New York, Fowler and Wells, 1856.
     192 p. illus., 3 pl. on 2 l.   DLC

471. —— —— Stereotyped, rev. and enl. New York, Fowler and Wells, n.d.
     192 p. illus., 3 pl. on 2 l.   NN

472. —— —— Stereotyped ed. rev. and enl. New York, Samuel R. Wells, n.d.
     192 p. illus., 3 pl. on 2 l.   NN,NPV
     Both this issue and the preceding still carry the original 1853 copyright.
     The form of imprint suggests this is the latest issue of the book.

Franklin, William Buel, 1823–1903
See Meigs, Montgomery Cunningham.

473. Frederick, Frank Forrest, 1866–
     Architectural rendering in sepia . . . New York, William T. Comstock, 1892.
     40 p. 13 pl. (part double)   DLC,MB,NN,NNC-A,OU,PP

474. French, Benjamin Franklin, 1799–1877
     History of the rise and progress of the iron trade . . . New York, Wiley and
     Halsted, 1858.
     179 p.   CSmH,CtY,IU,MBAt,MH,MWA,MdBE,MnU,
                             MoS,NN,NNC,NHi,PPFrankl

475. Fryer, William John, 1842–1907, *ed.*
     Architectural ironwork. A practical work for iron workers, architects and
     engineers, and all whose profession or business connects them with archi-
     tectural ironwork. Showing the organization mechanical and financial of a
     foundry and shops . . . New York, John Wiley and sons, 1876.
     220 p. illus., 2 pl.   CU,CtHWatk,MB,MoS,NN,NNC-A,OCi,
                             PPFrankl,Vi

476. —— Laws relating to buildings in the city of New York . . . Law limiting the
     height of dwelling houses in New York . . . N[ew] Y[ork], The Record and
     Guide, 1885.
     84 p. illus.   DLC

477. —— —— N[ew] Y[ork], The Record and Guide, [1892].
                                           DLC,MH,PP
     Omits: Law limiting the height . . . but adds a complete directory of
     architects in New York city, Brooklyn, Jersey City, and Newark.

478. —— Laws relating to buildings in the city of Brooklyn . . . N[ew] Y[ork], The
     Record and Guide [c1894].
     172 p. illus.   DLC

479. Fuller, Albert W.
    Artistic homes in city and country . . . Boston, J. R. Osgood & co., 1882.
        2 p. l. 44 pl.   CtHWatk,DLC,MB,MBAt,MSaE,NN,PPM

480. —— —————— rev. and enl. ed. Boston, J. R. Osgood & co., 1884.
        3 p. l. 75 pl.   DLC,MB,OCl
    With a new 1884 copyright.

482. —— —————— [4th] rev. and enl. ed. Boston, Ticknor and company, 1886.
        4 p. l. 77 pl.   MB
    With a new 1886 copyright.
    "Preface to the fourth and revised edition: . . . most of the old plates have
    been replaced by new ones, and several are illustrated from photographs
    of the buildings themselves . . . To Mr. Wm. Prettyman and Richard
    Prescott I am indebted for articles on Decoration and Sanitary matters,
    and to my partner, Mr. Wm. Wheeler, for valuable assistance in per-
    fecting many of the recent designs . . . Albany, N. Y., Feb. 1, 1886."
    No copy of the presumptive [3d] edition has been located.

483. —— —————— 5th and rev. ed. Boston, Ticknor and company, 1891.
        4 p. l. 70 pl.   DLC,MB,NN,NNC-A,OCl,Vi
    William Arthur Wheeler was joint author of this edition, which carries
    a new 1891 copyright.

484. Gallier, James, 1798–
    American builder's general price book and estimator . . . New York, Stanley
    & co., 1833.
        iv, 128, l. 72, 17 p.   CSmH,CtY,DLC,MH,MWA,NcD,
                                                NN,NHi,OO,PPM
    "Sold by Lafever and Gallier, architects."
    Includes Building laws.

485. —— —————— Boston, Marsh, Capen & Lyon, 1834.
        [3]–15 p.   MB
    Paper cover bound in.

486. —— —————— 2d ed. Boston, M. Burns, 1836.
        130 l. 79 p. front.   CSmH,MBAt,MH,MWA,NNC-A,NHi

487. —— Autobiography of James Gallier architect. Paris, Printed by E. Briere, 1864.
        150 p.   NNC-A,LNT
    Although not an American imprint, this important biographical work can
    hardly be omitted from this list.

    Gambrill, Charles D.
    See Richardson, Henry Hobson

488. Gardner, Eugene Clarence, 1836–1915
    Commonsense in church building . . . New York, Bicknell and Comstock, 1880.
        166 p. 7 plans   DLC,MB,MBAt,PPL

489. —— Farm architecture; houses and barns: a lecture . . . Holyoke, 1882.
        47 p. illus.   CtY

490. —— Homes and all about them . . . Boston, J. R. Osgood and company, 1885.
        710 p. front., illus., 56 pl.   DLC,MB,MH,OCl

491. —— Homes and how to make them . . . Boston, James R. Osgood and com-
    pany, 1874.
        314 p. incl. illus., 5 pl. front.   CU,CtY,DLC,IU,MBAt,MHi,MWA,
                                                        NNCoo,OO

492. —— —————— Boston, James R. Osgood and company, 1875.
        314 p. incl. illus., 5 pl., front.   MiU,MoS

Gardner, Eugene Clarence
493. Homes and how to make them . . . Boston, James R. Osgood and company, 1878.
      314 p. incl. illus., 5 pl., front.   MSaE,MoS,NN,NNC-A,NNMM

494. —— Home interiors . . . Boston, James R. Osgood and company, 1878.
      268 p. front., illus., 48 pl.   CU,CtY,DLC,IU,MB,MH,MWA,
                                    MoS,NjP,NN,OCl,PPFrankl

495. —— The house that Jill built, after Jack's had proved a failure. A book on home architecture . . . New York, Fords, Howard & Hulbert, 1882.
      249 p. illus., 20 pl.   CtMW,CtY,DLC,IU,MB,MBAt,MH,
                                    MWA,MnU,MoS,OCi,OCl
      In "Our continent" library, [v. 6].
      There was a 3d ed. edition in 1896. No copies of the presumptive 2d edition have been located, though one is listed in the 1904 catalogue of the MdBE.

496. —— Illustrated homes: a series of papers describing real houses and real people . . . Boston. James R. Osgood and company, 1875.
      287 p. incl. illus., 36 pl.   CU,DLC,IU,MB,MBAt,MH,MWA,MoS,
                                    NjP,NN,NNC-A,NNCoo,OCl,OO,PP,PPL,Vi

497. —— Town and country school buildings . . . New York and Chicago, E. L. Kellogg & co., 1888.
      128 p. illus.   DE,DLC,DSG,IU,MnU,NNC-A,PPL

498. Garnsey, George O
      The American glossary of architectural terms; being a concise and comprehensive compilation of all the terms used in the practice of architecture and the building arts . . . Chicago, Ill. [The Clark & Langley co.] 1887.
      [96] p. front., (part.) illus.   CtY,DLC,PPD

499. —— —— Chicago, The National builder publishing co., 1892.
      [88] p. front., (part.) illus.   MB,PPFrankl

500. —— —— 3d ed. Chicago, The National builder publishing co. [1892].
      [88] p. front., (part.) illus.   CtY,ICJ
      "Preface to the third edition" dated 1892.

501. —— The national builder's album of beautiful homes, villas, residences, and cottages . . . Chicago, The National builder publishing co., °1891.
      [5], 115 p. illus.   ICJ,NNC-A
      Vol. I only.

502. Gash, John
      Catechism of architecture . . . San Francisco, Wm. Doxey, 1893.
      40 p.   CU

503. Gaudard, Jules, 1833–
      Foundations . . . New York, D. Van Nostrand, 1878.
      104 p. illus.   CU,CtY,ICJ,MH,MWA,MiH,MnU,NN,OU

504. —— —— 2d ed. New York, D. Van Nostrand, 1891.
      104 p. illus.   IU,MB,NN

General congregational convention
    See Congregational churches in the U.S.

Gerhard, William Paul, 1854–
    See Brunner, Arnold William

505. Gibson, Louis Henry, 1854–
Convenient houses, with fifty plans for the housekeeper. Architect and house-
wife; a journey through the house; fifty convenient house plans; practical
house building for the owner; business points in building, how to pay for
a home . . . New York, Thomas Y. Crowell & co., [1889].
4, 321 p. front., illus., 6 pl.　　　DLC,ICJ,IU,MB,MH,MoS,NN,NNC-A,
NNCoo,NNMMo,OCi,OCl,OO,OU,PPFrankl
The NNC-A copy carries on the binding: "By Louis H. Gibson, author
of Beautiful Houses," which indicates this edition was sometime in print,
as *Beautiful houses* is dated [c1895].

506. Gilbert, Bradford Lee,　　–1911
Architectural sketches . . . [New York] 1890.
56 l. incl. illus., pl.　　　　　　　　　　　　　　　　　　DLC

507. —— Sketches of public buildings . . . [New York? c1882].
Cover title, 5 l. 7 pl.　　　　　　　　　　　　　　　　　DLC

508. Gilman, E
The economical builder: a treatise on tapia and pisé walls . . . Washington,
Jacob Gideon, jr., printer, 1839.
10 l. 23 p. 10 l. 1 fold. col. pl.　　　　　　　　　　　　NNC-A

509. Goforth, William Davenport, 1866–
Old colonial architectural details in and around Philadelphia . . . New York,
Wm. Helburn, c1890.
2 p. l. 50 pl.　　　　　　　　CU,CtY,DLC,ICA-B,IU,MB,MH,NN,NNC-A,
NNMM,OCl,OU,PP
William John McAuley was joint author.

510. Gould, Lucius D　　, 1814–
The American house carpenter's and joiner's assistant; being a new and easy
system of lines, founded on geometrical principles, for cutting every description of joints, and for framing the most difficult roofs . . . New York, Daniel
Burgess & co., 1853.
136 p. 44 pl.　　　　　　　　　　　　　　　　　　　　MH

511. —— —— 2d ed. New York, Daniel Burgess & co., 1855.
141 p. 48 pl.　　　　　　　　　　　　　　　　　　　　DLC

512. —— —— 2d ed. New York, Ivison & Plimney, 1857.
141 p. 48 pl.　　　　　　　　　　　　　　　　　　　　NNC-A

513. —— Carpenter's and builder's assistant . . . New York, A. J. Bicknell & co.,
1874.
70 p. 23 pl.　　　　　　　　　　　　　　　　DLC,MnU,NN,PPFr

514. —— —— New York, Bicknell & Comstock, 1879.
69 p. 27 pl.　　　　　　　　　　　　　　　　　　DLC,MH,OCi
With title: The new carpenter's and builder's assistant . . . rev. and enl.

516. —— —— 4th rev. ed. New York, William T. Comstock, 1882.
78 p. 36 pl.　　　　　　　　　　　　　　　　　　　　DLC
No copies of the presumptive 3d ed. have been located.

518. —— —— 6th ed. New York, William T. Comstock, 1888.
78 p. 36 pl.　　　　　　　　　　　　　　　　　　　　NNCoo
With the 1874 title and a new 1888 copyright.
No copies of the presumptive 5th edition have been located.

519. —— —— 7th ed. New York, William T. Comstock, 1890.
78 p. 36 pl.　　　　　　　　　　　　　　　　　　　　NNC-A

Gould, Lucius D
520. Carpenter's and builder's assistant . . . 8th rev. ed. New York, William T. Comstock, n.d.
        78 p. 36 pl.   PPD
        With the 1888 copyright, but not certainly before 1895.
        There was a 9th edition in 1897. Gould also wrote treatises on stair building.

521. Green, Samuel W
        Complete history of the New York and Brooklyn bridge . . . New York, S. W. Green's son, 1883.
        96 p.   CtY,MB,MH,PU

522. Greenough, Horatio, 1808–1852
        Aesthetics at Washington, No. 1 . . . Washington, printed by Jno. T. Towers, 1851.
        22 p.   MB,NN,NNMM

523. ——— Travels, observations and experience of a Yankee stone-cutter . . . Part 1. New York, G. P. Putnam & co., 1852.
        222 p.   DLC,NN
        "By Horace Bender" (*pseud.*) No more parts were published. This includes the important article *American architecture*, which first appeared in the North American review in 1843, *Structure and organization*, and *Criticism in search of beauty*. H. T. Tuckerman's *Memorial of Horatio Greenough*, 1853, also includes most of this material.

524. Gregg, David A
        Architectural rendering in pen and ink . . . Boston, Ticknor & co. [ʳ1891–92].
        4 pts. in 2 v., pl.   DLC,NN,PPD

525. Grimshaw, Robert, 1850–
        Hints on house building . . . New York, Practical publishing co., 1887.
        32 p.   PPFrankl

526. ——— ——— 2d and enl. ed. New York, Practical publishing co., 1889.
        77 p.   MB,MoS,OO,PP

527. Guastavino, Rafael
        Essay on the theory and history of cohesive construction applied especially to the timbrel vault. Read before the Society of arts, Massachusetts institute of technology . . . Boston, Ticknor and company, 1892.
        149 p. 4 fold. pl.   ĐLC,IU,OU

528. ——— ——— 2d ed. Boston, Ticknor and company, 1893.
        149 p. 4 fold. pl.   NN,NNC-A

529. ——— Lecture written for the congress of architects, in connection with the Columbian exposition, on cohesive construction, its past, its present, its future? . . . Chicago, 1893.
        cover title, 16 p.   NNC-A

530. Guillaume, L
        Guillaume's Interior architecture . . . New York, A. J. Bicknell & co., 1875.
        1 p. l. 12 pl.   DLC

531. Hale, Benjamin
        Introduction to the mechanical principles of carpentry . . . Boston, Richardson & Lord, and P. Sheldon, Gardiner, Me. P. Sheldon, printer. 1827.
        182 p.   NHi

532. Hall, John
A series of select and original modern designs for dwelling houses, for the use of carpenters & builders: adapted to the style of building in the United States . . . Baltimore, Printed by John Murphy, 1840.
32 p. 24 pl.   MdBP,ViU
Hall, described as "architect" in this title, published in the same year *The cabinet maker's assistant* and also *A new and correct method of hand-railing.*

533. ── ──── 2d ed. Baltimore, Printed by John Murphy, 1840.
32 p. 24 pl.   NHi

534. ── ──── 2d ed. Baltimore, John Murphy, Philadelphia, James Fullerton, Pittsburg, George Quigley, 1848.
32 p. 24 pl.   DLC,Md,MdBP,NHi
A page of advertisements, etc., precedes the title page.

535. Hallett, William T.
Specifications for frame houses varying in cost from two thousand to twenty thousand dollars . . . New York, A. J. Bicknell & co., 1875.
2 p. l., 31 (i.e., 33), 7 numb. l.   DLC

537. ── ──── 3d ed. New York, A. J. Bicknell and Wm. T. Comstock, 1881.
[2], 26, 7 p.   DLC,MB,PP
With a new copyright of 1881.
No copies of the presumptive 2d ed. have been located.

538. ── ──── 4th ed. New York, William T. Comstock, 1883.
[4], 26 (i.e., 28), [7] p.   DLC,NNC-A

539. ── ──── 5th ed. New York, William T. Comstock, 1893.
[2], 26, 7, [6] p.   PPD

540. Halsted, Byron David, 1852–1918
Barn plans and outbuildings . . . New York, Orange Judd and company, 1881.
235 p. front., illus.   DLC,IU,MnU,MoS,NN,OCl,PU

541. ── ──── New York, O. Judd and company, 1882.
235 p. front., illus.   NNC-A

542. ── ──── New York, O. Judd and company, 1886.
235 p. front., illus.   CU,DLC,MB

543. Hamlin, Alfred Dwight Foster, 1855–1926
. . . History of architectural styles: Evolution, development and relations of the historic types . . . [Albany, N. Y., University of the State of New York extension department, 1894].
15 p.   MB,NN,OO
At head of title: New York state education department syllabus no. 49.

544. Hammond, George W   ?
A mill-built dwelling house . . . [Boston, Parkhill, printers] 1892.
28 p. incl. front., pl.   DLC,MB
Partly reprinted from the *American architect and building news.* A description of the summer home of G. W. Hammond at Yarmouthville, Me.

545. Hammond, J   H
The farmer's and mechanic's practical architect . . . Boston, J. P. Jewett and company, Cleveland, H. P. B. Jewett, 1858.
224 p. incl. front., illus., pl.   CtHWatk,DLC,MBHo,MH,MSaE,
MWA,NNC-A,OCl,PPL

546. Hannaford, Samuel, and sons
   Selections from executed work and sketches . . . ₍Cincinnati, Benton, Boyd &
   Harvey, 1894₎.
      2 p. l. ₍46₎ pl.   OCi,OU

547. Harney, George E
   Stables, outbuildings and fences . . . New York, Geo. E. Woodward ₍ᶜ1870₎.
      vi, ₍90₎ p. 62 pl.   DLC,MB,MH,MWA,MnU,NN,NNC-A,
                                                                 NNMM,NHi,PP
      Added lithographic t.-p. reads: Barns, outbuildings and fences.
      See also Downing, Andrew Jackson

548. Hart, Joseph Coleman
   Designs for parish churches in the three styles of English church architecture
   . . . New York, Dana and company, 1857.
      111 p. illus., 42 pl.   DLC,MWA,NNC-A,PP,RIBA

549. Hartshorne, Henry, 1823–1897
   Our homes . . . Philadelphia, P. Blakiston, 1880.
      150 p. illus.   CtY,DLC,DSG,MoS,NN,OCl,PP,PPFrankl
      American health primers. No. IX.
      A treatise on household sanitation.

550. —— —— Philadelphia, P. Blakiston, 1882.
      150 p. illus.   ICJ,MH,MoS,PPD

551. —— —— Philadelphia, P. Blakiston, 1885.
      150 p. illus.   MnU

552. Harvey, T. W., lumber co., *Chicago, pub.*
   Architectural designs₁ Chicago, T. W. Harvey lumber co., 1889.
      39 p. illus.   MB
      2 pts in 1 v.

553. Hatfield, Robert Griffith, 1815–1879
   The American house carpenter, a treatise upon architecture, cornices and
   mouldings, framing, doors, windows, and stairs together with the most important principles of practical geometry . . . New York & London, Wiley and
   Putnam, 1844.
      254, 32 p. illus.   DLC,PPCC

554. —— —— 2d ed. New York & London, Wiley and Putnam, 1845.
      272, 32 p. illus.   ICA-B,MnU,NN,NNC-A,NHi
      With a new preface to the 2d edition.

555. —— —— 3d ed. New York, John Wiley, 1849.
      272, 32 p. illus.   MeB,PPFrankl

556. —— —— 4th ed. New York, John Wiley, 1850.
      272, 32 p. illus.   MiU

557. —— —— 5th ed. New York, John Wiley, 1852.
      272, 32 p. illus.   DLC
      With a new preface to the 5th edition.
      Offered for sale by Fowlers and Wells for $2.00 in 1855.

558. —— —— 7th ed. rev. and enl. New York, Wiley & Halsted, 1857.
      398, 36 p. illus.   IU,MB,MBAt,MnM,OO,PPFrankl
      With title *The American carpenter. A treatise on the art of building
      and the strength of materials.*
      No copies of the presumptive 6th edition have been located.
      With a new preface to the 7th edition.

Hatfield, Robert Griffith
559. The American house carpenter . . . 7th ed. rev. and enl. New York, John Wiley & son, 1867.
398, 36 p. illus.   DLC,MoS

560. —— —— 7th ed. rev. and enl. New York, John Wiley & son, 1868.
398, 36 p. illus.   CtMW

561. —— —— 7th ed. rev. and enl. New York, John Wiley & son, 1869.
398, 36 p. illus.   IU

562. —— —— 7th ed. rev. and enl. New York, John Wiley & son, 1874.
398, 36 p. illus.   MnU,MoS,NNC

563. —— —— 8th ed. rewritten and enl. New York, John Wiley & sons, 1880.
685 p. front., illus., 16 pl.   CtY,DLC,ICJ,MB,MH,NN
With new 1880 copyright. Edited by O. P. Hatfield.

564. —— —— 9th ed. New York, John Wiley & sons, 1883.
685 p. front., illus., 16 pl.   CU,NN

565. —— —— 10th ed. New York, John Wiley & sons, 1886.
685 p. front., illus., 16 pl.   OCi

566. —— —— 11th ed. New York, John Wiley & sons, 1889.
685 p. front., illus., 16 pl.   NNC-A,OCi,PU

567. —— —— 12th ed. New York, John Wiley & sons, 1892.
685 p. front., illus., 16 pl.   MiH
There was a later issue in 1895.

568. —— Plans of the Parish house [New York, 1848?]
cover title, 7 pl.   NN (2 copies)
This was the house of Henry Parish on Union Square at Broadway and
17th Street to which he moved in 1848 or 1849.
Hatfield also wrote technical works such as *Experimental tests for building
stones, Fireproof floor* and *Theory of transverse strains,* published in the
sixties and seventies.

569. Haupt, Herman, 1817–1905
General theory of bridge contruction . . . New York, D. Appleton & co., Philadelphia, G. S. Appleton, 1851.
268 p. 14 pl.   DLC,ICJ,NWM,Vi

570. —— —— New York, D. Appleton & co., 1853.
268 p. 14 pl.   DLC,MnU,NN

571. —— —— New York, D. Appleton & co., 1856.
268 p. 14 pl.   NN

572. —— —— New York, D. Appleton & co., 1862.
268 p. 14 pl.   MnU

573. —— —— New York, D. Appleton & co., 1865.
268 p. 14 pl.   NN

574. —— —— New York, D. Appleton & co., 1869.
268 p. 14 pl.   IU

575. —— —— New York, D. Appleton & co., 1870.
268 p. 14 pl.   NN

576. —— —— New York, D. Appleton & co., 1871.
268 p. 14 pl.   MnU,NNC-A

Haupt, Herman
577. General theory of bridge construction . . . New York, D. Appleton & co., 1886.
268 p. 14 pl. NN
General Haupt wrote many other engineering works even less relevant than
this to the present list.

578. Haviland, John, 1792–1852
The builder's assistant, containing the five orders of architecture, selected
from the best specimens of the Greek and Roman with the figured dimensions of their height, projection, and profile, and a variety of mouldings,
modillions & foliage, on a larger scale, both enriched and plain; with working drawings showing their method of construction: selected from a number of beautiful examples, copied from the antique. For the use of builders,
carpenters, masons, plasterers, cabinet makers, and carvers: and for whom
are sixty original designs, with their plans, elevations and sections . . .
Philadelphia, John Bioren, 1818, 1819, 1821.
3 v. 150 pl. (part fold.)   CSmH (v. 2 only),MoS (v. 1, 2 only),NNC-A,
                               NNGS,NNMM,NHi,PP (v. 1 only),PPFrankl,PPL
"engraved by Hugh Bridport, artist."
Haviland was born in England and came to Philadelphia in 1816. It will
be noted that this is the earliest book to offer Greek as well as Roman
orders. Bound in Vol. III of the NHi copy is *House carpenters' book of
prices and rules*, Philadelphia, 1819. 50 p.

579. —— —— 2d ed. Baltimore, Fielding Lucas, Jr. [1830].
4 v. 150 pl. (part fold.) CtY,DLC,MWA,NHi
All the plates are in v. 4.
With title: *The practical builders' assistant.*

580. —— A communication to the county commissioners . . . Philadelphia, 1849.
The copy of this item, once held by PHi has been lost.

581. —— A description of Haviland's design for the new penitentiary, now erecting
near Philadelphia, accompanied by a bird's eye view . . . Philadelphia, Robert
Desilver, 1824.
12 p. PHi,PPAmP,PPL
A. J. Wall seems to have misread the faded date on the PPL copy as 1821.

582. —— An improved and enlarged edition of Biddle's Young carpenter's assistant.
See Biddle, Owen
This work was much enlarged by Haviland in the 1833 edition.

583. —— Obituary notice of John Haviland. Philadelphia, Printed by Isaac Ashmead,
1852.
14 p. front. MH,PP,PPL
On title page in brackets: From the Journal of prison discipline . . . vol.
vii, July, 1852.

584. —— Plans for the halls of justice, New York . . . New York, 1835.
12 lithographs NHi,PPAmP

585. *Haweis, Mary Eliza (Joy), 1852–1898
Beautiful houses . . . New York, Scribner and Welford, 1882.
115 p. front.   CtY,MBAt,MH,MnU,NN,NNC-A,NNMM,NHi,
                   NPV,OCi,OCl,PP

586. *Heck, Johann Georg,   , *comp.*
The art of building in ancient and modern times . . . New York, D. Appleton & co., 1856.
220 p. 60 pl. NNC-A

49

*Heck, Johann Georg
The plates are in a separate atlas.
This material appeared earlier in v. 4.—*Architecture,* of the *Iconographic encyclopedia of science, literature and art,* New York, R. Garrigue, 1851–52. 6 v. The entire work was arranged by Heck and translated from the German by S. F. Baird. Later editions of the *Encyclopedia,* 1857 and ᶜ1885, include the same material.

587. Heins & LaFarge, architects
Description of the design for the cathedral of Saint John the divine . . . Philadelphia, Globe printing house, 1891.
25 p. 9 pl.   NHi(imp.)
Edition limited to 25 copies for private distribution.

588. Henderson, H   A   M
Manual of Kentucky school of architecture . . . Frankfort, Ky., Printed at the Kentucky Yeoman office. S. I. M. Major, Public printer, 1876.
136 p. illus.   H.R.H.

589. *Henrici, Olaus Magnus Friedrich Erdmann, 1840–1918
Skeleton structures, especially in their application to building of steel and iron bridges . . . New York, D. Van Nostrand, 1867.
96 p. 4 pl. (1 fold.)   CU,CtY,DLC,IU,MH,NNCoo,PP

590. Hills, Chester
The builder's guide; or, A practical treatise on the several orders of Grecian and Roman architecture, together with the Gothic style of building; constituting a complete exposition of the most modern and approved methods adopted by skilful architects in the various departments of carpentry, joinery, masonry and sculpture, embracing all their necessary details, and a plain and comprehensive arrangement, particularly adapted to the wants of the less experienced . . . Hartford, D. W. Kellogg & Co., 1834.
2 v. in 1. front., 35, 34 pl. (part double)   CtY,MH,NHi,NNCoo,NNMM
The plates are lithographed.
The second volume includes one plate of shop fronts, several of house plans and elevations, and two plates of churches. Two of the houses are Gothic but not the churches. There are, however, five plates of Gothic details from the works of the elder Pugin.

591. ——— ——— New York, Daniel Appleton & co., 1836.
2 v. in 1. front., 33, 34 pl. (part double)   NNC-A,PU-FA

592. ——— ——— Hartford, Case, Tiffany and Burnham, 1846.
96 p. front., illus., 50 pl. (part double)   MWA,NN,NNC-A,PPL
"rev. and imp. with additions of villa and schoolhouse architecture.
By H. Austin . . . and Henry Barnard . . ." The frontispiece and plates 1–4 are villas by Austin. Pp. 89-96, figs. 1–38 are Barnard's schoolhouses. Plates 1–5, 7, 24–29, 32 and 33 of vol. 1 and plates 12–18 and 23–26 of vol. 2 of the 1st edition are omitted.

593. ——— ——— 2d rev. ed. Hartford, Case Tiffany and Burnham, 1847.
96 p. front., illus., 50 pl. (part double)   CtHWatk,DLC,ICA-B,MH,
                                                                      NNMM,NPV,PP,PPD

594. Historic churches of America; their romance and their history . . . illustrated by etchings, photogravures and other reproductions . . . with full letter text by by sixteen competent authorities, compiled from the chronicles, legends and traditions of the most famous churches, meeting houses, missions and cathedrals in the United States and adjoining countries. Philadelphia, H. L. Everett, [ᶜ1890].
160 p. illus., pl.   CSmH,MB,MdBE,NN,NNC-A,NHi,OCl,PP
Publication in 20 parts apparently extended through the years 1891–94.

595. Hobbs, Isaac H., and son, *architects, Philadelphia.*
    Hobbs's Architecture: containing designs and ground plans for villas, cottages and other edifices, both suburban and rural, adapted to the United States, with rules for criticism and introduction . . . Philadelphia: J. B. Lippincott & co., 1873.
    189 p. incl. 84 pl.   DLC,IU,MB,MBAt,MH,MSaE,NNC-A,
                                                            PPFrankl,PPM,RIBA

596. —— —— 2d ed. rev. and enl. Philadelphia, J. B. Lippincott & co., 1876.
    265 p. incl. front., illus., 122 pl.   DLC,MB,MH,NN,NNC-A,PPM

597. Holly, Henry Hudson, 1834–1892
    Church architecture illustrated with thirty-five lithographic plates from original designs . . . Hartford, Conn., M. H. Mallory and company, 1871.
    258 p. incl. 35 pl.   DLC,ICA-B,MB,MoS
    Added lithographic title page illustrated in color.

598. —— Holly's country seats: containing lithographic designs for cottages, villas, mansions, etc., with their accompanying outbuildings; also, country churches, city buildings, railway stations, etc., etc., . . . New York, D. Appleton & company, 1863.
    171 p. 36 pl.   CSmH,CtY,DLC,ICA B,MB,MBHo,MI I,MSaE,
                                        MiU,MoS,NN,NNC-A,NNMM,PPFrankl

599. —— —— New York, D. Appleton & company, 1866.
    171 p. 36 pl.   NN,NNC

600. —— Modern dwellings in town and country adapted to American wants and climate with a treatise on furniture and decoration . . . with one hundred original designs comprising cottages villas and mansions. New York, Harper & brothers, 1878.
    219 p. front., illus.   CU,CtY,ICA-B,MB,MBAt,MH,MSaE,MWA,MiU,
                                        MoS,NjP,NN,NNC-A,NNCoo,NNMM,
                                        NcD,OU,PP,RP,ViU

601. —— —— New York, Harper & brothers, n.d.
    219 p. front., illus.   NjP,OCl
    With the original 1878 copyright.

    Homes in city and country
    See Sturgis, Russell, and others

602. Hopkins, David S.
    Houses and cottages. Containing thirty-three designs costing from $800.00 to $1500.00, mostly of low cost. Grand Rapids, Mich., D. S. Hopkins, ᶜ1889.
    [67] p. illus.   DLC

603. —— —— 2d ed. Grand Rapids, Mich., D. S. Hopkins, ᶜ1890.
    [67] p. illus.   DLC,ICA-B

604. —— Houses and cottages; a collection of house and cottage designs. Grand Rapids, [D. S. Hopkins, ᶜ1889–   ].
    v. illus.   DLC,NNC-A(v. 4 only),OCl(v. 4–9)
    Book 12: 2d edition

605. —— Cottage Portfolio. 12 designs of low cost homes . . . New York, F. A. Hodgson, 1886.
    1 p. l. 12 pl.   DLC
    Cover title.

606. Hopkins, John Henry, 1792–1868

Essay on Gothic architecture, with various plans and drawings for churches designed chiefly for the use of the clergy . . . Burlington, [Vt.] Printed by Smith & Harrington, 1836.

vi, 46 p. 13 pl.   CtY,DLC,ICA-B,MB,MBAt,MH,MdBP,
                               NN,NNC-A,NNMM,OO,PPL

Added lithographic title page.

607. Horrors in architecture and so-called works of art in bronze in the city of New York . . . By an admirer of art whose name is of no consequence to the reader. New York, 1886.

20 p.   NNC-A

608. Horton, Caroline W

Architecture for general students . . . New York, Hurd & Houghton, 1874.

287 p. illus., 8 pl.   CtY,DLC,IU,MBAt,MH,NN,NNC-A,
                               NPV,OCl,OO,PP

609. *Hosking, William, 1800–1861, and others

Treatises on architecture, building, masonry, joinery and carpentry . . . New York, D. Appleton and company, 1852.

157 p. 36 pl.   MH,NNMM

From the *Encyclopedia Brittanica*, 7th ed.

This material first appeared as a separate work, Edinburgh, 1832.

Contents—Architecture and building by W. Hosking, Masonry and joinery by T. Tredgold, Carpentry by T. Young.

610. The house and its surroundings. New York, D. Appleton & co., 1879.

96 p. illus.   CtY,DSG,MB,MH,MnU,NM,OCl,PPD,ViU

Health primers. No. 3. edited by J. L. Down and others.

611. —— —— New York, D. Appleton & co., 1881.

96 p. illus.   NN

612. —— —— New York, D. Appleton & co., 1886.

96 p. illus.   NPV

613. —— —— New York, D. Appleton & co., 1889.

96 p. illus.   NN

614. —— —— New York, D. Appleton and Company, 1894.

96 p. illus.   ICJ

615. Howe, Hezekiah, 1775–1839

Architecture. Part I. Ancient architecture. New Haven, Hezekiah Howe, 1831.

74 p. plates   MSaE,NN,NHi,PU

Copyrighted by Howe and printed by Howe, who was presumably also the author or compiler.

616. Hunnewell, James Frothingham, 1832–1910

The historical monuments of France . . . Boston, James R. Osgood & company, 1884.

336 p. 23 pl.   CtHWatk,DLC,IU,MH,MLy,MWA,MoS,NN,
                               PPL,PPM,OU

617. —— The imperial island; England's chronicle in stone . . . Boston, Ticknor and company, 1886.

445 p. 65 (i.e., 63) pl., incl. front.   ICA-B,IU,MH,MWA,MiU,
                               MnU,NN,NNC

London edition the same year.

618. Hunt, Richard Morris, 1828–1895
    Designs for the gateways of the south entrances to the Central Park . . .
    New York, D. Van Nostrand, 1866.
      36 p. 9 pl.   CtY,DLC,ICJ,MB,MBAt,MH,NN,
                                        NNC-A,NHi,PU,RIBA

Huntington, Daniel, 1816–1906
    See Ludlow, *Miss*

Huss, George Martin
    See Description of drawings for . . . Saint John the divine

619. Hussey, Elisha Charles
    Home building. A reliable book of facts, relating to building, living, materials,
    costs. At about 400 places from New York to San Francisco . . . in 1875 . . .
    45 original designs of building . . . [New York, Leader & Van Hoesen, c1876].
      viii, p. 42 l. 197–416 p. illus., 42 pl.   MH,MWA,PP

620. —— —— [New York, Leader & Van Hoesen, c1877]
      viii, p. 42 l. 97–416 p. illus., 42 pl.   DLC,MB,MoS,NN,NNC-A,OCl

621. —— Hussey's National cottage architecture; or, Homes for everyone. Chiefly
    low-priced buildings for towns, suburbs and country . . . New York, Geo.
    E. Woodward, 1874.
      24 p. 63 pl.   DLC,ICJ,MB,MBAt,MH,MBaE,MWA,NN,
                                     NNC-A,OCi,OCl,PPM

622. Illsley, Charles E.
    Architectural competitions . . . Minneapolis, 1887.
                                          . RIBA

623. —— Houseplanning at home . . . St. Louis, C. B. Woodward company, 1894.
      112 p. illus.   DLC

624. Ingram, J   S
    The Centennial exposition described and illustrated . . . Philadelphia, Hub-
    bard bros. [etc.], [c1876].
      770 p. incl. front., illus.   CSmH,IU,InI,NcD,MB,MH,MWA,
                                       MnU,MoS,NN,PP,PPL
    There has been no attempt to include other descriptive accounts of the
    1876 Centennial exposition in Philadelphia, of which there must be ten
    or more, easily to be found in the Philadelphia libraries and often else-
    where as well.

627. International correspondence schools, Scranton, Pa.
    . . . History of architecture. 3d ed. Scranton, Pa., International text book
    co. [c1889].
      187, [1], 6 p. illus.   OU
    At head of cover title: Instruction paper . . . 103.
    No copies of the presumptive 1st and 2d editions have been located.

628. Jacques, Daniel Harrison, 1825–1877
    The house: a pocket manual of rural architecture: or, How to build country
    houses and out-buildings; embracing the origin and meaning of the house;
    the art of house-building, including planning, style, and construction; de-
    signs and descriptions of cottages, farmhouses, villas, and out-buildings, of
    various cost and in the different styles of architecture, etc., etc.; and an ap-
    pendix containing recipes for paints and washes, stucco, rough cast, etc.;
    burnt brick, balloon frames and the concrete or gravel wall . . . with numer-

Jacques, Daniel Harrison
    ous original plans designed by F. E. Graef, architect, and others, New York, Fowler and Wells, 1859.
        176 p. illus.   DLC,MB,MSaE,MWA,NNC-A,NHi
        "By the author of 'The garden,' 'The farm,' etc.," but undoubtedly by Jacques.
        At head of title: Rural manuals, No. 1.

629. —— —— rev. ed. New York, Geo. E. & F. W. Woodward, 1866.
        176 p. illus.   CU,DLC,MB,MH,MoS,NNC-A,PPL
        With title: The house: a manual of rural architecture . . . With numerous original plans, by D. H. Jacques.

630. —— —— rev. ed. New York, G. E. & F. W. Woodward, 1867.
        176 p. illus.   NN,PPM

631. —— —— rev. ed. New York, Geo. E. Woodward, 1868.
        176 p. illus.   IU

632. —— —— rev. ed. New York, Geo. E. Woodward, 1869.
        176 p. illus.   MSaE,NNC-A

633. Jarves, James Jackson, 1818–1888
    Art hints. Architecture, sculpture and painting . . . New York, Harper & brothers, 1855.
        398 p.   CSmH,CtY,DLC,MB,MBAt,MH,MWA, MdBP,MnU,MoS,
                                NN,NNC,NNMM,NPV,OCi,OO,OU,PPFrankl

634. —— The art-idea; part second of confessions of an inquirer . . . New York, Hurd & Houghton, 1864.
        381 p.   CtY,MB,MBAt,MH,MiU,MoS,NjP,NN,NNC-A,PPL
        ". . . including an account of American architecture . . ." Part one. Heart experience, of *The confessions of an inquirer* appeared in 1857.

635. —— —— 2d ed. New York, Hurd & Houghton, 1865.
        381 p.   CtY,DLC,MH,MoS

636. —— —— 3d ed. New York, Hurd & Houghton, 1866.
        381 p.   CtY,IU,NNC-A,OCi,OClMA,OClWHi
        With title: *The art-idea: sculpture, painting and architecture in America.*

637. —— —— 3d ed. New York, Hurd & Houghton, 1870.
        381 p.   CSmH,DLC,MiOC,NjP

638. —— —— 4th ed. New York, Hurd & Houghton, 1877.
        381 p.   CSmH,NNMM,OCl,OU

639. —— —— 5th ed. Boston, Houghton, Mifflin and company, n.d.
        381 p.   DLC,PPD
        The DLC assumes a date in the nineties which seems unlikely.

640. —— Art thoughts, the experiences and observations of an American amateur in Europe . . . New York, Hurd & Houghton, 1869.
        379 p.   CU,CtMW,CtY,I,MH,MnU,MoS,NjR, NN,OCi,OCl,PPM

641. —— —— New York, Hurd & Houghton, 1870.
        379 p.   MB,OClMA,PPL

642. —— —— New York, Hurd & Houghton, 1871.
        379 p.   DLC,IU,MdBP,NNMM,PU

643. —— —— New York, Hurd & Houghton, 1875.
        379 p.   CtY,MB

Jarves, James Jackson
644. Art thoughts . . . Boston, Houghton, Mifflin and company, 1876.
379 p.   ICA-R

645. —— ——— Boston, Houghton, Mifflin and company, 1879.
379 p.   NNMM,PPPM

646. —— ——— Boston, Houghton, Mifflin and company, 1882.
379 p.   MB,MiOC,OU,PChhC

647. —— ——— Boston, Houghton, Mifflin and company, 1887.
379 p.   CtY,PPD
Jarves' other books touch only very incidentally on architecture.

648. *Jenkin, Henry Charles Fleeming, 1833–1885
Healthy houses, adapted to American conditions by G. E. Waring, jr. . . .
New York, Harper and bros., 1879.
122 p. 1 plan   CtY,MB,MBAt,MH,MoS,NN,PPCP
First appeared Edinburgh, 1878.

649. Johnson, John Butler, 1850–1902
Theory and practice of modern framed structures . . . New York, John
Wiley & sons, 1893.
527 p. illus., pl.   CtY,MH,MnU,NN,OU,PP

650. —— ——— 2d ed. New York, John Wiley & sons, 1893.
527 p. illus., pl.   PPFrankl

651. —— ——— 3d ed. New York, John Wiley & sons, 1894.
527 p. illus., pl.   CU,MB,MnU,MoS,NNC,PU-ETS

652. Johnson, Stephen William
Rural economy: containing a treatise on pise buildings; as recommended by
the board of agriculture in Great Britain, with improvements by the author;
on buildings in general: on the culture of the vine; and on turnpike roads,
with plates . . . New York, I. Riley & co., 1806.
viii, 246, [5] p. 8 pl.   CSmH,DLC,ICA-B,MBAt,MBHo,MWA,
                                NjHi,NjP,NjR,NHi,NN,NNC-A,NNS,PPL,WHi
Printed by William Elliot, New Brunswick, N. J. The author, a New
Brunswick lawyer, is sometimes confused with Samuel W. Johnson, 1830–
1909.

653. Johnson, William K.
Modern homes . . . Chicago [1894?].
[4] p. 52 designs (i.e., plates)   MB,OCl
Johnson is described in the title as "architect." The suggested date is that
used at the MB.

654. Johnson, William   , translator
The practical draughtsman's book of industrial design and machinist's and
engineer's drawing companion forming a complete course of mechanical engineering and architectural drawing . . . New York, Stringer & Townsend,
1854.
196 p. illus., 54 pl. (1 fold., 2 col.)   NNCoo
"Translated from the French of M. Armengaud the elder, and Armengaud, the younger, and Amouroux, civil engineers. Rewritten and arranged
with additional matter and plates, etc."
First appeared Ostende, 1850.
Advertised in the Scientific American as appearing in 1853 in 13 parts
at 37½ cents each.
Offered by the publishers for $6.50 in 1854.

Johnson, William

655. The practical draughtsman's book . . . New York, Stringer & Townsend, [1857].
196 p. illus., 54 pl. (1 fold, 2 col.)   MH,MnM

656. —— —— Philadelphia, Henry Carey Baird, 1864.
196 p. illus., 54 pl. (1 fold., 2 col.)   CtHWatk,MnU

657. —— —— Philadelphia, Henry Carey Baird, 1870.
196 p. illus., 54 pl. (1 fold., 2 col.)   NNC

658. —— —— Philadelphia, Henry Carey Baird, 1872.
200 p. illus., 54 pl. (1 fold., 2 col.)   NNCoo,PP

659. Johonnot, James, 1823–1888
Country school-houses; containing elevations, plans, and specifications . . .
and a treatise on schoolhouse architecture . . . with numerous designs by S.
E. Hewes . . . New York, Ivison and Phinney, 1859.
230 p. illus., 19 pl.   IU,NN

660. —— —— New York, Ivison, Phinney, Blakeman & co., Chicago, S. C. Griggs
& co., 1866.
220 p. illus., 70 figs. on pl.   MH,MnU

661. —— Schoolhouses . . . Architectural designs by S. E. Hewes. New York, J. W.
Schermerhorn & co., 1871.
271 p. incl. 42 pl. (2 col.)   CU,DLC,MH,NN,NNCoo,PPL
36 "plates" are printed on both sides and are merely full-page illustrations.

662. —— —— New York, J. W. Schermerhorn & co., 1872.
271 p. incl. 42 pl. (2 col.)   NN

663. Jones, Alvin Lincoln
Under colonial roofs . . . Boston, Charles B. Webster, 1894.
237 p.   CtY,MB,MBAt,MH,NHi

664. *Jones, Owen, 1809–1874
Grammar of ornament . . . New York, J. W. Bouton, 1880.
157 p. illus., 112 pl. (part col.)   NPV,OO
Added title page illustrated in colors.
First published London[1856].
With contributions by J. B. Waring, J.O. Westwood, and M. D. Wyatt.

665. Julien, Alexis A
The decay of the building stones of New York city . . . [New York, 1883?].
pp. 67–168   OO
Reprinted from papers read before the New York Academy of sciences,
Jan. 29 and April 30, 1883.

666. Kelt, Thomas,   , *comp.*
Mechanic's textbook and engineer's pocket guide . . . Boston, Phillips, Sampson & co., 1849.
403 p. illus.   MoS
With "Valuable hints to the young mechanic" by John Frost.

667. —— —— Boston, Phillips, Sampson & co., New York, James C. Derby, 1850.
403 p. illus.   MWA

668. —— —— Boston, Phillips, Sampson & co., New York, James C. Derby, 1854.
403 p. illus.   PPWa(imp.)
With title: *Mechanic's textbook and engineer's practical guide.*

669. —— —— Boston, Phillips, Sampson & co., New York, James C. Derby, 1856.
403 p. illus.   NcD

Kelt, Thomas
670. Mechanic's textbook and engineer's pocket guide . . . Boston, Phillips, Sampson & co., New York, James C. Derby, 1857.
403 p. illus. PU

671. —— —— Boston, Crosby & Ainsworth, 1866.
403 p. illus. DLC,NN

672. —— —— Boston, Nichols and Hall, 1872.
178 p. illus. MB,MoS

673. Kennion, John W
The architects' and builders' guide. An elaborate description of all the public, commercial, philanthropic, literary and ecclesiastical buildings already constructed, and about to be erected next spring in New York and its environs, with their cost respectively, and the names of the architects and builders . . . New York, Fitzpatrick & Hunter, 1868.
3 pts. xxxi, 70, 140, 108 p. illus., 2 pl. DLC,ICA-B,NN,NHi

674. Kent, William Winthrop, 1860–
Architectural wrought iron ancient and modern . . . New York, William T. Comstock, 1888.
34 p. illus., 36 pl. DLC,MB,MoS,NN,NNC-A,PP

675. King, David
Historical sketch of the Redwood library and athenaeum in Newport, Rhode Island . . . Boston, John Wilson and sons, 1860.
53 p. NNC-A

676. —— —— Providence, R. I., Providence press co., 1876·
12 p. NNC-A

677. King, David H
The King model dwellings, situated on 138th and 139th Streets, Seventh and Eighth Avenues [New York, S. Lees, printer, 1891?].
[23] p. illus. NNC-A

678. King, David W
Homes for home builders or practical designs for country, farm and village . . . New York, O. Judd co., 1886.
251 p. illus. IU,MoS,NN,PPM

679. Kirby, Henry P   –1915
Architectural compositions . . . Boston, Bates, Kimball & Guild [c1892].
1 p. l. 50 pl. CU,DLC,ICA-B,MH,MnU,NNC-A,OCl,PPD

680. Kirby, J   H
Kirby's Domestic architecture, containing twenty-three original designs, consisting of elevations, plans and constructive details, all drawn to a working scale . . . Philadelphia, Pa. [King & Baird, printers, c1874].
2 p. l. 28 pl. DLC,MiGr,PPM
Kirby was a Syracuse, N. Y., architect.

681. —— Modern cottages . . . Syracuse, N. Y.[Hall & McChesney, printers, 1886].
128 p. illus., 32 pl. MWA

682. —— Portfolio of cottages . . . Syracuse, n.d.
24 pl. MnU

Kirkham, Guy
The best security . . . Springfield, Clark W. Bryan co. [1894].
33 p. incl. illus., pl. DLC

683. Knapen, D   M
       Mechanic's assistant . . . New York, D. Appleton & co., 1849.
          276 p. illus.   DLC

684. —— —— New York, D. Appleton & co., 1850.
          276 p. illus.   CtY

685. —— —— New York, D. Appleton & co., 1856.
          276 p. illus.   PPFrankl

686. Lafever, Minard, 1797–1854
       The architectural instructor, containing a history of architecture from the
       earliest ages to the present time . . . also the Greek and early Roman classic
       orders . . . with a large number of original designs of cottages, villas, and
       mansions . . . and further designs of churches, monuments and public build-
       ings together with a glossary of architectural terms . . . New York, George
       P. Putnam, 1856.
          526 p. 112 pl.   CtY,ICA-B,IU,MB,MH,MWA,NjP,
                                     NN,NNC-A,NNMM,NHi,NNCoo,NRU,PPM
       The copyright date of this issue is 1854 suggesting that there may have
       been an earlier one, but none has been located.

687. —— The beauties of modern architecture . . . New York, D. Appleton & Co., 1835.
          2 p. l. [65]–139, [1]– [96] p. 48 pl.   CtY,ICA-B,NNC-A,NHi,OO,PP
       "Architectural history. Extracts from Elmes' Dictionary" occupies pp.
       .[65]–128; "Glossary of names and terms used in architecture," from the
       Encyclopedia Brittanica, seventh edition, pp. [129]–139.

689. —— —— 3d ed. New York, D. Appleton & co., 1839.
          176 p. 48 pl.   CtY,DLC,MH,MoS,NHi,NjP,NN,NNCoo,RIBA
       No copy of the presumptive 2d ed. has been located.

690. —— —— new ed. New York, D. Appleton & co., 1849.
          176 p. 48 pl.   NHi,OClMA,PPFrankl

691. —— —— new ed. New York, D. Appleton & co., 1855.
          176 p. 48 pl.   DLC,MB,MH,MdBP
       Offered for sale by Fowlers and Wells in 1855 for $4.00.

692. —— The modern builder's guide . . . New York, Henry C. Sleight, Collins &
       Hannay, 1833.
          146 p. front., pl. 1–53, 56–88   CtY,ICJ,MdBP,MH,MoS,NHi,NNC-A
                                                                       NNMM,PU
       The frontispiece might be considered to be rather an engraved title page
       with "Design for a country villa." The title page mentions "87 copper
       plates" so plates 54 and 55 are not to be considered as missing.

693. —— —— New York, William D. Smith, 1841.
          119 p. front., pl. 1–53, 56–88   NHi,NN,OO,PPCC

694. —— —— New York, Paine & Burgess, 1846.
          119 p. front., 89 pl.   ICA-B,ICJ,MH,NHi,OU
       With a new 1846 copyright. The preface of the first, 1833, edition is
       repeated, confusingly signed and dated: New York, 1846, as if this were
       the first edition. Plates 54 and 55 are added, with designs for a Classical
       and a Gothic church, the former Ionic, the latter based on the National
       Scotch church in London. Plate 89, with a plan and elevation of a country
       residence, is also added.

695. —— —— New York, Cady & Burgess, 1849.
          119 p. front., 89 pl.   MH

696. —— —— New York, Cady & Burgess, 1850.
          119 p. front., 89 pl.   .PPFrankl

Lafever, Minard
697. The modern builder's guide . . . New York, Daniel Burgess & co., 1853.
   119 p. front., 89 pl.   DLC,MnU

698. —— —— New York, Daniel Burgess & co., 1855.
   119 p. front., 89 pl.   MoS

699. —— The modern practice of staircase and hand-rail construction, practically
   explained, in a series of designs . . . With plans and elevations for ornamental
   villas . . . New York, D. Appleton & co., 1838.
   47 p. 15 pl. (2 col.)   DLC,NHi

700. —— The young builder's general instructor; containing the five orders of architecture selected from the best specimens of the Greek and Roman . . . and
   a variety of mouldings, and fancy pilasters, square and circle head front
   doors . . . Newark, N. J., Printed by W. Tuttle & co., 1829.
   175 p. 67 pl.   CtY,DLC,ICA-B,NHi,NN,NNC-A,NNMM,OO

701. Lakey, Charles D.
   Lakey's village and country houses, or cheap homes for all classes . . . New
   York, American builder publishing co., 1875.
   2 p. l. 84 pl.   CtY,DLC,MB,MH,MWA,NNC-A,OCl

702. Lamb, Martha Joanna Reade (Nash), 1829–1893, ed.
   The homes of America . . . New York, D. Appleton and company, [c1879].
   256 p. incl. front., illus.   CtY,DLC,MB,MBAt,MH,MSaE,MdBE,MnU,
             MoS,NN,NNC-A,NHi,NPV,OCi,OCl,PP,PU

703. Landrin, Henri C
   Treatise on steel . . . Philadelphia, Henry Carey Baird, 1868.
   352 p. illus.   MH,MdBE,MoS,NNC,NPV,PP,PPL
   First appeared Paris, 1859.

704. Lang, William Bailey
   Views, with ground plans, of the Highland cottages at Roxbury . . . Boston,
   printed by L. H. Bridgham and H. E. Felch, 1845.
   2 p. l. 81. 9 pl.   DLC,MB,MBAt,MH,MHi,MWA,
                 NN,NNC-A,PPL,Vi

705. *Langley, Batty, 1696–1751
   The builder's jewel; or, The youth's instructor, and workman's remem-
   brancer. Explaining short and easy rules, made familiar to the meanest
   capacity, for drawing and working I. The five orders of columns entire; or
   any part of an order, without regard to the module or diameter. And to
   enrich them with their rusticks, flutings, cablings, dentules, modilions, &c.
   Also to proportion their doors, windows, intercolumniations, porticoes and
   arcades. Together with fourteen varities of raking, circular, scrolled, compound, and contracted pediments; and the true formation and accadering
   of their raking and returned cornices; and mouldings for capping their
   dentules and modilions. II. Block and cantaliver cornices, rustick quoins,
   tabernacle frames, pannelling, and centering for groins, trussed partitions,
   girders, roofs, and domes. With a section of the dome of St. Paul's, London
   . . . 1st Amer. ed. Charlestown, Printed by S. Etheridge, for Samuel Hill,
   [i.e., Hall] engraver, Boston [1800].
   46 p. 100 pl.   MH,MHi,MWA,NNMM,PP,RPJCB(imp.)
   Thomas Langley, 1702–1751 was joint author.
   As Etheridge began printing in Charlestown only in 1799 and this work
   is announced as just published in the Salem Gazette, March 7, 1800, the
   date is practically fixed as early in the year 1800.
   First appeared London, 1741. There was a London edition as late as 1808
   and there had been over a dozen there altogether.
                        MoS

*Langley, Batty
706. Examples from ancient masonry in the proportions and orders of the most eminent
     masters . . . Boston and New York, Geo. H. Polley & co., n.d.
       [6] p. 73 pl.   NNC-A
       First appeared London, 1733. This reprint, "selected by John A. Fox,
       architect. Boston," may well be later than 1895. It is probably the
       first example of the reprinting of eighteenth-century sources as models
       for the Colonial Revival.

     Langley, Thomas, 1702–1751
       See Langley, Batty

707. Latrobe, Benjamin Henry, 1764–1820
       A private letter to . . . Congress . . . on . . . public buildings of the United
       States at Washington . . . Washington city, printed by S. H. Smith, 1806.
       32 p.   DLC,MBAt,NN,NNC-A,PHi

708. Latrobe, John Hazlehurst Boneval, 1803–1891
       The Capitol and Washington at the beginning of the present century. An
       address delivered . . . before the American institute of architects in Wash-
       ington, D. C. . . . 1881 . . . Baltimore, Steam press of W. K. Boyle, [1881].
       30 p. 3 pl.   DLC,MB,MdBE,NN,NNC-A,OU,PPAmP
       J. H. B. Latrobe also wrote a *Picture of Baltimore,* Baltimore, F. Lucas,
       jr. [1832].

709. Leahy, William Augustine, 1867–
       The Catholic churches of Boston and vicinity and St. John's seminary,
       Brighton . . . Ed. de luxe. Boston, McClellan, Hearn and co., 1892.
       43 l. 39 pl.   DLC,MB,NHi
       "A folio of photogravures with notes and historical information."

710. Lee, Charles Alfred, 1801–1872
       Hospital construction with notices of foreign military hospitals . . . Albany,
       N. Y., Steampress of C. Van Benthuysen, 1863.
       32 p.   DLC,DSG,MBAt
       Reprinted from the Transactions of the Medical society of the state of
       New York.

711. *Lefèvre, André-Paul-Emile, 1834–1904
       Wonders of architecture . . . New York, Charles Scribner & co., 1870.
       264 p. incl. front., illus., pl.   CtY,DLC,MB,MBAt,MH,MSaE,
                                                      MiOC,OCl,PPFrankl
       First appeared Paris, 1865.
       Translated from the French and with an added chapter on English archi-
       tecture by R. Donald.

712. —— —— New York, Charles Scribner & co., 1871.
       264 p. incl. front., illus., pl.   CU,DLC

713. —— —— New York, Scribner, Armstrong & co., 1872.
       264 p. incl. front., illus., pl.   MB,MdBE,ScC

714. —— —— New York, Charles Scribner & co., 1886.
       264 p. incl. front., illus., pl.   CU,InI,MnU,NN,PP

715. —— —— New York, Charles Scribner's sons, n.d.
       264 p. incl. front., illus., pl.   Vi

716. Leffel, James, and company
       Leffel's House plans containing elevations, plans and descriptions of houses
       costing from $500 to $3,000 and adapted to families having good taste and
       moderate means. New York, J. Leffel & co., 1884.
       223 p. illus.   DLC,MB,OCi

717. Leicht, Alfred F.
    A few sketches of picturesque suburban homes . . . [New York, ᶜ1892].
    [20] p. illus.   DLC

718. Leland, E   H
    Farm homes in-doors and out-doors . . . New York, Orange Judd co., 1881.
    204 p. 2 pl.   IU,MB,MH,NN

719. ——— ——— New York, Orange Judd co., 1882.
    204 p. 2 pl.   DLC,MBHo

720. Lent, Franklin Townsend, 1855–
    Sound sense in suburban architecture, containing hints, suggestions and bits
    of practical information for the building of inexpensive country houses . . .
    Cranford, N. J., F. T. Lent, 1893.
    98 p. front. illus.   DLC,MB,NNC,NNC-A,NPV,OCi,PPL

721. ——— ——— Cranford, N. J., F. T. Lent, 1894.
    97 p. front. illus.   DLC,MB,MoS,PP
    With title: Sensible suburban residences, containing suggestions, hints
    and practical ideas, sketches, plans, etc., for the building of country
    homes.

722. Leuchars, Robert B
    Practical treatise on the construction, heating and ventilating of hot houses;
    including conservatories, greenhouses, graperies . . . Boston, Jewett & co.,
    1851.
    366 p. front., illus., 48 pl.   CU,DLC,ICJ,MB,MH,NN,
                                                NPV,OCi,PPFrankl
    Leuchars is described on the title page as "garden architect."

723. ——— ——— Boston, Jewett & co., 1854.
    366 p. front., illus., 48 pl.   PP,PPL

724. ——— ——— New York, C. M. Saxton, 1857.
    366 p. front., illus., 48 pl.   MB,MoS,PPFrankl

725. ——— ——— New York, A. O. Moore & co., 1859.
    366 p. front., illus., 48 pl.   DLC

726. ——— ——— New York, Orange Judd & company, n.d.
    366 p. front., illus., 48 pl.   DLC,IU,NN
    This still carries the original 1850 copyright.

727. Levy, Albert
    Albert Levy's architectural photographic series [New York] A. Levy
    [ᶜ1883–   ].
    v. photos.   CU(Series 5 only),DLC,MB(Series 30,33),MnU(Series
               25 only),MoS(Series1,2,9,10,16,31,33),PPFrankl(Series 2,10)
    The different series have different subtitles: 2, for example, "Country
    dwellings;" 10, "Seashore cottages and country houses," etc.

728. *Liénard, Michel
    Specimens of the decoration and ornamentation of the XIXth century . . .
    Boston, James R. Osgood and company, 1875.
    3 v. in 1. 127 pl.   CtY,DLC,MB
    First appeared Liége, 1866.

729. ——— ——— New York, J. O'Kane, n.d.
    1 p. l. 6 p. 127 pl.   DLC,PPD
    With title: Liénards' Specimens of decorations and ornamentation. Prob-
    ably issued in the early eighties.

730. Little, Arthur
    Early New England interiors . . . Salem, Marblehead, Portsmouth and Kittery
    . . . Boston, A. Williams & co., 1878.
        45 l. 36 pl.   CU,DLC,InI,MB,MBAt,MH,MSaE,MWA,
                                        MdBE,Nh,NNC-A,NHi,OCi,OCl,OU,PPPM,Vi

731. Lloyd, Augustus Parlett
    Treatise on the law of building and buildings . . . Boston and New York,
    Houghton, Mifflin & co., 1888.
        618 p.   DLC,ICJ,IU,IaAS,MB,MdBE,MnU,NcD,NN,PPBAss.

732. ——— ———— 2d ed. Boston and New York, Porter & Coates, 1894.
        537 p.   DLC,InI,MB,MH,PPBAss

733. *Loftie, William John, 1839–1911
    Inigo Jones and Wren; or, The rise and decline of modern architecture in
    England . . . New York, Macmillan and co., 1893.
        284 p. 49 pl., incl. front.   CU,CtNlC,DLC,InI,MB,MH,MnU,
                                        NNC-A,OCi,OCl,PP
    There was also a London edition in 1893.
    Most of Loftie's other books are properly guidebooks and English imprints
    as well. *A plea for art in the house* [c1876] is also not relevant here.

734. Long, Robert Cary,   –1849
    Ancient architecture of America. A discourse delivered before the New York
    historical society at the meeting April 3rd., 1849 . . . New York, Bartlett &
    Welford, 1849.
        37 p. 11 (i.e. 9,) pl.   DLC,ICJ,MB,MH,MdBE,NHi,NN,NNC-A
    This early discussion of Mayan and Aztec remains also appeared in New
    York historical society proceedings, 1849.

735. Long, Stephen Harriman, 1784–1864
    Description of the Jackson bridge, together with directions to builders of
    wooden or frame bridges . . . Baltimore, Printed by Lands & Nielson, 1839.
        24 p. illus., 2 pl.   DLC,PP

736. ——— Description of Col. Long's bridges, together with a series of directions to
    bridge builders . . . Concord, N. H., Printed by J. F. Brown, 1836.
        72, [4] p. illus., 7 pl.   DLC

737. ——— ———— Philadelphia, Printed by W. F. Geedes, 1841.   DLC

    ——— Specifications of a brace bridge, and of a suspension bridge . . . Philadelphia,
    1839.
        11 p. 4 pl.   DLC

    Loos, Richard Conover
        [Architectural designs]
        The existence of a 4th ed., 1896, and a 5th ed., 1898, in the DLC presupposes
        a 1st, 2d, and 3d edition. Two of these, at least, should have been previous
        to 1895. No locations of these presumptive editions have been reported.

740. Loring, Sanford E
    Principles and practices of architecture. Comprising forty six folio plates of
    plans, elevations and details of churches, dwellings, stores constructed by the
    authors. Also an explanation and illustration of the French system of apart-
    ment houses, and dwellings for the laboring classes together with copious
    text . . . Chicago, Cleveland [etc.] Cobb, Pritchard, and co., 1869.
        62 p. front., 45 pl.   DLC,MB,MBAt,NNC-A,NNCoo,OCl
    William Le Baron Jenney was joint author.

741. Lossing, Benson J
Outline history of the fine arts . . . Part I. Architecture . . . New York, Harper and brothers, 1842.
33 p.   NHi,NNC-A

742. *Loudon, John Claudius, 1783–1843
Encyclopedia of cottage, farm, and villa architecture and furniture . . . new ed. New York, R. Worthington, 1883.
1317 p. illus.   DLC,MdBE,PPD
First appeared London, 1833. This is from the London new ed., 1850, edited by Mrs. Loudon.

743. Ludlow, Miss
A general view of the fine arts . . . New York, George P. Putnam, 1851.
477 p.   DLC,MH,NN,NNC-A
"With an introduction by D. Huntington"; pp. 338–430 deal with architecture in a separate section.

747. —— —— 5th ed. New York, A. S. Barnes & co., Cincinnati, H. W. Derby, 1854.
477 p.   DLC
No copies of the presumptive 2d, 3d, and 4th editions have been located.

748. —— —— New York, A. S. Barnes & Burr, 1862.
477 p.   DLC,NN,PU
The original title appears at the head of the title page. The new title reads: *Manual of the fine arts, critical and historical*. Miss Ludlow's name is omitted, but Huntington is still mentioned as the author of the introduction.

749. —— —— New York, A. S. Barnes & co., 1866.
477 p.   MiOC

750. —— —— New York, and Chicago, A. S. Barnes & company, 1875.
476 p.   DLC

751. —— —— New York A. S. Barnes & co. [1879].
476 p. 6 pl.   MoS

752. Lupton, Nathaniel Thomas
On heating and ventilation with especial reference to the public school buildings of Nashville . . . with plans and tables by Wm. C. Smith. Nashville, Tenn. [?1878].
23 p. plans   NNC-A
Cover title.

753. McAlpine, William Jarvis, 1812–1890
Modern engineering. A lecture delivered on the 10th of February, 1869 . . . at the request of the American institute [of architects] Albany, Van Benthuysen steam printing house, 1874.
58 p.   DLC,NN

754. —— —— 2d ed. New York, D. Van Nostrand, 1874.
72 p.   MH,NN

McAuley, William John, 1867–
See Goforth, William Davenport

755. McClarren, Samuel T
Second annual souvenir of designs . . . [Pittsburgh? c1891].
Cover title, 23 pl.   DLC
No copies of the presumptive first or later Annual souvenirs have been located.

756. Mann, George R
    Selections from an architect's portfolio . . . [St. Louis] I. Haas & co., 1893.
    Cover title, 36 pl.
                                                                        MoS

757. Martin, George A   –1904
    Fences, gates and bridges . . . New York, Orange Judd co., 1887.
    188 p. illus.   DLC,IU,MB,MdBE,PPL

758. —— —— New York, Orange Judd co., 1892.
    188 p. illus.   NN,OO

759. —— Our homes; how to beautify them . . . New York, Orange Judd co., 1888.
    188 p. illus.   DLC,MnU

760. Mason, George Champlin, 1820–1894
    The old house altered . . . New York, G. P. Putnam's sons, 1878.
    179 p. illus.   CtMW,DLC,MB,MBAt,MnU,ESaE,MWA,
                                                            NHi,NNC-A,PP

761. —— Thoughts on architecture, its literature and practice. Newport, R. I., Mar-
    shall's, 1879.
    24 p.   NNC-A
    Mason was also the author of a series of guidebooks to Newport, of which
    the first appeared in 1848 and the latest in 1891. They were illustrated
    with fine views of architecture.

762. Massachusetts institute of technology. Department of architecture.
    Annual exhibition of the department of architecture . . . Boston, May, 1891.
                                                                        NN
    Cover title. The plates are numbered irregularly. [21] p. of advertisements
    at the end.

763. —— —— Boston, May, 1892.
    [13] p. 31 pl.   MB

764. —— Catalogue of drawings . . . Boston, The Elezevir press, 1892.
    [23] p. plates   MB,OO
    "Printed for the use of the students."

765. Matthews, Charles Thompson
    The renaissance under the Valois, a sketch of French architectural history
    . . . New York, William T. Comstock, 1893.
    23 p. illus., 41 pl.   DLC,MH,MiU,PP

766. Meigs, Montgomery Cunningham, 1816–1897
    Report on the construction of the new Pension building made to the secre-
    tary of the interior . . . Washington, Government printing office, 1883–87.
    5 v.   MB,NNC-A,(1887 vol. only),PP

767. *Meikleham, Robert,   , pseud. Robert Stuart
    Dictionary of architecture . . . Philadelphia, A. Hart, late Carey & Hart,
    1851.
    v. 1 and 2 in 1, 662 p. illus., 597 p. v. 3, pl.   IU,MoS,NjR,NN
    First appeared London [1830].
    NN copy bound as three volumes.

    —— —— New York, A. S. Barnes & co., Cincinnati, H. W. Derby, 1854.
    2 v. in 1, 662 p. illus., 597 p.   IU,MH,MWA,MiU
    With title: *The home cyclopedia, Cyclopedia of architecture, historical,
    descriptive, topographical, decorative, theoretical and mechanical . . .*

64

768. *Memes, John Smythe, 1795–1858
History of sculpture, painting and architecture . . . Boston, Allen and Goddard, 1831.
    xii, 299 p.   CU,CtMW,CtY,MB,NN,NcD,OCl,OU,RPD
    Vignette on title page.
    First published Edinburgh, 1829.
    The first general history of art published in America. Pp. [227]–299 deal with architecture.

769. —— —— Boston, Clapp and Broaders, 1834.
    299 p.   DLC,MB,MBAt,MH,MWA,NjP,PPL,PPM
    There may have been a later issue in 1848.

Miller, Charles Crosby
See Cummings, Marcus Fayette

770. Mills, Robert, 1781–1855
The American pharos; or, Lighthouse guide . . . Washington, Thompson and Homans, 1832.
    184 p.   DLC,PPA

771. —— —— rev. ed. Washington, William M. Morrison, 1845.
    189 p.   NNC,PPFrankl
    With title: The American lighthouse guide.

772. —— Design no. 1 for a marine hospital . . . Washington city, P. Haas' lithy [1837?].
    Cover title, 4 fold. pl.   DLC,MH,NN

773. —— Design no. 2 for a marine hospital . . . Washington, city, P. Haas' lithy [1837?].
                              DLC,MH,NN

774. —— Guide to the Capitol of the United States . . . Washington, 1834.
    64 p. front., plan   DLC,MB,MH(imp.)

775. —— —— Washington, P. Force, printer, 1841.
    50 p. 7 plans.   CSmH,DLC,NN,PPT.
    With title: *Guide to the national executive offices and capitol.*
    Titles continue to vary slightly in the subsequent editions.

776. —— —— Washington, P. Force, printer, 1842.
    58 p. 11 plans.   DLC,MBAt,NN

777. —— —— Washington, W. Greer, printer, 1847–48.
    94 p. 8 plans.   CSmH,DLC,PPL

778. —— —— Washington, J. C. Greer, printer, 1854.
    82, [4] p. front., illus.   CtHWatk,DLC,MH,MWA,NN,PP

779. —— Water-works for the metropolitan city of Washington . . . Washington, Printed by L. Towers, 1853.
    36 p.   DLC,PPL
    Prefatory note: "The following papers were originally published in the National intelligencer, 1849."
    Mills probably began a work on *The principles of architecture,* never finished or published.

780. Minifie, William, 1805–1880
A textbook of geometrical drawing, for the use of mechanics and schools, with illustrations for drawing plans and sections of buildings, and machinery . . . Baltimore, W. Minifie & co., 1849.
    127 p. 56 pl. (incl. front.) 8^0.   DLC,MH,MWA,NNMM

Minifie, William

781. A textbook of geometrical drawing . . . Baltimore, W. Minifie & co., 1849.
156 p. 48 pl. (incl. front.) 4^0. DLC
". . . abridged from the octavo edition," above.

782. —— —— 2d ed. Baltimore, W. Minifie & co., 1850.
127 p. front., 56 pl. 8^0. CtHWatk,DLC,NNCoo

783. —— —— 3d ed. Baltimore, W. Minifie & co., 1851.
127 p. front., 56 pl. 8^0. MdBM

784. —— —— Baltimore, W. Minifie & Co., 1852.
127 p. front., 56 pl. 8^0. PP

785. —— —— 5th ed. Baltimore, W. Minifie & co., 1854.
157 p. front., 56 pl. 4^0. NN
A new issue of the abridged edition, with the frontispiece and additional
plates of the octavo edition.

786. —— —— Baltimore, William Minifie, London, Trübner, 1855.
157 p. front., 56 pl. 4^0. IU
Also abridged.

787. —— —— new ed. Baltimore, William Minifie, 1857.
156, [10] p. front., 48 pl. 4^0. CtHWatk

788. —— —— 7th thousand, rev. New York, D. Van Nostrand, 1868.
162 p. 56 pl., incl. front. 8^0. DLC
With a new copyright of 1867.

789. —— —— 8th thousand, rev. New York, D. Van Nostrand, 1869.
162 p. 56 pl., incl. front. 8^0. IU

790. —— —— 4th ed. New York, D. Van Nostrand, 1870.
143 p. 48 pl., incl. front. 12^0. NNCoo

791. —— —— 5th ed. rev. and enl. New York, D. Van Nostrand, 1871.
178 p. 48 pl., incl. front. 12^0. DLC,NN

792. —— —— 9th thousand, rev. New York, D. Van Nostrand, 1873.
162 p. 56 pl., incl. front. 8^0. MnU
With the 1867 copyright.

793. —— —— 6th ed. rev. and enl. New York, D. Van Nostrand, 1875.
178 p. 48 pl., incl. front. 12^0. NN(imp.)

796. —— —— 9th ed. rev. and enl. New York, D. Van Nostrand, 1890.
178 p. 48 pl., incl. front. 12^0. MnU
No copies of the presumptive 7th and 8th editions have been located.

797. Minton, Hollins & co.
Minton's tiles for floors of churches, banks and other public buildings . . .
For sale by Miller and Coates, 279 Pearl Street, New York [?1870].
6 p. 13 col. pl. NNMM

798. Mitchell, Donald Grant
Rural studies with hints for country places . . . New York, Charles Scribner & co., 1867.
viii, 295 p. illus. NHi

Monographs on American architecture.
See Richardson, Henry Hobson.
See Upjohn, Richard Mitchell.
See Ware, William Robert.

799. Moore, Charles Herbert, 1840–1930
    Development and character of Gothic architecture . . . London & New
    York, Macmillan & co., 1890.
        333 p. illus.   CtMW,CtY,DLC,ICA-B,InI,IU,MH,MnU,NN,
                                    NNC-A,NNMM,NPV,NcD,OCi,OCl,OO,PP,PPL
        Printed in England. Except that Moore is an American this would be con-
        sidered an English imprint.

800. *Morris, William, 1834–1896
    The decorative arts . . . Boston, Roberts brothers [1878].
        50 p.   CtY,MB,NN,NNC-A,NNMM
        First London edition the same year.

801. —— Hopes and fears for art . . . Boston, Roberts brothers, 1882.
        217 p.   CtMW,CtY,DLC,ICA-R,MBAt,MH,MiOC,NN,
                                    NNC-A,NNMM,OCi,OCl,PP
        First London edition the same year.

802. Morse, Edward Sylvester, 1838–1925
    Japanese homes and their surroundings . . . Salem, Peabody academy of
    science [c1885].
        2 p. l. xxxiii, 372 p. illus.   MSaP,PPPM
        "Prefatory note," dated January, 1886, explains that this is an advance
        issue with added title page of the regular edition, below.

803. —— —— Boston, Ticknor and company, 1886.
        xxxiii, 372 p. illus.   CU,DLC,IU,MSaP,MWA,MnU,OO
804. —— —— [2d ed.] Boston, Ticknor and company, 1886.
        xxxiii, 372 p. illus.   DLC,I,MB,MH,MSaP,NN,NNC-A,
                                    NNMM,OCi,PPL

806. —— —— [4th ed.] Boston, Ticknor and company, 1888.
        xxxiii, 372 p. illus.   MH,MSaP,PNt
        No copy of the presumptive 3d ed. has been located.

807. —— —— [4th ed.] New York, Harper & brothers, 1889.
        xxxiii, 372 p. illus.   NN,PPD

808. —— —— New York, Harper & brothers, n.d.
        xxxiii, 372 p. illus.   MSaP,MoS
        Still with the original 1885 copyright. There was a later issue in 1895.
        Morse's paper: On the older forms of roofing tiles, is too special for in-
        clusion, as also his Latrines of the east, 1893.

809. *Moseley, Henry, 1801–1872
    Mechanical principles of engineering and architecture . . . 1st Amer. from
    2d London ed. New York, Wiley and Halstead, 1856.
        699 p. illus.   DLC,ICJ,MH,MoS,NN,OCi,PPFrankl
        "With additions by D. H. Mahan."
        First appeared before 1855, the date of the 2d London edition.

810. —— —— 1st Amer. from 2d London ed. New York, John Wiley, 1860.
        699 p. illus.   CtMW,MH,PPFrankl
811. —— —— 2d Amer. from 2d London ed. New York, John Wiley, 1866.
        699 p. illus.   CU,DLC,IU,NN,OU,PPFrankl
812. —— —— 2d Amer. from 2d London ed. New York, John Wiley & son, 1869.
        699 p. illus.   DLC,MB,NN,ViU
813. —— —— 2d Amer. from 2d London ed. New York, John Wiley & son, 1875.
        699 p. illus.   MH,OU,PSC
        Moseley's Illustrations of mechanics, New York, 1842, is not particu-
        larly relevant.

814. Moseley, Thomas W   H
    Iron: new enterprise in its manufacture and applications to building . . .
    Boston, 1863.
        24 p. fold. pl.   MnU

815. Morton, M   J
    Mantel designs, n.p., n.d.
        33 pl.   NNMM

816. *Narjoux, Félix, 1836–1891
    Notes and sketches of an architect taken during a journey in the north-
    west of Europe . . . Boston, James R. Osgood and company, 1877.
        442 p. illus.   CU,CtHWatk(imp.),IU,MB,MLy,MSaE,NN,
                                                  NNC-A,OCi,OCl,PP,Vi
    Translated from the French by John Peto.
    First appeared Paris, 1876. London edition, 1876.
    Some consider 11 of the 214 illustrations to be plates.

817. National architects' union
    Artistic one-story houses . . . New York, Philadelphia, National architects'
    union [1893?].
        [59] p. illus.   MB
    Possibly a part of the later issue of *Modern rural homes.*

818. —— Modern homes. The perspective views and building plans for sensible low-
    cost houses . . . Philadelphia, National architects' union [1889].
        [56] p. illus.   DLC
    Probably v. 2 of the *Modern rural homes,* below.

819. —— Modern rural homes. The perspective views and building plans for fifty-
    one sensible low-cost houses . . . Philadelphia, National architects' union
    [1889?].
        [101] p. illus.   MiU
    Copyright by A. C. Child.

820. —— Modern rural homes. The perspective views and building plans for thirty-
    five sensible low-cost houses . . . Philadelphia, National architects' union
    [1885?–1891].
        3 v. illus.   MSaE
    Copyright by A. C. Child.
    Modern homes, above, may be v. 2 of this.
    Sensible low-cost houses, v. 3, below, is probably v. 3 of this.

821. —— Picturesque houses for forest and shore. Perspective views and floor plans
    . . . Philadelphia, National architects' union [1891].
        28 l. illus.   DLC,MSaE
    Copyright by A. C. Child.

822. —— Sensible low-cost houses . . . New York, National architects' union [1893?].
        3 v. in 1, illus.   MB
    Possibly a later issue of the item above. *Colonial houses for modern homes,*
    n.d., may be a part of this, but the DLC has only a 1903 issue of *Colonial
    houses for modern homes,* and an earlier issue is doubtful.
    The contents are, however, v. 1, 35 houses costing from $400 to $1800;
    v. 2, 55 houses costing from $1800 to $4000; v. 3, 35 houses costing
    from $3000 to $9000.

823. —— Sensible low-cost homes. vol. 3 . . . Philadelphia, National architects' union
    [1891].
        [26] p. illus.   DLC
    Copyright by A. C. Child.
    Probably v. 3 of *Modern rural homes,* above.

National architects' union
824. Sensible low-cost barns and stables . . . New York, National architects' union, 1893.
  24 designs on 4 sheets.   MB

825. National building plan association, *Detroit.*
  Artistic homes; with a description of beautiful and economical residence buildings, churches, school houses, store fronts, etc. . . . [Buffalo, Matthews, Northrup & Co.] ©1888.
  [97] p. illus.   DLC,MiGr

826. *Nevill, Ralph Henry, 1865–1930
  Old cottage and domestic architecture in south-west Surrey . . . 2d ed. New York, Dodd Mead & Co., 1892.
  142 p. illus.   NN,NNMM,OCl
  First appeared Guildford, Surrey, England, 1889. There was probably no American 1st ed. The Guildford 2d ed. was 1891.

827. New York. Architectural league
  Catalogue of the . . . annual exhibition . . . New York, 1887–
  v. plates.   NNC-A
  This is a separate publication beginning with the third annual exhibition, 1887. The catalogues of the first two exhibitions are included in the Annual catalogues of the Salmagundi club and American Black and White society, 8th annual exhibition, New York, 1886, and 9th annual exhibition, New York, 1887.

828. New York. Metropolitan Museum of Art
  Tentative list of objects desirable for a collection of casts, sculptural and architectural. New York, Printed for the Committee, [at the Devinne Press] 1891.
  x p. 1 l. 121 numb. l.   CSmH,CtY,DLC,ICA-B,MH,MoS,NN, NNC-A,NNMM,OClMA,PPPM

829. *Nicholson, Peter, 1765–1844
  The carpenter's new guide; being a complete book of lines for carpentry and joinery . . . 7th ed. from the 6th London ed. Philadelphia, M. Carey & son, 1818.
  127 p. 84 pl.   NNMM
  First appeared London, 1792.

830. —— —— 8th ed. Philadelphia, M. Carey & son, 1818.
  127 p. 84 pl.   CtY,ICJ,MH,MWA,MoS,NNC-A,NNGS,NNSo,NWM

831. —— —— 9th ed. Philadelphia, John Grigg, 1827.
  127 p. 84 pl.   CtY,NHi,PP,PU

832. —— —— 10th ed. Philadelphia, John Grigg, 1830.
  127 p. 84 pl.   DLC,MH(imp.) NHi

835. —— —— 13th ed. Philadelphia, Grigg, Elliott and company, 1848.
  117 p. 83 pl.   DLC(imp.),MH,NHi
  ". . . with additional plans for various staircases . . . by William Johnston." No copies of the presumptive 11th and 12th editions have been located. The 2 v. edition, London and New York, George Virtue, which may be dated in the early forties, is English rather than American as it was printed abroad.

838. —— —— 16th ed. Philadelphia, Lippincott, Grambo & co., 1854.
  107 p. front., 80 pl.   DLC,ICA-B,IU,MB,NNC-A,NNMM,PPFrankl
  ". . . carefully and thoroughly revised by N. K. Davis. And containing numerous new, improved and original designs for roofs, domes, etc. by Samuel Sloan . . ." No copies of the presumptive 14th and 15th editions have been located.

*Nicholson, Peter

839. The carpenter's new guide . . . 16th ed. Philadelphia, J. B. Lippincott and company, 1860.
      107 p. front., 80 pl.   ICA-B,MdBP

840. —— —— 16th ed. Philadelphia, J. B. Lippincott and company, 1865.
      107 p. front., 80 pl.   MH

841. —— —— 16th ed. Philadelphia, J. B. Lippincott and company, 1867.
      107 p. front., 80 pl.   NN

842. —— Encyclopedia of architecture. A dictionary of the science and practice of architecture, building, carpentry, etc., from the earliest times to the present time, forming a comprehensive work of reference for the use of architects, builders, carpenters, masons, engineers, students, professional men and amateurs . . . New York, Martin and Johnson [a. 1858].
      2 v. 107, 125 pl.   CU,DLC,MWA,MoS,NN,NNC-A,
                                          NNMM,NHi(v. 1 only)
      Added engraved t.p.
      "Edited by Edward Lomax and Thomas Gunyon," and indeed rewritten by them. First appeared London, 1811–19, in 48 parts, under title: Architectural dictionary.
      This edition was probably issued in the mid-fifties as the Martin and Johnson firm became Johnson, Fry and company in 1858.
      The London and New York, George Virtue [1857–60] ed. was printed abroad and may be considered English rather than American.

843. —— —— new ed. New York, Johnson, Fry and company, n.d.
      2 v. 107, 125 pl.   CtY-F,DLC,ICA-B,MiU,PP
      Added engraved t.p.
      The DLC copy has an additional Atlas of plates.
      This edition must have been issued between 1858 and 1873, the years during which the firm Johnson, Fry and company, with address 27 Beekman Street, was in existence.

844. —— —— New York, Palliser, Palliser & co. [1887?].
      2 v. 107, 125 pl.   PPTU
      Before 1887 the Pallisers gave Bridgeport as their place of publication; later their own works were issued in New York by J. S. Ogilvie.

845. —— The mechanic's companion; or, The elements and practice of carpentry, joinery, bricklaying, masonry, slating, plastering, painting, smithing, and turning, comprehending the latest improvements and containing a full description of the tools belonging to each branch of business; with copious directions for their use. And an explanation of the terms used in each art; also an introduction to practical geometry . . . New York, W. C. Borradaile, 1831.
      333 p. 40 pl.   CtY,RP
      First appeared Oxford, 1825.

846. —— —— Philadelphia, James Locken, 1832.
      333 p. 40 pl.   MB,MH,MWA,NHi,NjR

847. —— —— Philadelphia, James Locken, 1842.
      333 p. 40 pl.   I,MH

848. —— —— Philadelphia, James Locken, 1845.
      333 p. 40 pl.   MdBP

849. —— —— Philadelphia, F. Bell, 1852.
      362 p. illus., 40 pl.   NN,NNC-A

850. —— —— Philadelphia, F. Bell, 1859.
      362 p. illus., 40 pl.   MBHo

*Nicholson, Peter

851. The mechanic's companion . . . Philadelphia, F. Bell, 1863.
362 p. illus., 40 pl.   NNC-A,PP

852. —— —— Philadelphia, Claxton, Remsen and Haffelfinger, 1868.
362 p. illus., 40 pl.

853. —— —— Boston, G. W. Cottrell, n.d.
362 p. illus., 40 pl.   CtY

854. —— The student's instructor in drawing and working the five orders of architecture . . . 6th ed. augm. and imp. New York, Railroad journal, 1837.
47 p. 41 pl.   MH,NN,NHi,PPFrankl
First appeared in England before 1804, the date of the 2d London edition. This is the 1st Amer. ed. Identical with the 3d London edition except for the interchange of plates 14 and 18.

855. Niernsee, John R
Report of the construction and embellishment of private dwellings in Vienna. . . . Washington, Government printing office, 1875.
26 p. pl.   DLC,MH,MiU,NNC,PP
At head of title: Vienna international exhibition, 1873.
In: U. S. Commission to the Vienna exhibition, 1873. Reports 1875–76, v. 4a.

856. Norman, John, 1748–1817, comp.
The town and country builder's assistant . . . explaining short and easy rules . . . for drawing and working the five orders of columns entire: or any part of an order, without regard to the module or diameter. And to enrich them with their rustics, flutings, cablings, dentules, modillions, &c. Also to proportion their doors, windows, intercolumniations, porticos, and arcades. Together with a variety of raking, circular, scrolled, compound and contracted pedements . . . Boston, N. E., Engraved, printed and sold by J. Norman [1786].
14 p. front., 60 pl.   DLC (imp.),MB,MH,MHi,NHi,NN,NNC-A,
      NNMM,RPJCB
"By a lover of architect," but evidently compiled by Norman.
The date of this first work on architecture compiled in America can be supplied from the date on the frontispiece as 1786. Norman, who issued the first architectural book in America, Swan's *The British architect*, in 1776, was born in England. He advertised in the *Pennsylvania Journal*, May 11, 1774, as "Architect and Landscape Engraver." Apparently he never practiced architecture here, but was active first in Philadelphia and after 1780 in Boston as an engraver. In 1792 he brought out the first American edition of William Pain's *The practical builder*. *The town and country builder's assistant* consists of material taken from English sources, the frontispiece, for example, is from Isaac Ware's *The complete body of architecture*, London, 1756. This date indicates about the same time lag of a generation as in the case of the American edition of Swan between 1st London and 1st American editions in the eighteenth century.

857. Norman, William,   , comp.?
The builders easy guide; or, Young carpenter's assistant: containing a great variety of useful designs in carpentry and architecture; as, the proportioning of the five orders, mouldings, &c. at large, with their enrichments; plans and elevations for houses, for town and country; designs for chimney-pieces, shop-fronts, door-cases, staircases, &c; design for a church with plan and elevation; design for a pulpit, bridge, &c. &c; with many other important articles and useful embellishments. Compiled from the latest and approved European publications. To which is added a list of the price of carpenter's

Norman, William
  work in the town of Boston . . . Boston, printed and sold by William Norman, 1803.
   8 p. 48 pl.   NNSo
   William Norman, presumably the compiler of this work, is described in the title page as "Book and Chart-seller." He later issued William Pain's *Builder's pocket treasure,* Boston, 1794, and Pain's *Practical house carpenter,* Boston, 1796, in which title page he is described as "Bookseller and stationer." As he had the same address as John Norman from 1798 to 1805 he was probably a relative and John Norman may well have engraved the plates in the three books William issued, if indeed John were not also the compiler of this one as well.
   The "list of the price of carpenter's work," mentioned in the title, as well as Plate 5 are lacking in the only known copy and Plate 21 is misnumbered 20.

858. Norton, Charles Eliot, 1827–1908
  . . . Dimensions and proportions of the temple of Zeus at Olympia . . . [Boston] 1877.
   pp. 145–170.   MH,NNC-A,RIBA
   At head of title: With the compliments of the author.
   From the Proceedings of the American academy of arts and sciences, vol. XIII.

859. —— Historical studies of church building in the middle ages . . . New York, Harper & brothers, 1880.
   331 p.   CSmH,CtY,DLC,ICA-B,InI,MB,MH,MdBE,MnU,NjP,NN,
               NNC-A,NNMM,NPV,OCl,OO,PP,PPL,RP,ViU

860. —— History of ancient art . . . Boston, A. Mudge & son, printers, 1891.
   2 v. in 1.   DLC,ICA-B,MH
   ". . . prepared by H. F. Brown and Wm. H. Wiggins, jr. from lectures delivered by . . . Norton at Harvard . . ."

861. —— Lectures on the history of the fine arts, 1875–76. [Cambridge? 1876?].
   42 p.   MH
   Notes taken by G. E. Woodberry and J. R. Wheeler.

862. —— Notes of travel and study in Italy . . . Boston, Ticknor & Fields, 1860.
   320 p.   CtHWatk,DLC,MB,MH,NNC,NjP,NIC,NN

863. —— —— Boston, Houghton, Mifflin and company, 1881.
   320 p. [l.] 13 p.   MH
   With the original 1859 copyright.

864. —— —— Boston, Houghton, Mifflin and company, n.d.
   320 p. [l.] 13 p.   MdBP,NN,NNC
   With the same 1859 copyright. It is not clear whether this issue preceded or followed that of 1881, but the form of the imprint implies 1876 or later.

865. —— —— Boston, Houghton, Mifflin and company, [c1887].
   320 p.   CtHWatk,DLC,MH

866. —— Painting and sculpture in their relation to architecture, as illustrated by the practice of the Italian artists of the thirteenth and fourteenth centuries . . . [Boston, D. Estes and C. E. Lauriat, 1880].
   [7] p.   MH

867. Oakeshott, George John
  Detail and ornament of the Italian renaissance . . . New York, Wm. Helburn, n.d.
   1 p. l. 40 pl. (part double)   NNMM
   First published London, 1888.

868. Oakey, Alexander F   , 1850–
    Building a home . . . New York, D. Appleton and company, 1881.
        115 p. illus.   CtY,DLC,MB,MBAt,MH,MSaE,MoS,
                                                                        NN,PP,PPL

869. ——— ——— New York, D. Appleton and company, 1882.
        115 p. illus.   MSaE,PP,Vi

870. ——— ——— New York, D. Appleton and company, 1883.
        115 p. illus.   NN

871. ——— ——— New York, D. Appleton and company, 1884.
        115 p. illus.   MB,NN,NNC,NNCoo,NPV,PPFrankl
    Oakey also wrote *Home grounds*, 1881, and *Architect and client*, a dis
    cussion of professional ethics.

872. Ogilvie, George W
    Architecture simplified or how to build a house. Chicago, George W. Ogilvie
    [c1885].
        10 p. illus.   MiU,MoS

873. O'Kane, James   , *pub.*
    Modern romanesque . . . carving and sculpture as applied to architecture
    . . . New York, J. O'Kane [1892].
        1 p. l. 20 pl.   CtHWatk,DLC,MB

874. Olmsted, Vaux and company
    Preliminary report upon the proposed suburban village at Riverside, near
    Chicago . . . New York, Sutton, Brown and co., printers, 1868.
        23 p.   MB,MH,NNC
    More relevant to architecture than Olmsted, Vaux and company's many
    other landscape reports of the sixties.
    See also Vaux, Calvert.

875. Ormsbee, Agnes Bailey
    The house comfortable . . . New York, Harper & brothers, 1892.
        232 p.   DLC,IU,InI,MB,MnU,MoS,NN,NNC-A,
                                                                OCl,OU,PP

876. Osborne, Charles Francis
    Notes on the art of house-planning . . . New York, William T. Comstock,
    1888.
        106 p. illus.   CtY,DLC,MB,MH,OCl,PPD

877. Otis, Calvin N
    Sacred and constructive art: its origin and progress . . . New York, G. P.
    Putnam & son, 1869.
        305 p.   CU,CtY,DLC,MB,NNC-A,NPV,PPL

878. Overman, Frederick, 1810–1852
    Mechanics for the mill wright, machinist, engineer, civil engineer, architect
    and student. Containing a clear and elementary exposition of the principles
    and practice of building machines . . . Philadelphia, Lippincott, Grambo &
    co., c1851.
        420 p. illus.   ICJ,MB,NN

879. ——— ——— Philadelphia, J. B. Lippincott & co., 1852.
        420 p. illus.   PPFrankl

880. ——— ——— Philadelphia, J. B. Lippincott & co., 1856.
        420 p. illus.   ViU

881. ——— ——— Philadelphia, J. B. Lippincott & co., 1858.
        420 p. illus.   DAU,MoS

Overman, Frederick
882. Mechanics for the mill wright . . . Philadelphia, J. B. Lippincott & co., 1860.
420 p. illus. NNC

883. —— —— Philadelphia, J. B. Lippincott & co., 1864.
420 p. illus. MH,MnU

884. —— —— Philadelphia, J. B. Lippincott & co., 1869.
420 p. illus. IU
Overman also wrote books on metallurgy, even less relevant to architecture than this.

885. Owen, Robert Dale, 1801–1877
Hints on public architecture, containing, among illustrations, views and plans of the Smithsonian institution: together with an appendix relative to building materials . . . New York and London, George P. Putnam, 1849.
119 p. illus., 15 pl. CtHWatk,CtY,DLC,ICA-B,MB,MBAt,MH, MSaE,MWA,NcD,NNC-A,NNCoo,NNMM,NPV,OO,PPFrankl

886. Owen, Harvey L
Bits of Canterbury cathedral . . . William T. Comstock, 1891.
1 p. l. 24 pl. DLC,NN,NNC-A

889. Page, Harvey L
Architectural designs . . . 3d ed. [Washington, Gibson bros. printers c1886].
10 p. illus., 36 pl. DLC
No copies of the presumptive 1st and 2d editions have been located.

892. —— —— 6th ed. 1000 [Washington, Gibson bros., printers, 1888].
8 p. illus., 36 pl. DLC
No copies of the presumptive 4th and 5th editions have been located.

893. —— Houses of moderate cost . . . Washington, Gibson bros., printers, c1889.
[39] p. incl. front., illus., pl. Vi

894. *Pain, William, 1730?–1790?
The builder's pocket treasure. In which not only the theory, but the practical parts of architecture are carefully explained . . . A new edition London Printed: Boston Reprinted, and sold by William Norman, 1794.
iv, 20 p. 55 pl. MB,MnU,NHi,NNMM
First appeared London, 1763.
The first architectural work issued by William Norman, q.v. The English editions of Pain had been popular and influential in America since before the Revolution.

895. —— The carpenter's pocket directory. The best methods of framing timber buildings . . . Philadelphia, J. H. Dobelbower and L. Thackara, 1797.
[32] p. 24 pl. MH,NN(imp.),NNC-A
First appeared before 1792, the date of a London "new edition."
Evans gives the collation as 68 p. 24 pl. without indicating where such a copy exists.

896. —— The practical builder; or, Workman's general assistant . . . 4th ed. rev. and corr. Boston, Printed and sold by John Norman, 1792.
8 p. 83 pl. CtY,MB,MH,MSaE,MWA,NHi,NN,NNMM, NNSo,RPD,RPJCB
First appeared London, 1774. London 4th ed., from which this 1st Amer. ed. is drawn, 1787.
The last architectural book issued by John Norman, q.v.

897. —— The practical house carpenter; or, Youth's instructor; containing a great variety of useful designs in carpentry and architecture . . . elevations and sections of houses for town and country, ledges, hothouses, greenhouses, stables, &c;

*Pain, William
    design for a church with plan, elevation, and two sections . . . 1st Amer.
    from 5th London ed., with additions. Boston, printed and sold by William
    Norman, 1796.
        16, 7 p. 148 pl.   MB,MH (imp.),MHi,MSaE,MWA,NNMM
        First appeared before 1788, the date of the 2d London ed. Possibly the
        1st London ed. carried a different title. The London 5th ed. was 1794.
        There are 146 numbered plates and two unnumbered plates, one facing
        plate 3 and one facing plate 65.

898. —— —— 6th ed. with additions. Philadelphia, Printed by Thomas Dobson,
    1797.
        v, 15 p. 146 pl.   DP,ICA-B,MWA,MoS,NHi,NN,NWM,
                                            PHi,PPCC,PU,RPJCB
        Some copies may have the full 148 plates mentioned in the title. This is
        of course the 6th edition in relation to the earlier London editions, but
        the [2d] American edition.

899. Paine, Timothy Otis, 1824–1895
        Solomon's temple and capitol, ark of the flood and tabernacle or the holy
        houses of the Hebrews . . . Boston and New York, Houghton, Mifflin and
        company, 1885.
        2 v. 42 pl.   CtY,PBa
        The preface states the work was begun in 1852. This is not a new edition
        of the 1861 work listed below, but much more extensive.

900. —— —— Boston and New York, Houghton, Mifflin and company, 1886.
        x, 198 p. 42 pl.   MB,MH,MdBE,PP
        Identical with the previous issue but bound as one volume.

901. —— Solomon's temple; or the tabernacle; first temple, house of the king . . .
    Boston, George Phinney, 1861.
        99 p. 21 pl.   MH,MoS,NNMM,OCi,PBa

902. —— —— Chicago, E. B. Myers and Chandler, 1868.
        [3], 99 p. 20 pl. (part col.)   MB

903. Palliser, Palliser & co., architects, Bridgeport and New York. i.e., Palliser, George,
    1849–1903, and Palliser, Charles
        George Palliser's Modern buildings [New York, 1891].
        122 p. illus.   DLC

904. —— Palliser's American architecture; or Everyman a complete builder . . . New
    York, J. S. Ogilvie, c1888.
        95 p. illus.   NN,OO

905. —— —— New York, Chicago, J. S. Ogilvie [1889].
        95 p. illus.   DLC,NNC-A

906. —— Palliser's American cottage homes . . . Bridgeport, Conn., Palliser, Palliser
    & co. [1877].
        2 p. l. 40 pl., incl. t.p.   DLC

907. —— —— Bridgeport, Conn., Palliser, Palliser & co., c1878.
        2 p. l. 40 pl. (incl. t.p.)   MB,MWA,OCi,PP,PPM
        Palliser's New cottage homes, below, includes much the same material.

908. —— Palliser's Commonsense school architecture . . . New York, J. S. Ogilvie,
    c1889.
        110 p. incl. front., illus.   DE,DLC,NN,NNC-A,RIBA

909. —— —— New York, J. S. Ogilvie, 1892.
        110 p. incl. front., illus., plates.   DLC
        Peerless series, no. 60.

Palliser, Palliser & co.

910. Palliser's Courthouses, village, town and city halls . . . New York, J. S. Ogilvie, ᶜ1889.
      108 p. incl. illus., 3 pl. (1 double and col.)   DLC

911. —— Palliser's Memorials and headstones . . . with the orders of architecture and miscellaneous designs and details . . . New York, J. S. Ogilvie publishing co., ᶜ1891.
      140 p. incl. illus., 94 pl. on 48 l.   DLC,MWA

912. —— Palliser's miscellaneous architectural designs and details . . . New York, J. S. Ogilvie [1891].
      96 p. incl. illus.   DLC

913. —— Palliser's Model dwellings . . . New York, J. S. Ogilvie [1893].
      128 p. illus.   DLC
      The peerless series, no. 68.

914. —— Palliser's Model homes for the people . . . Bridgeport, Conn., 1876.
      23 p. illus.   NNMM
      By George Palliser, architect.
      Advertising at the rear.

915. —— —— Bridgeport, Conn., Palliser, Palliser & co. [ᶜ1878].
      83 p. illus.   DLC,MB,MSaE,MNU,NjP,NjR,NN(96 p.),NNC-A,PP

916. —— —— 5th thousand, New York, Palliser, Palliser & co., 1883.
      84 p. incl. illus., 28 pl.   PPFrankl
      With a new 1883 copyright.

917. —— —— 10th thousand, Bridgeport, Palliser & co., ᶜ1887.
      84 p. incl. illus., 28 pl.   MH

918. —— —— 15th thousand, New York, Palliser, Palliser & co., n.d.
      84 p. incl. illus., 28 pl.   H.R.H.
      Still with the 1883 copyright.

919. —— Palliser's New cottage homes and details, containing nearly two hundred and fifty new and original designs in all the modern popular styles, showing plans, elevations, perspective views and details of low priced, medium and first class cottages, villas, farmhouses, town and country places, houses for the seashore, and south, and for summer and winter resorts, etc., etc. City brick block houses . . . New York, Palliser, Palliser & co. [ᶜ1887].
      [180] p. incl. 65 pl.   MB(imp.),MH,MWA,PP

920. —— —— New York, Palliser, Palliser & co. 1888.
      [4], [144], [6] p. incl. front., illus.   DLC,MnU,MoS,NNC-A,NNCoo

921. —— —— New York, Palliser, Palliser & co. [1891?].
      [791] p. illus.   NN

922. —— Palliser's Useful details . . . [Bridgeport? 1881?].
      2 p. l. 40 double pl.   DLC,PU
      "Introductory" dated: Bridgeport . . . 1881.

923. —— —— [Bridgeport? 1890?].
      2 p. l. 40 double pl.   DLC
      "Introductory" dated: Bridgeport . . . 1890.

924. —— Specifications for frame houses costing from five hundred to fifteen hundred dollars . . . Bridgeport, Conn., Palliser, Palliser and co., New Haven, Punderson and Crisand, printers, 1878.
      22 numb. l. 1 l.   DLC
      Cover title.

925. Parker, Francis Jewett, 1825–1909
    Church building and things to be considered, done, or avoided in connection therewith . . . Boston, Cupples, Upham and company, 1886.
        137 p. front., illus., 6 pl.   DLC,MB,MBAt,MCE,NcD,Nh,PPM

926. Patterson, W   M
    A manual of architecture: for churches, parsonages and schoolhouses . . . Nashville, Tenn., Publishing house of the Methodist Episcopal Church South, 1875.
        113 p. front., illus., 15 pl.   DLC,MoS,PP

927. Patton, William Mac Farland, 1845–
    Practical treatise on foundations . . . 1st ed. 1st thousand. New York, John Wiley & sons, 1893.
        402 p. illus., 22 fold. pl.   CU,CtY,MB,MH,MiH,MoS,NNC,
                                                       PP,PPFrankl,Vi

928. Peabody, Robert Swain, 1845–1917
    Notebook sketches . . . Boston, James R. Osgood & company, n.d.
        39 p.   CU,CtY,MB,MBAt,MWA,NHi
        Cover title.

    Pennsylvania. Department of public instruction
    See Burrowes, Thomas Henry

929. Pfeiffer, Carl, 1834–1888
    American mansions and cottages . . . Boston, Ticknor & co., 1889.
        5 pts. 102 pl.   DLC,IU,MBAt,MH,NNC-A(imp.)

930. —— Sanitary relations to health principles in architecture . . . [New York, Francis & Loutrel, printers, 187–   ].
        24 p.   CtHWatk,DLC,DSG,NN,NNC-A
        "A paper read at the annual meeting of the American public health association, 1873."

931. Philadelphia. The art club of Philadelphia
    Catalogue of the inaugural exhibition of architecture and the allied arts . . . Philadelphia, 1890.
        38 p. pl.   NNC-A,PP

932. —— —— Philadelphia, 1892.
        36 p. pl.   DLC,NNC-A,NNMM,PHi
        With title: Catalogue of the annual exhibition.

933. —— —— Philadelphia, 1893.
        26 p. pl.   MB,NNC-A,NNMM,PP
        With title: Catalogue of the third annual exhibition.

934. Philadelphia. Centennial exposition, 1876.
    Reports of the judges, architecture and engineering . . . Philadelphia, J. B. Lippincott & co., 1876–77.
        10 v.   PPFrankl

935. Philadelphia. Commissioners for the erection of public buildings.
    The new public buildings on Penn Square . . . Philadelphia [Press of H. B. Ashmead] 1880.
        38 p. front., 10 pl.   DLC,NNC-A

936. —— Plans of the new public buildings, Philadelphia . . . [Philadelphia, 1888?].
        10 pl.   NNC-A
        Several other similar pamphlets are perhaps of more political than architectural interest.

937. Philadelphia. Pennsylvania Academy of the Fine Arts
Catalogue of the architectural exhibition . . . Philadelphia [1894?].
194? p. illus. H.R.H.(imp.)
Advertising front and rear.

Picturesque sketches
See Ware, William Rotch.

938. Pierce & Dockstader
Modern buildings of moderate cost: containing forty-five plans and nine-
teen views of twenty different houses costing from $700 to $18,000, and
eight churches costing from $1000 to $20,000 . . . [Elmira, N. Y., Empire
printing house, ᶜ1886].
72 p. illus. DLC

939. —— Modern buildings . . . [Elmira, N. Y., Advertiser association, ᶜ1890].
3 p. l. 31 pl. DLC

940. A plea for the use of the fine arts in the decoration of churches. New York, John
F. Trow, printer, 1857.
56 p. MB,NN,NNC-A,PP
Cover title: Christian art.

941. Polley, George Henry, 1846–1930, *comp.*
Artistic furniture and architectural interiors . . . Boston and New York,
Geo. H. Polley & co. [ᶜ1892].
1 p. l. 61 pl. DLC,OCi

942. —— Spanish architecture and ornament . . . Boston and New York [Geo. H.
Polley & co., ᶜ1889].
1 p. l. 50 pl. DLC,IU,NNMM,MB,MSaE,MoS,PP

The Pompeia
See Smith, Franklin Webster

943. Poole, William Frederick, 1821–1894
The construction of library buildings . . . Washington, Government print-
ing office, 1881.
26 p. CSmH,CtHWatk,DLC,IU,MBAt,MH,MWA,
MnU,NN,NNC,PP
In: U. S. Bureau of education. Circular No. 1. 1881.

944. —— Remarks on library construction . . . Chicago, Jansen McClurg & co., 1884.
34 p. CtY,DLC,ICJ,MB,MBAt,MH,MdBP,
NN,NNC-A,NHi,PPL

945. —— Report on the progress of library architecture . . . resolutions . . . concern-
ing . . . the library of congress . . . Boston, American library association,
1882.
16 p. DLC,MB,MdBP,NN,PPL
There are also various periodical articles by Poole on similar topics.

946. Pope, Thomas
A treatise on bridge architecture, in which the superior advantages of the
flying pendent lever bridge are fully proved. With an historical account of
different bridges erected in various parts of the world . . . New York, 1811.
288 p. 18 pl. DAU,DLC,ICJ,IU,MB,MH,NjR,NN,
NNC-A,NHi

947. Potter, Edward Tuckerman, 1831–1904
World pictures in capitals . . . Philadelphia, J. B. Lippincott & co., 1869.
21 p. 8 pl. DLC,NN,NNC-A,PP

Potter, Edward Tuckerman
948. The capitals of the Banker screen in the First Reformed Dutch church, Schenectady,
N. Y. . . . New York, Photographed by Geo. G. Rockwood, 1864.
7 p. 12 pl.   MWA,NN,PP
A rather early example of illustration with real photographs.

949. —— Notes relating to concentrated residence in various countries . . . Newport,
Daily News job print, 1888.
29 p.   NNC-A

950. Powell, George Townsend, 1843–1927
Foundations and foundation walls for all classes of buildings . . . New York,
Bicknell & Comstock, 1879.
119 p. illus.   DLC,MnU,MoS,OCi,PPFrankl
This and later editions include Baumann's important *Art of preparing
foundations,* first published 1873.

951. —— —— rev. and enl. [ed.] New York, William T. Comstock, 1884.
166 p. illus.   DLC,DSG,IU,MnU,OU,PU

952. —— —— 3d ed. New York, William T. Comstock, 1889.
166 p. illus.   MiH,NNC-A,PPFrankl,ViU

953. —— —— 4th ed. New York, William T. Comstock, 1889.
166 p. illus.   CtY,MB,MnU,NNC,OU,PP
There was a 5th ed. in 1896.

954. Pratt, S
. . . First Chicago grand opera festival at the exposition building, com-
mencing April 6, 1885 . . . Chicago, Printed by Skeen and Stuart stationery
co., 1885.
64 p. illus.   ICA-B
At head of title: Official souvenir.
Although issued as a programme, this constitutes an excellent monograph
on this important work of Sullivan with description, drawings, and plans
of the Grand opera festival auditorium.

955. *Prentice, Andrew Noble
Renaissance architecture and ornament in Spain . . . Boston, Geo. H. Polley
& co., 1894.
2 p. l. 60 pl.   NPV
First published London [1893]. The undated American editions are presumably of 1895 or later.

956. Price, Bruce, 1845–1903
. . . A large country house . . . New York, William T. Comstock [c1887].
13 p. illus., 24 pl.   DLC,MB,MH,NN,NNC-A,NNCoo,PPD
At head of title: Modern architectural practice, no. 1.

957. *Prignot, Eugène, and others
Mantels and side walls . . . New York, J. O'Kane, 4 College Pl., n.d.
1 p. l. 32 pl.   CtNlC

958. Purdy, Corydon Tyler
. . . The steel construction of buildings. A lecture delivered before the college of mechanics and engineering of the university of Wisconsin, March
2, 1894 . . . Madison, Wis., The university, 1894.
pp. 41–67   CU,CtY,DLC,ICJ,IU,MB,MH,MnU,
                                       MoS,NNC,OO,OU,PBm,ViU
At head of cover title: Bulletin of the university of Wisconsin. Engineering series, vol. 1. no. 3.

959. Putnam, John Pickering, 1847–1917.
    Architecture under nationalism . . . Boston, The Nationalist educational asso-
    ciation, 1890.
        64 p.   ICJ,MB,MBAt,MH
        "Published by permission of the *American architect*."

960. —— —— 2d ed. Boston, Ticknor & co., 1891.
        64 p.   NN

961. —— The open fireplace in all ages . . . Boston, James R. Osgood and company,
    1881.
        xii, [2] p. 11, 202 (i.e., 212) p. front., illus., 35 pl.   DLC,ICA-B,
                  MB,MBAt,MH,MdBE,MoS,NNC,NHi,NPV,OCl,PPFr

962. —— —— new ed. enl. Boston, James R. Osgood and company, 1882.
        2 p. l. xiv, 204 p. illus., pl.   CtHWatk,CtY,ICJ,ICU,IU,NN

963. —— —— new ed. rev. and enl. Boston, Ticknor & co., 1886.
        xiv, 207 p. illus., 55 pl.   NNC-A,MB
        With an "Introduction to the second edition."

964. Randall, Gurdon P
    Book of designs for schoolhouses . . . Chicago, Knight & Leonard, printers,
    1884.
        96 p. front., pl.   DLC,I

965. —— Descriptive and illustrated catalogue containing plans in perspective of col-
    leges, schoolhouses, churches and other public buildings . . . Chicago, Hor-
    ton & Leonard, 1866.
        36 p. front., pl.   DLC

966. —— —— [2d ed. rev.] Chicago, Horton & Leonard, 1866.
        37 p. front., pl.   DLC,MSaE,MnHi

967. —— —— Supplement . . . Chicago, Horton & Leonard, 1866.
        14 p. front.   DLC,MnHi

968. —— The great fire of Chicago and its causes. What are and what are not fire-
    proof buildings, and how to build them . . . Chicago [1871].
        16 p.   DLC
        Cover title.

969. —— A handbook of designs containing plans in perspective for: . . . , court
    houses, universities, academies, schoolhouses, churches, dwellngs . . . Chi-
    cago, Church, Goodman and Donelley, printers, 1868.
        46 p. 30 pl.   CtHWatk,DE,DLC,ICHi,IU,MB,MH
        Probably a new edition of the *Descriptive and illustrated catalogue,* above,
        incorporating the *Supplement.*

970. —— How to build schoolhouses . . . Chicago, G. K. Hazlitt & co., 1882.
        29 p.   DLC

971. Ranlett, William H
    The architect, a series of original designs for domestic and ornamental villas,
    connected with landscape gardening, adapted to the United States . . . New
    York, William H. Graham, 1847–49.
        2 v. 60 pl.   CtY(v. 2 only),DLC,ICA-B,ICJ,IU,MB,MH,MSaE,
                MWA,MdBP,NHi,NN(v. 1 only),NNC-A(v. 2 only),
                NNCoo,NNMM(v. 1 only; see note),NWM,OO
                (Pts. 2,7,8 of v. 2 lacking),PPFrankl
    It is not evident whether vol. 1 first appeared in parts, but of vol. 2, no.
    1 appeared in February 1848. Later numbers did not appear monthly, as

Ranlett, William H
    nos. 9 and 10, at least, were not out until into 1849. Nos. 1–3 carry the
    imprint of Graham, later numbers were published by Dewitt & Daven-
    port, whose imprint appears on vol. 2 when issued as a whole. DLC and
    NNMM report a variant issue of vol. 1 with added title page bearing the
    imprint Dewitt & Davenport, 1849. This is not the same as vol. 1 of the
    issue below.

972. —— —— New York, Dewitt & Davenport, 1851.
    2 v. 60 pl.   NN(v. 1 only),NNC-A(v. 1 only),NNMM(v. 2 only)
    This issue still carries the cover date 1847 and the original 1847 copy
    right. Offered for sale by Fowlers and Wells for $12.00 in 1855.

973. —— The city architect. A series of original designs for dwellings, stores and
    public buildings adapted to cities and villages . . . New York, Dewitt & Daven-
    port, 1856.
    2 pts. illus., 10 pl.   ICJ,NNC-A,OO
    Apparently only the first two parts of volume 1 were ever issued.

    Raynerd, Daniel
    See Benjamin, Asher

974. *Redgrave, Gilbert Richard, 1844–   , trans.
    Outlines of historic ornament . . . New York, Scribner & Welford, 1884.
    170 p. illus.   DLC,NNC-A,NNMM,OCi,PHC
    "Translated from the German."

975. Reed, Samuel Burrage
    Cottage houses for village and country homes. Together with complete plans
    and specifications . . . New York, Orange Judd company, 1883.
    136 p. illus.   CU,DLC,MB,MH,NN,OCl,OO,PPM
    "Most of these plans were originally contributed to successive numbers
    of the *American agriculturist* since the publication of 'House plans for
    everybody'; consequently are of recent date."

976. —— —— New York, Orange Judd company, 1884.
    136 p. illus.   IU,MBHo,NNC-A

977. —— —— New York, Orange Judd company, 1886.
    136 p. illus.   MnU,NNCoo
    There was an edition as late as 1895.

978. —— Dwellings for village and country with general descriptions and detailed esti-
    mates . . . Thirty five dwellings. New York, Orange Judd company, 1885.
    121 p. illus.   MB,NNC-A,NNMM,OCl,Vi

979. —— —— New York, The author, 1885.
    121 p. illus.   DLC,ICJ,MB,MnU

980. —— House plans for everybody. For village and country residences, costing from
    $250 to $8,000 . . . New York, Orange Judd company [1878].
    243 p. illus.   DLC,IU,MB,MH,NNCoo

982. —— —— 3d ed. New York, Orange Judd company, 1879.
    243 p. illus.   ICA-B
    No copy of the presumptive 2d ed. has been located.

984. —— —— 5th ed. New York, Orange Judd company, 1881.
    243 p. illus.   MB,NN
    No copy of the presumptive 4th ed. has been located.

985. —— —— 5th ed. New York, Orange Judd company, 1883.
    243 p. illus.   MoS,PP

Reed, Samuel Burrage
986. House plans for everybody . . . 5th ed. New York, Orange Judd company, 1884.
DLC

987. Reid, David Boswell, 1805–1863
A college of architecture and its relation to professional education and to the improvement of public health . . . Hartford, F. C. Brownell, 1857.
pp. 629–641 DLC,NNC-A
Reprinted from *Barnard's American journal of education*, December, 1856.

988. —— Ventilation in American dwellings . . . New York, John Wiley, 1858.
124 p. illus., 30 pl. CU,CtHWatk,MWA,MoS,NN,PPFrankl
Based on a paper in the Smithsonian institution annual report for 1856, Washington, 1857.

989. —— ———— New York, John Wiley, 1864.
124 p. illus., 30 pl. NPV

990. Reminiscences of Carpenters' hall, in the city of Philadelphia and extracts from the ancient minutes of the proceedings of the Carpenters' company. Philadelphia, Crissey and Markley, printers, 1858.
41, 21, 57 p. 2 pl. NNC
The last 57 pages give catalogue of Carpenters' company library books in 1857.

991. *Révoil, Henry-Antoine, 1822–1900
Romanesque architecture in the south of France . . . New York, Helburn & Hagen, n.d.
3 v. pl. NNMM (v. 2, 3 only), MiU,MnU
First appeared Paris, 1868–73, in 60 parts. Probably printed abroad and issued here in the nineties, possibly after 1895.

992. —— Romanesque ornament, with construction and details . . . Boston, George H. Polley & co., n.d.
60 pl. NNMM
Possibly 1895 or later.

993. Reynolds, Louis Ethan
A treatise on handrailing . . . New Orleans, Printed by Hinton & co., 1849.
95 p. 20 pl. LNT,NcD,NNC-A
One of the very few Southern publications connected with building.

994. *Richardson, Charles James, 1806–1871
House building, from a cottage to a mansion; a practical guide to members of building societies and all interested in selecting or building a house . . . 2d ed. corr. and enl. New York, G. P. Putnam's sons, 1873.
504 p. illus. MB,MH,MSaE,MdBE,MoS,NN,NNC, NNCoo,PPFrankl
First appeared London, 1870, with title: Picturesque designs for mansions, villas, lodges. The London 2d and 3d editions have the title: *The Englishman's house*. This is presumably the 1st American edition.

995. Richardson, Henry Hobson, 1838–1886
The Ames memorial building[s], North Easton, Mass. . . . Boston, Ticknor & company, 1886.
23 p. MoS,NNC-A (imp.)
At head of cover title: Monographs of American architecture, issued in connection with the American architect and building news, III.

996. —— ———— Boston, Ticknor & company, n.d.
23 pl. ICA-B,OCl
It is not clear whether the undated issues of these monographs follow or precede the dated ones.

Richardson, Henry Hobson
997. Austin hall, Harvard law school, Cambridge, Mass. . . . Boston, James R. Osgood
and company, 1885.
18 pl.   ICA-B(imp.),MBAt,MH,OCl,OO
At head of cover title: Monograpais of American architecture [etc.] I.

998. —— —— Boston, Ticknor & company, 1886.
18 pl.   IU,NN,NNC-A(imp.),OU

999. —— —— Boston, Ticknor & company, n.d.
18 pl.   MoS,RIBA

1000. —— The Billings library the gift to the university of Vermont of Frederick
Billings . . . Boston, The Heliotype printing co. [188–?].
11 pl. (2 col.)   DLC,ICJ,NN,NNC-A
Cover title.
Generally dated [1895] and listed under: University of Vermont. There
is no apparent justification for so late a date.

1001. —— Description of drawings for the proposed new county buildings for Allegheny county, Penn. . . . Boston, Printed for private circulation, 1884.
48 p. illus.   MH

1002. —— Trinity church, Boston . . . Boston, Ticknor & company, 1888.
23 pl.   ICA-B,MBAt,MH,MoS,NN,NNC-A(imp.),OCl,OU,RIBA
At head of cover title: Monographs of American architecture [etc.] V.
"Gambrill and Richardson, architects."

1003. Riddell, John
Architectural designs for model country residences, illustrated by colored
drawings of elevations and ground plans. Accompanied by general descriptions and estimates. Prepared expressly for persons who contemplate building, and artisans throughout the United States . . . Philadelphia, John Riddell, Lindsay & Blakiston, 1861.
2 p. l. 14 l. 20 col. double pl.   IU,MWA,MdBP,OCi,PP

1004. —— —— Philadelphia, John Riddell, J. B. Lippincott & co., 1864.
[25] p. 22 col. double pl.   CU,ICA-B,MH,PPFrankl
With a new 1864 copyright.

1005. —— —— Philadelphia, T. B. Peterson & bros., 1867
[28] p. 20 col. double pl.   DLC,NNC-A,OCl

1007. —— The practical carpenter and joiner. Illustrated by cardboard models mounted
on linen. 2d ed. rev. and enl. Philadelphia, Claxton, Remsen & Haffelfinger,
1874.
43 p. front., 37 pl.   NNMM
No copy of the presumptive 1st edition has been located. Riddell also published *The scientific stair-builder*, Philadelphia, 1854. This is included because of its unusual illustrations.

1008. Ripley, M   M
The world's worship in stone, temple, cathedral, and mosque . . . Boston,
Estes and Lauriat, 1880.
176 p. front., illus., pl.   DLC,MH,NNC-A,OCl
There are 150 engravings.

1009. —— —— Boston, Estes & Lauriat, 1881.
176 p. front., illus., pl.   ICA-B,PP,PPPM

1010. —— —— Boston, Estes & Lauriat, 1882.
176 p. front., illus., pl.   MBAt,NNMM,PP

83

Ripley, M   M

1011. The world's worship in stone . . . Boston, Estes & Lauriat, 1883.
       176 p. front., illus., pl.   MB,PPTU,Vi

1012. —— —— Boston, Estes & Lauriat, n. d.
       176 p. front., illus., pl.   CtY,MoS,NNMM
       With the original 1879 copyright.

1013. Ritch, John Warren, 1822–
       . . . The American architect comprising original designs of country resi-
       dences adapted to the taste and circumstances of the merchant, the farmer
       and the mechanic . . . New York, C. M. Saxton, 1847–[49].
           [No. 1]–[No. 24] 96(?) pl.   MB(incomplete),H.R.H.(nos. 5, 7, 9–14)
           The description is taken from the cover of No. 5, the earliest part lo-
           cated. The authors are given as "Ritch & Grey, architects." On No. 7 the
           author appears as "John W. Ritch, architect"; No. 9 has "Ritch & Grey"
           again; Nos. 10–14, "John W. Ritch" alone. As No. 5 is dated Oct[ober]
           and No. 7 Dec[ember], the monthly publication of the parts may be pre-
           sumed to have run from June 1847 through May 1849, as the total num-
           ber of "designs" in later editions is 24 and one appeared in each part. The
           1847 copyright is in the name of Jones & Newman. Each part cover title
           carries at the head "Price 25 cts. $3 pr. annum. Published monthly"
           as well as the number of the part and sometimes the month of issue. The
           rear covers carry a prospectus of the work; an advertisement of the lithog-
           raphers, Jones & Newman; and one of J. W. Ritch, or of Ritch & Flem-
           ing (on Nos. 13, 14), "Architects and superintendents of Buildings."
           Saxton's address is given on Nos. 5–14 as 205 Broadway.

1014. —— —— New York, C. M. Saxton, 1848.
       24 l. 48 pl.   NHi
       At head of title: Jones & Newman's architectural publications, First Series.

1015. —— —— New York, C. M. Saxton [1849–50?].
       [96 p.] 96 pl.   MSaE
       At head of title: Jones & Newman's architectural publications.
       Saxton's address is given as 121 Fulton Street which establishes the sug-
       gested date, rather than 1857, as supplied by the MSaE, which is certainly
       too late. See the sequence of issues below. Binding title: American archi-
       tect—Sec. series.

1016. —— —— New York, C. M. Saxton [1850–51?].
       2 v. [96] p. 96 pl.   CtY,MdBP,OO,H.R.H.
       At head of title: Jones & Newman's architectural publications.
       The title after the word "designs" varies from that of the parts, reading:
       "of cheap country and village residences, with details, specifications, plans
       and directions and an estimate of the cost of each design . . ." Saxton's
       address is given as 123 Fulton Street, establishing the suggested date.
       Vol. 2 of the H.R.H. copy had binding title: American architect—second
       series. Vol. 1 has lost its binding title. The OO copy apparently has bind-
       ing titles vol. 1: American architect—first series; vol. 2, the same as
       H.R.H. copy.

1017. —— —— New York, C. M. Saxton [1850–51?].
       3, 71 p. 96 pl.   DLC,NN,NNC-A
       Identical except for collation with the issue listed just above. The DLC
       supplies the date as 1852 without explanation.

1018. —— —— New York, C. M. Saxton [1851–56?].
       [69] p. 96 pl.   MB,MSaE,MWA,MiU,NN,NHi(imp.)
       At head of title: Saxton's architectural publications.
       Saxton's address is given as 152 Fulton Street, where the firm was located
       in the years 1851–56, thus suggesting the date.

Ritch, John Warren
The MiU copy is said to be a "New edition" but is presumably either of this or one of the other four issues listed here.
The NHi copy has 24 1., 48 pl. Binding title: American Architect First Series.

1019. —— —— New York, C. M. Saxton, Barker & company [1859–64?].
71 p. 96 pl.   MH
The publisher's address is given as No. 25 Park Row, at which address the firm was located from 1859 through 1864.
The various issues of this work are extremely difficult to distinguish: it may be that some of the holders do not have the specific issues here attributed to them.

1020. Robinson, Charles Morrison, 1867–
Architectural suggestions illustrated with a number of designs for public and private buildings . . . [Philadelphia, Craig, Finley & co., printer] 1893.
1 p. l. 60 pl.   DLC
Snyder was joint author.
See also Smith, George T, and Robinson, Charles Morrison

1021. Roebling, John Augustus, 1806–1869
Long and short span railway bridges . . . New York, D. Van Nostrand, 1869.
30 p. 13 pl.   DLC,IU,MB,MH,NjP,NIC,NN,NNC,PU
A memoir by Roebling of the Niagara Falls suspension bridge is included in Engineering papers, No. 1, 1886.

1022. *Rosengarten, A
Handbook of architectural styles . . . New York, D. Appleton & company, 1876.
501 p. illus.   MB,NjP,NN,OO
Translated from the German by W. Collett-Sanders.

1023. *Ruskin, John, 1819–1900
An inquiry into some of the conditions at present affecting "the study of architecture in our schools . . . New York, John Wiley and son, 1866.
29 p.   CtY,ICA-B,InI,MH,NcD,NNC-A
Originally read before the Ordinary general meeting of the Royal institute of British architects, May 15, 1865, and first published in the Sessional papers of the R.I.B.A., 1864–65, v. XIX, pp. 19–40. This unauthorized American edition precedes any separate English publication, as is also true of the 1873 American edition of The poetry of architecture.
The ICA-B copy is bound with the 1880 issue of Lectures on architecture and painting. There is, of course, a separate title page. Such binding together of issues of Ruskin material of various dates is probably more frequent than the notes indicate.

1024. —— —— New York, John Wiley and son, 1869.
29 p.   PP

1025. —— —— New York, John Wiley and son, 1872.
29 p.   MB

1026. —— —— New York, John Wiley and son, 1875.
29 p.   DLC,MSaE,MnU
The MSaE copy is bound with The seven lamps of architecture and other Ruskin material. Separate title page.

1027. —— —— New York, John Wiley and sons, 1882.
29 p.   IU,OO
Bound with Lectures on architecture and painting. Separate title page.

*Ruskin, John
1028. An inquiry . . . New York, John Wiley and sons, 1884.

      29 p.   ICA-B,PU
      Bound with *The seven lamps of architecture* and other Ruskin material as
      vol. 14 of the [*Works*]. Separate title page.

1029. —— —— New York, John B. Alden, 1885.

      29 p.   CtMW,NN
      Bound with *The seven lamps of architecture* and other Ruskin material
      in vol. 1 of the [*Works*]. Separate title page.

1030. —— —— New York, John Wiley and sons, 1885.

      29 p.   CtMW,NN,OCL,PPL
      Bound with *The seven lamps of architecture* and other Ruskin material.
      Binding indicates this as vol. 7 of the [*Works*]. Separate title page.

1031. —— —— New York, John Wiley and sons, 1886.

      29 p.   CtMW,MB
      Identical with the 1885 Wiley issue.

1032. —— —— New York, John Wiley and sons, 1889.

      29 p.   PP

1033. —— —— New York, John Wiley and sons, 1891.

      29 p.   PP
      Bound with *Lectures on architecture and painting*.

1034. —— —— Philadelphia, Renwee, Wattley and Walsh, [1891?].

      pp. [339]–358   ICA-R
      Bound with *The seven lamps of architecture* and other Ruskin material
      in vol. 5 of the *Complete works*. Other vols. of this edition of the *Com-
      plete works* are dated 1891. The various issues of the Brantwood edition
      are omitted here. Printed in England and carrying an English as well
      as an American place of publication and publisher's name, they are not,
      as the works of a foreign author, here considered American imprints.
      The appearance of the authorized Brantwood edition in America must
      explain the cessation of Wiley issues around 1890. Except for the Renwee,
      Wattley and Walsh edition, some of the volumes of which carry the date
      1891, undated editions are also omitted, as all, presumably, are of 1895
      and later. They are mostly, however, definitely American.
      These omissions apply to all the Ruskin items in this list, which includes
      all his writing most directly concerned with architecture. The Cook and
      Wedderburn bibliographical notes to the *Library edition* do not cover the
      material listed here, considering it pirated. The *Inquiry* above and *The
      poetry of architecture* would seem to be first separate editions. The 1860
      American edition of the whole of *Stones of Venice* also precedes the first,
      1874, English edition of the work as a whole. But the English editions of
      the separate volumes, in 1851 and 1853, are, of course, the first.

1035. —— Lectures on architecture and painting, delivered at Edinburgh, in November,
      1853 . . . New York, John Wiley, 1854.

      189 p. 15 pl., incl. front.   CtMW,CtY,MB,MBAt,MH,MPly,
                                                  MWA,MeB,MdBP,NN,PU
      This unauthorized American edition appeared the same year as the first
      London edition, as was also true of *The seven lamps of architecture*, 1849,
      and of *The stones of Venice. The foundations*, 1851, a conspicuous tribute
      to the early popularity of Ruskin in America. The rapid succession of
      issues of these works in America cannot be accurately compared with the
      infrequent English editions. Very probably the English editions were large
      and the American issues small. Yet the number of American issues in the
      fifties remains surprising, and the early American appearance of the *Inquiry*
      in 1866 and *The poetry of architecture* in 1873, suggests an insatiable
      appetite for Ruskin's architectural writing.

*Ruskin, John
1036. Lectures on architecture and painting . . . New York, John Wiley and Oliver S. Halsted, 1856.
189 p. 15 pl., incl. front.   CU,CtY,MH,NjP,NN,NNC,OCi

1037. —— —— New York, John Wiley, 1859.
189 p. 15 pl., incl. front.   MH,MWelC,NPV,OO

1038. —— —— New York, John Wiley and son, 1864.
189 p. 15 pl., incl. front.   MH

1039. —— —— New York, John Wiley and son, 1866.
189 p. 15 pl., incl. front.   DLC,InI,PVC

1040. —— —— New York, John Wiley and son, 1870.
189 p. 15 pl., incl. front.   InI,PU

1041. —— —— New York, John Wiley and son, 1872.
189 p. 15 pl., incl. front.   MH
Bound with An inquiry . . .

1042. —— —— New York, John Wiley and son, 1875.
189 p. 15 pl.   DLC,MSaE,MnU
Bound with The seven lamps of architecture and other Ruskin material.
Separate title page.

1043. —— —— New York, John Wiley and sons, 1880.
189 p. 15 pl.   ICA-B
Bound with the 1866 issue of An inquiry into some of the conditions
at present affecting "the study of architecture in our schools." Separate
title page.

1044. —— —— New York, John Wiley and sons, 1882.
189 p. 15 pl.   CU,IU,MdBE,NN,OO
The IU and OO copies are bound with An inquiry . . . Separate title page.

1045. —— —— New York, John Wiley and sons, 1884.
189 p. 15 pl.   ICA-B,PU
Bound with The seven lamps of architecture in vol. 14 of the [Works].
Separate title page.

1046. —— —— New York, John B. Alden, 1885.
129 p. 15 pl.   CtMW,MdBE,NN,OO
Bound with The seven lamps of architecture and other Ruskin material
in vol. 1 of the [Works]. Separate title page.

1047. —— —— New York, John Wiley and sons, 1885.
189 p. 15 pl.   CtMW,MoS,NN,OCl,PPL
Bound with The seven lamps of architecture and other Ruskin material.
Binding indicates this as vol. 7 of the [Works]. Separate title page.

1048. —— —— New York, John Wiley and sons, 1886.
189 p. 15 pl.   CtMW,MB,PP
Identical with the 1885 Wiley issue.

1049. —— —— New York, John Wiley and sons, 1889.
189 p. 15 pl.   PP(imp.),PPD

1050. —— —— New York, John Wiley and sons, 1890.
189 p. 15 pl.   ICA-B,InI,MB

1051. —— —— New York, John Wiley and sons, 1891.
189 p. 15 pl.   PP(imp.)
Bound with An inquiry . . .

*Ruskin, John

1052. Lectures on architecture and painting . . . Philadelphia, Renwee, Wattley and
Walsh, [1891?].
   pp. [211]–337. 15 pl.   ICA-R
   Bound with *The seven lamps of architecture* and other Ruskin material
   as vol. 5 of the *Complete works*. Other vols. of this edition of the *Complete works* are dated 1891.

1053. —— —— The opening of the crystal palace . . . New York, John B. Alden,
1885.
   16 p. Bound with other Ruskin material in [vol. 10] of the *Works*   NNC-A
   Separate title page.

1054. —— The poetry of architecture: cottage, villa, etc. To which is added suggestions on works of art. By "Kata Phusin," conjectured nom-de-plume of John
Ruskin . . . New York, John Wiley and son, 1873.
   246 p. illus.   I,MB,MBAt,MH,MPly,MdBE,NN,
                                                             NPV,OCi,PBm
   This material first appeared serially in the *Architectural magazine*, London,
   in 1837–38. This unauthorized American edition preceded any English
   publication in book form.

1055. —— —— New York, John Wiley and sons, 1877.
   246 p. illus.   CtY,DLC,IU,PCH

1056. —— —— New York, John Wiley and sons, 1880.
   246 p. illus.   MB,PPGi

1057. —— —— New York, John Wiley and sons, 1883.
   246 p. illus.   Vi

1058. —— —— New York, John Wiley and sons, 1885.
   246 p. illus.   CtMW,NN,OCl,PPD
   Bound with *The seven lamps of architecture* and other Ruskin material.
   Binding indicates this as vol. 7 of the [*Works*]. Separate title page.

1059. —— —— New York, John Wiley and sons, 1886.
   246 p. illus.   CtMW,MB
   Identical with the 1885 issue.

1060. —— —— New York, John Wiley and sons, 1889.
   246 p. illus.   PP

1061. —— —— New York, John Wiley and sons, 1890.
   246 p. illus.   CtY,MB

1062. —— —— Philadelphia, Renwee, Wattley and Walsh, [1891?].
   pp. [3]–178, illus.   ICA-B
   Bound with other Ruskin material in vol. 4 of the *Complete works*.
   Other vols. of this edition of the *Complete works* carry the date 1891.

1063. —— —— New York, Bryan, Taylor & co., 1894.
   pp. [3]–178, illus.   InI,PP
   Bound with other Ruskin material in vol. 4 of *Complete works*, "Edition
   de luxe . . . limited to 750 copies."

1064. —— The seven lamps of architecture . . . New York, John Wiley, 1849.
   186 p. 14 pl.   CtY,MB,MH,NjP,NN,NNC-A,PU
   This unauthorized edition appeared the same year as the first London
   edition. It was, of course, Ruskin's first book on architecture; and its
   immediate appearance in America is an indication of the interest in architecture at this time, and of the fact that the early volumes of *Modern
   painters* had already established a market here for Ruskin's work. Wiley

*Ruskin, John
     maintained the precedent of American editions in the same year as the
     first London edition with all Ruskin's architectural works except for vols.
     2 and 3 of the *Stones of Venice.*

1065. —— —— New York, John Wiley, 1852.
          186 p. 14 pl.   MBAt,MH,NN

1066. —— —— New York, John Wiley, 1854.
          186 p. 14 pl.   MH

1067. —— —— New York, Wiley & Halsted, 1857.
          186 p. 14 pl.   CU,CtMW,MH,MPly,NN,NNMM

1068. —— —— New York, John Wiley, 1859.
          186 p. 14 pl.   CSmH,DLC,MWA,NjP,NN,NPV,PPA

1069. —— —— New York, John Wiley, 1863.
          186 p. 14 pl.   NNC

1070. —— —— New York, John Wiley & son, 1865.
          186 p. 14 pl.   MH,NN,PPFrankl

1071. —— —— New York, John Wiley & son, 1866.
          186 p. 14 pl.   DLC

1072. —— —— New York, John Wiley & son, 1868.
          186 p. 14 pl.   PHatU

1072. —— —— New York, John Wiley & son, 1871.
          186 p. 14 pl.   DLC,OO,PU

1073. —— —— New York, John Wiley & son, 1874.
          186 p. 14 pl.   MB,MH,MWelC

1074. —— —— New York, John Wiley & sons, 1876.
          186 p. 14 pl.   MSaE
          Bound with other Ruskin material.
          Separate title page.

1075. —— —— New York, John Wiley & sons, 1877.
          186 p. 14 pl.   PP

1076. —— —— New York, John Wiley & sons, 1880.
          206 p. 14 pl.   DLC,MH,OCi
          The Crowell issue with the 1880 copyright is probably later than 1895.

1077. —— —— New York, John Wiley & sons, 1882.
          206 p. 14 pl.   CU

1078. —— —— New York, John Wiley & sons, 1884.
          206 p. 14 pl.   DLC,ICA-B,MH,NNC-A,PU
          Bound with other Ruskin material as vol. 14 of the [*Works*].   Separate
          title page.

1079. —— —— New York, John B. Alden, 1885.
          210 p. 14 pl.   CtMW,MdBE,NN,PP
          Bound with other Ruskin material as vol. 1 of the *Works*. Separate title page.

1080. —— —— New York, John Wiley & sons, 1885.
          206 p. 14 pl.   CtMW,ICA-B,NN,OCl,OO,PPL
          Bound with other Ruskin material. Binding indicates this as vol. 7 of the
          [*Works*]. Separate title page.

1081. —— —— New York, John Wiley & sons, 1886.
          206 p. 14 pl.   CtMW,CtY,ICA-B,ICN,MB
          Identical with the 1885 Wiley issue.

*Ruskin, John
1082. The seven lamps of architecture . . . New York, John Wiley & sons, 1889.
206 p. 14 pl.   CtY,PP
Identical with the 1885 Wiley issue.

1083. —— —— New York, John Wiley & sons, 1890.
206 p. 14 pl.   NN
Identical with the 1885 Wiley issue.

1084. —— —— New York, John Wiley & sons, 1891.
206 p. 14 pl.   PU
Identical with the 1885 Wiley issue.

1085. —— —— Philadelphia, Renwee, Wattley and Walsh, n.d.
pp. [3]–210, 14 pl.   ICA-R
Bound with other Ruskin material as vol. 5 of the *Complete works.* Other
vols. of the *Complete works* are dated 1891.

1086. —— —— New York, Bryan, Taylor & co., 1894.
210 p. 14 pl.   PP,PPE
In *Complete works,* "Edition de luxe . . . limited to 750 copies."

1087. —— The stones of Venice . . . New York, John Wiley, 1851 [vol. 1.]
435 p. illus.   CtMW,DLC,MB,MBAt,MH,MWA,MdBE,
                                 MdBP,NjP,NN,OO,PU,ScC
This unauthorized American edition of the first volume, "The foundations,"
of the *Stones of Venice* appeared the same year as the first London edition.
It is textually identical with the London edition even to the "List of plates,"
but the plates are omitted, although the text cuts are included.

1088. —— —— New York, John Wiley, 1860.
3 v. illus.   CtMW (v. 2, 3 only),CtY,CU,DLC,MH,MWA (v. 2 only),
                                 NjP,NN,NNC
The first American edition of the whole work, including "Volume the
second. The sea stories" and "Volume the third. The fall," which had both
first appeared in London in 1853. No edition of the work as a whole appeared in London until 1874. The plates of the English editions are lacking
in this 1860 edition as in the 1851 edition of vol. 1.

1089. —— —— New York, John Wiley, 1864.
3 v. illus.   DLC

1090. —— —— New York, John Wiley & son, 1865.
3 v. illus.   MH,PU

1091. —— —— New York, John Wiley & son, 1867.
3 v. illus.   OCl

1092. —— —— New York, John Wiley & son, 1872.
3 v. illus.   MH,PU

1093. —— —— New York, John Wiley & son, 1873.
3 v. illus.   MB,MH

1094. —— —— New York, John Wiley & son, 1875.
3 v. illus.   MSaE,PHatU

1095. —— —— New York, John Wiley & sons, 1877–78.
3 v. illus.   PU-F

1096. —— —— New York, John Wiley & sons, 1880.
3 v. illus.   CU,ICA-B,InI,NjP,NNC-A

1097. —— —— New York, John Wiley & sons, 1881.
3 v. illus.   MH

*Ruskin, John

1098. The stones of Venice . . . New York, John Wiley & sons, 1882.
  3 v. illus.   CU,ICA-R
  Vol. 5, 6, 7 of the [Works].

1099. —— —— New York, John Wiley & sons, 1883.
  3 v. illus.   PP

1100. —— —— New York, John Wiley & sons, 1884.
  3 v. illus.   IU,NPV,OU,PU,Vi

1101. —— —— New York, John Wiley & sons, 1885.
  3 v. in 2., illus.   CtMW,MB,NN
  Bindings indicate this as vol. 5, 6 of the [Works].

1102. —— —— New York, John B. Alden, 1885.
  3 v. in 2., illus.   MdBE (lacks v. 3),NNC-A,OO
  Vol. 1 and 2 form [vol. 5] of the Works; vol. 3 is bound with other Ruskin
  material in [vol. 6] of the Works.

1103. —— —— New York, John Wiley & sons, 1886.
  3 v. in 2., illus.   CtMW,MB
  Identical with the 1885 Wiley issue.

1104. —— —— New York, John Wiley & sons, 1887.
  3 v. in 2., illus.   NPV (v. 1 and 2 in 1 only),PP

1105. —— —— New York, John Wiley & sons, 1888.
  3 v. in 2., illus.   DLC,NPV,OO

1106. —— —— New York, John Wiley & sons, 1889.
  3 v. in 2., illus.   OCi,PP (v. 2 only)
  Identical with the 1885 Wiley issue. The United States book company issue
  with the 1889 copyright is probably later than 1895.

1107. —— —— New York, John Wiley & sons, 1890.
  3 v. in 2., illus.   DLC,MPly,PVC
  Identical with the 1885 Wiley issue.

1108. —— —— Philadelphia, Renwee, Wattley and Walsh, 1891.
  3 v. illus.   ICA-R
  Vol. 1, 2, 3 of the [Works].

1109. —— —— Illus. holiday ed. Boston, Estes and Lauriat, 1894.
  3 v. illus., 25, ?, 12 pl.   MoS (v. 1, 3 only)

1110. —— —— New York, Bryan, Taylor & co., 1894.
  3 v. illus.   PP,PPE
  Vols. 1, 2, 3 of the Complete works, "Edition de luxe . . . limited to 750
  copies."

1111. —— The two paths, being lectures on art and its application to decoration and
  manufacture delivered in 1858–59 . . . New York, John Wiley, 1859.
  217 p. front., illus., 1 pl.   CU,CtMW,CtY,DLC,InI,
  MB,MH,MWA,NjP,NN,NNC-A,OCl,PPGi
  This unauthorized American edition appeared in the same year as the first
  London edition. It includes: Lecture IV., The influence of the imagination
  in architecture; and Lecture V., The work of iron in nature art and policy.
  Otherwise it is no more particularly relevant to architecture than many
  other Ruskin items not included in this list.

1112. —— —— New York, John Wiley & son, 1865.
  217 p. front., illus., 1 pl.   MH
  Bound with The Political economy of art.

*Ruskin, John
1113. The two paths . . . New York, John Wiley & son, 1866.
217 p. front., illus., 1 pl.

DLC,I

1114. —— —— New York, John Wiley & son, 1869.
217 p. front., illus., 1 pl.
Included with other Ruskin material in vol. 1 of the [Works].

PHatU,PU

1115. —— —— New York, John Wiley & son, 1870.
217 p. front., illus., 1 pl.

CtMW

1116. —— —— New York, John Wiley & son, 1872.
217 p. front., illus., 1 pl.

MB,PU

1117. —— —— New York, John Wiley & son, 1875.
217 p. front., illus., 1 pl.

ICA-R,MB

1118. —— —— New York, John Wiley & sons, 1876.
217 p. front., illus., 1 pl.

DLC,PU-F

1119. —— —— New York, John Wiley & sons, 1881.
217 p. front., illus., 1 pl.

PPAppr

1120. —— —— New York, John Wiley & sons, 1883.
217 p. front., illus., 1 pl.
In vol. 12 of the [Works].

ICA-B,MBAt,NN

1121. —— —— New York, John Wiley & sons, 1884.
217 p. front., illus., 1 pl.

ICA-B,PU

1122. —— —— New York, John Wiley & sons, 1885.
217 p. illus., 1 pl.

CtMW,IU,NN,PPL

Bound with other Ruskin material. Binding indicates this as vol. 8 of the
[Works]. Separate title page.

1123. —— —— New York, John B. Alden, 1885.
151 p. Bound with other Ruskin material in [vol. 9] of the Works. MdBE

1124. —— —— New York, John Wiley & sons, 1886.
217 p. illus. 1 pl.
Identical with the 1885 issue.

CtMW,MB

1125. —— —— New York, John Wiley & sons, 1887.
217 p. front., illus., 1 pl.

PP

Bound with other Ruskin material. Separate title page.

1126. —— —— New York, John Wiley & sons, 1888.
217 p. front., illus., 1 pl.

MoS

1127. —— —— New York, John Wiley & sons, 1891.
217 p. front., illus., 1 pl.

PP

1128. —— —— Philadelphia, Renwee, Wattley and Walsh, 1891.
pp. 7–151 illus.

ICA-R

Bound with other Ruskin material in vol. 13 of the [Works].

1129. —— —— New York, Bryan, Taylor & co., 1891.
pp. 7–151 illus.

PP

Bound with other Ruskin material in Complete works, "Edition de luxe
. . . limited to 750 copies."

—— Works

As the relevant items have all been listed separately and their place in various
issues of the [Works] as far as possible indicated, no attempt has been made
to list issues of the [Works] as such.

1130. San Francisco News letter, *comp.*
    Artistic houses of California. Issued with San Francisco News letter, San Francisco, F. Marriott, publisher, 1887–88.
      52 pl.   CU

1131. Sanders, James Harvey, 1832–1899
    Practical hints about barn building. Chicago, J. H. Sanders publishing co., 1892.
      284 p. illus.   DLC,CU
    There are 82 full-page illustrations.

1132. —— —— Chicago, J. H. Sanders publishing co., 1893.
      284 p. illus.   MB

1133. Scattergood, David
    Handbook of the State house at Philadelphia. Philadelphia, The author, 1890.
      64 p. illus.   NNC-A
    Scattergood also prepared and published a *Handbook of Girard College* in 1888.

1134. Schneider, T   F
    Selections from work of T. F. Schneider, architect. Washington, D. C., 1894.
      1 p. l. 46 pl.   ICA-B,NN

1135. Schuyler, Montgomery, 1843–1914
    American architecture . . . New York, Harper & brothers, 1892.
      211 p. illus.   CU,CtY,DLC,IU,InI,MB,MH,MdBF,MoS,NHi,NN,
                                NNC-A,NNCoo,NPV,OCi,OO,PP,Vi

1136. Schweinfurth, Julius Adolph, 1858–1931
    Sketches abroad . . . Spain, Italy, France and the So. Kensington museum, Boston, Ticknor and co., 1888.
      2 p. l. 30 pl.   DLC,ICA-B,MBAt,MoS,NN,NNC-A,NNMM,OCi

1137. Scott, Frank J
    The art of beautifying suburban home grounds of small extent . . . plans for residences and their grounds . . . New York, D. Appleton & co., 1872.
      618 p. pl.   NHi,NNC-A
    Advertising at rear.

1138. *Scott, Sir George Gilbert, 1818–1878, and others
    Examples of modern architecture, ecclesiastical and domestic . . . churches and chapels, schools, colleges, mansions, town halls, railway stations . . . 1st American from the latest English ed. Boston, James R. Osgood and company, 1873.
      2 p. l. 64 pl. (part fold.)   DLC,MBAt,OO,PU

1139. Scott, Thomas H.
    Souvenir designs . . . [Pittsburgh, ᶜ1892].
      cover title, [46] p. illus.   DLC

1140. *Sganzin, Joseph Mathieu, 1750–1837
    An elementary course of civil engineering . . . 1st American from the 3d French ed. Boston, Hilliard, Gray, Little & Wilkins, 1827.
      220 p. 6 fold. pl.   DLC,ICJ,MB,MWA,MoB,NN,NNC,
                                  NWM,PPL
    First appeared before 1809, the date of the 2d Paris edition.

1141. —— —— 2d ed. Boston, Hilliard, Gray, Little & Wilkins, 1828.
      232 p. 6 fold. pl.   DLC,MB,OCl,PU

1142. —— —— 3d ed. Boston, Hilliard, Gray and company, 1837.
      232 p. 6 fold. pl.   IU

1143. Shaw, Edward
   Civil architecture; or, A complete theoretical and practical system of building, containing the fundamental rules of the art of geometry and mensura-
tion . . . also the five orders of architecture: with a great variety of beautiful
examples selected from Vitruvius, Stuart, Chambers and Nicholson: with
many useful and elegant ornaments and rules for projecting them . . . Boston, Shaw and Stratton, 1830. Vol. 1, parts 1, 2.
   76 p. 25 pl.   MB,MWM
   These two sections are apparently all that ever appeared of the first edition.

1144. —— —— Boston, Lincoln & Edmands, 1831.
   176 p. 95 pl.   MSaE,(imp.),NNMM,NHi
   Title varies slightly.

1145. —— —— 2d ed. enl. Boston, Marsh, Capen & Lyon [1832].
   192, 9 p. 97 pl.   IU,MH,MWA,NNMM,NHi,PPCC
   Plate 41 of the preceding edition is omitted; plates 44, 55, and 74 are new.

1146. —— —— 3d ed. rev. and enl. Boston, Marsh, Capen & Lyon, 1834.
   208 p. pl. 1–35, A, 36–100   DLC,NHi,PU

1147. —— —— 4th ed. rev. and enl. Boston, Marsh, Capen & Lyon, 1836.
   208 p. pl. 1–35, A, 36–100   CtHWatk,CtY,ICA-B,NN,NNC-A,
                           NHi,OU,ViU

1149. —— —— 6th ed. rev. and impr. Boston, John P. Jewett and company;
Cleveland, Ohio, Jewett, Proctor and Worthington, 1852.
   191 p. 102 pl.   CSmH,ICA-B,MH,NNCoo,NNMM,OCi,OO,PPM
   Plates 35, 40, 42, 43, 57, 60, 61, 64, 68–70, 84, 85, and 96–101 are all
new. The title of this edition, which carries a new 1852 copyright, begins Shaw's Civil architecture. It contains "a treatise on Gothic architecture, with plates, &c. by Thomas W. Silloway and George M. Harding, architects," which continues to appear with later editions (pl. 96–101).
No copy of the presumptive 5th edition has been located.
With an "advertisement to the sixth edition."

1153. —— —— 10th ed. Boston, John P. Jewett and company, Cleveland, Ohio,
Jewett, Proctor and Worthington, 1856.
   191 p. 102 pl.   ICJ,MoS,PPL
   The title begins Civil architecture, being a complete . . .
   No copies of the presumptive 7th, 8th, and 9th editions have been located.

1154. —— —— 11th ed. Philadelphia, Henry Carey Baird, 1870.
   191 p. 102 pl.   MH,MiOC,NNCoo
   With a new copyright of 1869 and a preface to the 11th edition.
   Identical with the 6th edition.

1155. —— —— 11th ed. Philadelphia, H. C. Baird & co., 1876.
   191 p. 102 pl.   MWA,MiH,NjP,NNC-A

1156. —— The modern architect; or, Every carpenter his own master. Embracing
plans, elevations, specifications, framing, etc. for private houses, classic dwellings, churches, &c., to which is added the new system of stair building
. . . Boston, Dayton and Wentworth, 1854.
   128 p. front., 64 pl.   ICA-B,MBAt,MH,MWA,NNMM,OO,PP
   The new lien law of Massachusetts, iv p., is bound in after the plates.
   The first 52 plates, including two Gothic house designs and two Gothic
church designs, are identical with those in Rural architecture, 1843, below.

1157. —— —— Boston, Dayton and Wentworth, 1855.
   128 p. front., 64 pl.   NN,NNC-A
   The new lien law of Massachusetts, iv p., is bound in after the plates.

Shaw, Edward
1158. The modern architect . . . Boston, Dayton and Wentworth, 1856.
      128 p. front., 64 pl.   NNMM,OCl

1159. —— Operative masonry; or, A theoretical & practical treatise on building . . .
      Boston, Marsh, Capen & Lyon, 1832.
      140 p. 40 pl. 8⁰.   DLC,MB,MH,MWA,NN,NNNC-A,NHi,PP
      Plates 30–33 give Gothic vaulting details.

1160. —— —— Boston, Benjamin B. Mussey, 1846.
      192 p. 44 pl. 4⁰.   CU,DLC,MBAt,MH,MoS,NNMM,NHi,PPFrankl
      The title of this quarto edition, which carries a new 1845 copyright, reads
      Practical masonry; or, A theoretical & operative treatise on building . . .
      In general the material of the 1832 octavo plates is doubled up on the
      quarto plates. Plates 24 and 29–44 are new, but plate 24 is identical with
      plate 49 in Shaw's *Rural architecture*, 1843, below.

      —— Practical masonry, *see* Operative Masonry, above.

1161. —— Rural architecture; consisting of classic dwellings, Doric, Ionic, Corinthian
      and Gothic, and details connected with each of the orders; embracing plans,
      elevations parallel and perspective, specifications, estimates, framing, etc. for
      private houses and churches. Designed for the United States of America . . .
      Boston, James B. Dow, 1843.
      108 p. 52 pl.   ICA-B,MH,NNMM,NHi,OCi,OO,PU
      Plates 41–44 show Gothic details; plates 45 and 46 show two Gothic house
      designs, the second built for David Sears in Brookline, Mass.; and plates 51
      and 52 offer two Gothic churches. All the plates of *Rural architecture* ap-
      pear also in *The modern architect*, 1854, 1855, 1856, above. Shaw also pre-
      pared a new edition of the Boston carpenters' *Rules of Work* in 1836.

1162. Sheldon, George William, 1843–1914, *ed*.
      Artistic country seats: types of recent American villas and cottage architec-
      ture, with instances of country club-houses. New York, D. Appleton and
      company, 1886–[87].
      2 v. in 5 pts., illus. 50, 50 pl.   ICA-B,MB,MnU,NN,NNC-A,
                                                      NNMM,OCi,PP

1163. Shields, J   E
      A treatise on engineering construction . . . New York, D. Van Nostrand,
      1877.
      138 p. 3 pl.   DLC,IU,MB,MH,MiH,NNC,NjP,PPM

1164. Shinn, Earl, 1837–1886, Strahan, Edward, *pseud*.
      Mr. Vanderbilt's house and collection . . . Holland ed. Boston, New York and
      Philadelphia, George Barrie, 1883–84.
      2 v. illus., [125] pl., [37] col. pl.   CtY,IU,MB,NN,NNC,NNMM,
                                                   OCl,PP,PPPM
      Often entered under: Vanderbilt, William Henry.
      Shinn also wrote a book on old Philadelphia, *A century after*, 1875, as
      well as descriptions of works of art in other American collections.

1165. —— —— Japan ed. Boston, New York and Philadelphia, George Barrie,
      1883–84.
      4 v. illus., [125] pl., [37] col. pl.   ICA-R,IU,MH,MnU([v. 5]),
                                          MoS,NN,NNC-A,NNMM,NHi,NPV,OCi

1166. Shinn, George Wolfe, 1839–1910
      Church architecture . . . Reprinted from "The Churchman." New York,
      American church building fund commission, 1882.
      16 p. illus.   MH,NN

Shinn, George Wolfe
1167. King's Handbook of notable Episcopal churches in the United States . . . Boston, Moses King corporation, 1889.
    286 p. illus.   DLC,MCE,MH,MWA,MiGr,NcD,NN,
                                                  NNC-A,NNMM,NHi,PP

1168. Sholl, Charles
Working designs for ten catholic churches . . . New York, D. & J. Sadlior & co., 1869.
    [73] p. 35 pl.   CtMW,MB,NNC-A,NNMM

1169. Shoppell, Robert W   , *comp.*
Artistic modern houses of low cost. 60 designs illustrated and described . . . New York, Co-operative building plan association, 1881.
    31 p. illus.   MB

—— —— New York, Co-operative building plan association [1883].
    31 p. illus.   H.R.H.

1170. —— . . . Building designs. New York, Co-operative building plan association, n.d.
    6 v. 26, 22, 24, 28, 28, 21 pl.   CU(v. 4–6 only),MiU(v. 1–4 only)
Cover title. Running title: *Shoppell's Modern houses.*
v. 1. $1000 houses. v. 2. $1500 houses. v. 3. $2000 houses. v. 4. $3000 houses. v. 5. $4000 houses. v. 6. $6000 houses. Presumably a collection of plates from the quarterly *Shoppell's Modern houses,* 1886– , re-issued with a cover title about 1889.

1171. —— How to build, furnish, and decorate. Consisting of elevations and plans for houses, barns, and every description of outbuilding, accompanied with clear and concise instructions; also, a complete treatise on house furnishing and decoration. Six hundred and fifty illustrations. New York, Co-operative building plan association [1883].
    [106], 38, [60] p. illus.   DLC,OU,MiU
"Barns and outhouses" (with special title page) [60] p. at end. Usually entered under the publisher.

1172. —— How to build a house . . . New York, Co-operative building plan association [1883?].
    [48] p. illus.   H.R.H.
At head of title page: No. 1.

1173. —— —— New York, Co-operative building plan association, c1883.
    [106], 38, [62], 20 p. illus.   CtHWatk,DLC,MB,MiGr,NNC-A,OO
This issue has a 20 p. supplement at the end.

1174. —— Modern houses; beautiful homes . . . embellished by more than one thousand illustrations. New York, Co-operative building plan association [1887].
    xx, 366 p. incl. illus., col. pl.   DLC,MPly,NNC-A
This is to be distinguished from *Shoppell's Modern houses,* an architectural quarterly, New York, 1886– . The publisher's announcements suggest the complete work was to consist of 9 nos. in 2 v. 440 p. illus.

1175. —— Shoppell's Building plans for modern low-cost houses . . . illustrated by Stanley S. Covert and Francis K. Kain, architect, New York, Co-operative building plan association, c1884.
    36 p. illus.   ICA-B,NN

1176. —— —— New York, Co-operative building plan association, 1884.
    48 p. 167 designs.   MB
Frances S. instead of Francis K. Kain.

Shoppell, Robert W

1177. Shoppell's Model houses. Selected designs from Shoppell's Modern houses with full descriptions and estimates of cost . . . New York, Co-operative building plan association [c1890].
300 p. illus.   NNCoo,OO

1178. —— [Shoppell's Modern houses] [New York, Co-operative building plan association, x. 1888].
2 v. 183 pl. (part col.)   NNC-A
Running title. Probably not a separate item, but rather a casual collection of plates from *Building designs,* together with other plates from the quarterly Shoppell's Modern houses, 1886–   , or else a portion of Shoppell's *Modern houses, beautiful homes.*

1179. —— Stables and carriage houses; building designs. [New York, Co-operative building plan association, 1889].
8 p. 19 pl.   CU,MH,NN,OCi
Cover title.

1180. Short, R   Thomas
Proper homes and how to have them . . . 1st ed. [New York] c1887.
13 p.   DLC

1181. Sidney, J   C
American cottage and villa architecture, a series of views and plans of residences actually built: intended as models for those about to build, as well as architects, builders, etc., with hints on landscapes gardening, laying out of grounds, planting of trees, etc. . . . New York, D. Appleton & co., 1850.
4 pts. 6, 5, 5, 6 pl.   MSaE
Prospectus on back cover reads: "The work will be issued monthly . . . and will be completed in ten parts. Each number will contain at least three Designs . . ." Five parts were offered for sale by Fowlers and Wells for 50 cents each in 1855. No other parts have been traced. Very likely no more than four or five were ever issued.

1182. Silloway, Thomas William, 1828–1910
Textbook of modern carpentry . . . Boston, Crosby, Nichols and company, 1858.
180 p. 20 pl.   DLC,MB,MBAt,MH,NjR,NN,NNC-A,PU

1183. —— ———— Boston, Woolworth, Ainsworth & co., n.d.
180 p. 20 pl.   MB
Silloway, with George M. Harding, was the author of a *Treatise on Gothic architecture* which appeared in the 6th and later editions of Edward Shaw's *Civil architecture.* Silloway also wrote guidebooks, such as *The cathedral towns,* 1883, with Lee L. Powers.

1184. Silsbee, E   A
An informal talk on architectural and art topics . . . Salem, Essex Institute, 1880.
22 p.   MSaE,MWA,NNMM
Also appeared in the *Bulletin* of the Essex Institute, XII, 1880, pp. 56–73, Salem, 1881.

Simonds, Florence
See Corroyer, Edouard Jules.

1185. Skillings, David Nelson,   , and Flint, D   B
D. N. Skillings, and D. B. Flint's illustrated catalogue of portable sectional buildings. Patented Nov. 19, 1861 [Boston, Printed by A. Holland, 1862].
53 p. illus.   DLC,MB,MBAt,MH,NN,NNC,NNMM

97

1186. Sloan, Samuel, 1815–1884
    American houses: a variety of original designs for rural buildings . . . Phila-
    delphia, printed by Henry B. Ashmead, 1861.
       6 p. 16 l. 29 pl. [27 col.]   MH,NNC-A,PP,PPM
       The title page mentions 26 (*sic*) colored plates.

1187. —— —— Philadelphia, Henry Carey Baird [ᶜ1861].
       6 p. 14 l. 26 col. pl.   DLC,MH,NNMM,OCl

1188. —— City and suburban architecture; containing numerous designs and details
    for public edifices, private residences, and mercantile buildings . . . Phila-
    delphia, J. B. Lippincott & co., 1859.
       104 p. 136 pl. (part col.) incl. col. front.   CU,CtHWatk,DLC,MB,
                       MWA,MH,MdBP,NNC-A,OCi,OCl,OO,PPFrankl

1189. —— —— Philadelphia, J. B. Lippincott & co., 1867.
       102 p. 131 pl. (part col.)   IU,MH,NNCoo,NN,NNMM

1190. —— City homes, country houses and church architecture; or, The American
    builders journal . . . Philadelphia, Claxton, Remsen & Heffelfinger, 1871.
       792 p. illus., 82 pl.   DLC,ICA-B,MB
       A reissue in book form of the *Architectural review and American build-
       er's journal*, vol. 1, originally published monthly from July 1868 through
       June 1869.

1191. —— Description of design and drawings for the proposed Centennial buildings, to
    be erected in Fairmount Park . . . Philadelphia, King & Baird, printers, 1873.
       8 p.   PHi
       Compare another pamphlet by "Americanus."

1192. —— The model architect. A series of original designs for cottages, villas,
    suburban residences, etc. accompanied by explanations, specifications, estimates
    and details. Prepared expressly for the use of projectors and artisans through-
    out the United States . . . Philadelphia, E. G. Jones & co., [ᶜ1852].
       2 v. front., 113, 96 pl. (part col.)   DLC,ICA-B,ICJ,MB,MWA,
                      MdBP,MoS,NN,NNC-A(imp.) NNCoo,NWM,OO,PP,PPL-R
       Offered for sale by Fowlers and Wells for $15.00 in 1855.

1193. —— —— new ed. Philadelphia, E. H. Butler & co., 1860.
       2 v. 113, 93 pl. (part col.)   IU,MH,OCi,OO,PP
       "with new drawings and large additions."
       New 1859 copyright.

1194. —— —— new ed. Philadelphia, E. H. Butler co., 1865.
       2 v. 113, 93 pl. (part. col.)   CU

1195. —— —— new ed. Philadelphia, J. B. Lippincott & co., 1868.
       2 v. 113, 93 pl. (part col.)   NN,PU-F

1196. —— —— new ed. Philadelphia, J. B. Lippincott & co., 1873.
       2 v. 113, 93 pl. (part col.)   MB

1197. —— Sloan's Constructive architecture; a guide to the practical builder and
    mechanic. In which is contained a series of designs for domes, roofs and
    spires . . . choice examples of the five orders of architecture . . . Philadelphia,
    J. B. Lippincott & co., 1859.
       148 p. illus., 66 pl., incl. front. (part col.)   CU,DLC,MB,MdBP,MH,
                          NN,NNC-A,NNCoo,OCi,PP

1198. —— —— Philadelphia, J. B. Lippincott & co., 1866.
       148 p. illus., 66 pl., incl. front. (part col.)   ICA-B,IU,MWA,NjP,
                                  NN,NNC-A

Sloan, Samuel

1199. Sloan's Constructive architecture . . . Philadelphia, J. B. Lippincott & co., 1873.
148 p. illus., 66 pl., incl. front. (part col.)   MH

1200. —— Sloan's Homestead architecture, containing forty designs for villas, cottages, and farmhouses, with essays on style, construction, landscape gardening, furniture, etc., etc. . . . Philadelphia, J. B. Lippincott & co., 1861.
355 p. incl. illus., [52] pl. (1 col.)   DLC,ICJ,IU,MBHo,MH,MWA,
                                                              NNC-A,PU-F

1201. —— —— 2d ed. Philadelphia, J. B. Lippincott & co., 1867.
355 p. illus., incl. 51 pl. (2 col.)   DLC,IU,MH,NcD,NN,NNC-A,
                                                                 OCl,PP
With a new copyright of 1866.

1202. —— —— 3d ed. Philadelphia, J. B. Lippincott & co., 1870.
355 p. illus., incl. 51 pl. (2 col.)   MB,MH

1203. —— Specifications for the erection of a new banking house for the Philadelphia
Savings Fund Society . . . Philadelphia, J. B. Lippincott & co., 1868.
16 p.   PHi
"by Samuel Sloan and Addison Hutton, architects."

1204. *Smeaton, A   C
Builder's pocket companion, containing the elements of building, survey-
ing and architecture. With practical rules and instructions connected with
the subject . . . Philadelphia, Henry Carey Baird, 1850.
273 p. illus.   MH,PPFrankl
First appeared London, 1825.

1205. —— —— Philadelphia, Henry Carey Baird, 1852.
273 p. illus.   MB,PU

1206. —— —— Philadelphia, Henry Carey Baird, 1853.
273 p. illus.   NcD

1207. —— —— Philadelphia, Henry Carey Baird, 1854.
273 p. illus.   MoS
Offered for sale by Fowlers and Wells for $1.00 in 1855.

1208. —— —— Philadelphia, Henry Carey Baird, 1856.
273 p. illus.   PPL
There were further editions after the Civil War. This is one of the
earliest and most popular books of tabulated information for architects
and builders. Others are omitted from this list.

1209. *Smith, Charles H   J
Parks and pleasure grounds, with practical notes on country residences,
villas . . . Philadelphia, Henry Carey Baird, n.d.
290 p.   MB,NPV
Preface dated Edinburgh, 1852.

1210. —— —— New York, C. M. Saxton and company, 1853.
367 p.   DLC,MB,MH,NNMM
With title: *Landscape gardening; or, Parks and pleasure grounds.* With
notes and additions by Lewis Falley Allen.

1211. —— —— New York, C. M. Saxton and company, 1856.
367 p.   IU,MB,MH
With the 1853 title.

1212. Smith, Frank L
  A cosy home: how it was built . . . Boston, Press of T. O. Metcalf & co.,1887.
  96 p. illus.   DLC,MB

1213. —— . . . Suburban homes; or, Examples of moderate cost houses for Wollaston
  Park . . . [1st ed.] Boston, Wood, Harmon & co., 1890.
  48 p. incl. illus.   DLC
  Advertising matter interspersed.

1214. Smith, Franklin Webster
  A design and prospectus for a national gallery of history and art at Washington. Washington, Gibson bros., c1891.
  112 p. illus.   MBAt,MH,MWA,NN,NNC-A,NPV

1215. —— The Pompeia. A reproduction of the house of Pansa in Pompeii . . . at
  Saratoga Springs, [Saratoga Springs, N. Y.?] 1889.
  24 p.   NN

1216. —— —— [Saratoga Springs, N. Y.?] 1890.
  47 p. illus.   MH,NN,NNMM

1217. —— —— New York, American publishing company, 1890.
  34 p. pl.   DLC
  With title: *Catalogue of the Pompeia.*

1218. —— —— [Saratoga Springs, New York.?] 1891.
  47 p. illus.   RIBA
  With the 1889 title.

1219. Smith, George T   and Robinson, Charles Morrison
  Art in house building. Twenty designs of modern dwellings . . . costing
  from $600 upwards, including designs of a church & schoolhouse . . .
  [Pittsburgh, printed by J. Eichbaum & co.,], c1890.
  60 p. illus.   DLC,MSaE
  Smith and Robinson were architects in Altoona, Pa.
  See also Robinson, Charles Morrison.

1220. Smith, John Jay, 1798–1881
  See Walter, Thomas Ustick.
  Smith's *Designs for monuments and mural tablets,* 1846, is hardly relevant
  to this list.

1221. Smith, Oliver P
  The domestic architect: comprising a series of original designs for rural and
  ornamental cottages, with full and complete explanations and directions to
  the builder, embracing the elementary principles of the Grecian and the cottage styles, with primary rules for drawing and shading, and the rudiments
  of linear perspective . . . Buffalo, Derby & co., Chicago, D. B. Cooke & co.,
  1852.
  125 p. 42 pl.   MiU,NBu,NNMM

  —— —— Buffalo, Phinney & co., New York, Ivison & Phinney, 1854.
  125 p. 42 pl.   ICA-B,OO

1222. *Smith, Thomas Roger, 1850–1903
  Greek architecture . . . and Greek sculpture by George Redford, with an
  introduction by William H. Goodyear. Meadville, Pa., Flood and Vincent, 1892.
  145 p. illus.   IU,MB,MH,MiU,MnU,MoS,NN,
                                                         OCi,OO,PP
  Chautauqua Literary & Scientific Circle, Studies, 1892–93.
  Although several of T. R. Smith's other works carry New York as well
  as London on the title page and an American as well as an English publisher's name, they were printed in England and are properly to be considered as English imprints.

1223. Smith, Walter
Examples of household taste, illustrated. New York, R. Worthington, [?1853].
x, 521 p. illus.   NNMM
The industrial art of the international exhibition. Vol. II.

1224. Smith, Willam C
The new state prison of Tennessee . . . a paper read before the Engineering association of the South, at Nashville, Tennessee, December 13, 1894 . . . Nashville, Brandon printing co., n.d.
22 p. illus.   OU

1225. Smithmeyer, John L
Our architecture and its defects. A critical essay: prepared for the Association of architects of Washington, D. C., and delivered there, December 22, 1879 . . . Washington, D. C., C. W. Brown, printer, 1880.
CtY,DLC,ICN,MB,NNC-A

1226. —— Strictures on the Queen Anne style of architecture . . . Washington, C. W. Brown, printer, 1881.
12 p.   DSG,NN,OO

1227. —— Suggestions on library architecture, American and foreign, with an examination of Mr. Wm. F. Poole's scheme for library buildings . . . Washington, Gibson brothers, printers, 1883.
31 p.   CtY,DSG,I,MB,MBAt,MH,
                                            MdBP,Nh,NN,PPL
Smithmeyer published other papers of a technical nature as well as a description of the National Library Building (Library of Congress), of which he was the chief architect, in the *American library association papers*, in 1881.

Soderholtz, Eric Ellis
See Corner, James M
See Crane, Edward Andrew

1228. Spooner, Shearjashub, 1809–1859
Anecdotes of painters, sculptors and architects, and curiosities of art . . . New York, G. P. Putnam & co., 1850.
3 v.   NN

1229. —— —— New York, G. P. Putnam & co., 1853.
3 v.   CU,IU,MWA,NN,NNCoo,PP

1230. —— —— New York, G. P. Putnam & co., 1854.
3 v.   DLC,ICA-R,NNC,NNC-A,PVC

1231. —— —— New York, J. W. Bouton, 1865.
3 v.   CtY,I,InI,MB,MH,NNC,NNC-A,
                                            NHi,OCi,OCl

1232. —— —— New York, R. Worthington, [1880].
3 v.   DLC,PSC

1233. —— —— New York, A. W. Lovering, [c1880].
3 v. in 1.   InI,NN,NNMM

1234. —— An appeal to the people of the United States in behalf of art, artists and the public weal . . . New York, [J. J. Read, printers] 1854.
27 p.   DLC,MB

1235. —— A biographical and critical dictionary of painters, engravers, sculptors and architects . . . New York, G. P. Putnam & co., 1852.
1131 p. 24 pl.   NN

101

Spooner, Shearjashub
1236. A biographical and critical dictionary . . . New York, G. P. Putnam & co., 1853.
        1131 p. 24 pl.   CtY,DLC,MBAt,MH,MoS,NjP,NjR,
                                            NN,NNC,NNCoo,PP,PPPM,PU

1237. —— —— New York, J. W. Bouton, 1865.
        2 v. 24 pl.   CU,CtHWatk,CSmH,DLC,InI,MB,MH,
                                         MdBP,NN,NNC-A,NNCoo
With title: *A biographical history of the fine arts.*

1238. —— —— New York, Frederick Leypoldt & Henry Holt, 1867.
        2 v. 24 pl.   CtY,NNMM,OCi

1239. —— —— 5th ed. Philadelphia, George Gebbie, 1873.
        2 v. 24 pl.   I,MB,MH,MdBP,NjP,NN,OClMA

1240. Stevens, John Calvin,   and Cobb, Albert Winslow
        Examples of American domestic architecture . . . New York, William T.
        Comstock, 1889.
           30, [25], 32–40 p. l. incl. front., illus., 50 pl.   CtHWatk,DLC,
                                ICA-B,MB,MH,MWA,NN,NNC-A,OCl,PPL-R

1241. Stone, Edwin Martin, 1805–1883
        The architect and monetarian; a brief memoir of Thomas Alexander Tefft
        . . . . Providence, S. S. Rider and brother, 1869.
           64 p.   CtY,DLC,IU,MBAt,MH,MWA,NN,
                                          NHi,NPV,PPAmP,RPAt,RIBA

Strahan, Edward, *pseud.*
See Shinn, Earl

1242. Strickland, William, 1787–1854, *ed.*
        Reports, specifications, and estimates of public works in the United States
        of America; comprising the Philadelphia gas works; reservoir dam across
        the Swatara; twin locks on the Schuylkill canal; Delaware breakwater; Phila-
        delphia water works; dam and lock on the Sandy and Beaver canal; dam on
        the James River and Kanawha canal, Virginia; locks of eight feet lift on
        the same; aqueducts across Rivanna River and Byrd Creek on the same;
        superstructure, etc., of farm bridges, on the same; lock gates and mitre
        sills . . .Explanatory of the atlas folio of detailed engravings elucidating
        the engineering works herein described. London, J. Weale, 1841.
           2, 168 p. Atlas of 40 pl.   MH,MdBP,NNC-A (Atlas only)
           This is unquestionably an English imprint, but the importance of the
           work seems to justify its inclusion in the list. Strickland is described as
           "architect and engineer." Two civil engineers, Edward H. Gill and Henry
           R. Campbell, were co-editors and the works described are largely engi-
           neering rather than architecture.

1243. —— The tomb of Washington at Mt. Vernon . . . Philadelphia, Carey and Hart,
        1840.
           76 p. 5 pl.   DLC,MB,MWA,MdBP,Nh,NN,PHi,PP,ViU
           This precedes by seventeen years the appearance of the first of Wine-
           berger's more popular guides to Mount Vernon, which are omitted from
           this list.

*Stuart, Robert
  See Meikleham, Robert

1244. Sturgis, Russell, 1836–1909
        French architecture in the first half of the eighteenth century . . . Rochester,
        N. Y., Cutler manufacturing co., n.d.

Sturgis, Russell
    23 p. illus., 14 pl.   DLC,NNC-A
    Cover title.
    Very possibly of 1895 or later.

1245. —— Homes in city and country . . . New York, Charles Scribner's sons, 1893.
    214 p. front., illus., 14 pl.   CtNlC,DLC,ICA-B,IU,MB,MBAt,
                                    MH,MdBE,MiGr,NNC-A,NNCoo,NHi,NPV,PP
    Contents: The city house in the east and south, by Russell Sturgis; the
    city house in the west, by John W. Root; the suburban house, by Bruce
    Price; the country house, by Donald G. Mitchell; small country places,
    by Samuel Parsons, jr; Building and loan associations, by W. A. Linn—
    all previously published as articles in Scribner's magazine.

1246. Sullivan, Louis Henry, 1856–1924
    Emotional architecture as compared with classical. Chicago, 1894.
    pp. 32–34.   NNC-A
    From *Inland architect*, v. 24, no. 4, Nov. 1894.

1247. —— Inspiration, an essay. Read at the third annual convention [of the Western
    association] of architects, at Chicago, November 17, 1886 . . . Chicago,
    [Inland architect press] 1886.
    36 p.   ICA-B
    Sullivan's other publications are of 1895 or later.

1248. *Swan, Abraham
    The British architect: or, The builders treasury of staircases. Containing,
    I. An easier, more intelligible, and expeditious method of drawing the five
    orders, than has hitherto been published . . . II. Likewise staircases . . . III.
    Designs of arches, doors, and windows. IV. A great variety of new and
    curious chimneypieces . . . V. Corbels, shields, and other beautiful decora-
    tions. VI. Several useful and necessary rules of carpentry . . . Philadelphia,
    Printed by R. Bell for J. Norman, 1775.
    2 p. l. vi, 17 p. 60 pl.   DLC(2 copies, both imperfect),MH,MWA,
                                       NNC-A,NNMM,NHi,PPCC,PPFrankl,PHi
    First appeared London, 1745.
    The first book on architecture published in America. Swan is described
    as "architect" in the title, although in the London title he was called
    "carpenter." Norman is described as "architect engraver." There had
    been London editions, after the first, in 1750 and 1758; but the work
    was a generation old when republished in America.

1249. —— The British architect; or, The builders treasury of staircases . . . Boston.
    Printed typographically by John W. Folsom for John Norman, engraver, 1794.
    2 p. l. iv, 12 p. 60 pl.   MB,MWA,NNCoo,NHi,NNMM,PPFrankl

1250. —— A collection of designs in architecture, containing plans and elevations
    of houses, for general use . . . In two volumes. Each containing sixty plates
    . . . Vol. I, No. I. Philadelphia, Printed by R. Bell, 1775.
    4 p. 10 pl.   NN
    First appeared London, 1757.
    Of the American edition, announced in "Proposals" dated June 26, 1775,
    in *The British architect* to appear by subscription in monthly numbers,
    only the first, dedicated to John Hancock, is known.

1251. Sylvester, William Allen
    Modern house carpenter's companion and builder's guide . . . Boston, A.
    Williams and company, 1882.
    114 p. incl. illus., pl.   DLC
    This is possibly of a more general architectural relevance than the ordi-
    nary run of works on carpentry of the period after the Civil War.

Sylvester, William Allen
1252. Modern house carpenter's companion . . . Boston, A. Williams and company, [c1883].
114 p. incl. illus., pl.   MoS

1253. —— —— 3d thousand. Boston, Cupples, Upham & co., 1883.
210 p. 45 pl.   MB,MH,MdBE

1254. Tabor, Clarence H
Modern homes . . . Chicago, The author, 1889.
      DLC,MB,OCl

1255. Thayer, Rufus H   , *comp.*
History, organization and functions of the office of the supervising architect of the Treasury department . . . Washington, Government printing office, 1886.
54 p.   DLC,NN,NNC-A
Treas. dept. doc. no. 817.
M. E. Bell was the Supervising Architect in 1886.

1256. Thomas, T   , jr.
The working man's cottage architecture, containing plans, elevations and details, for the erection of cheap, comfortable, and neat cottages . . . New York, R. Martin, 1848.
64 p. 11 pl.   NN,NNC-A,NNCoo,NHi,PPL-R,ScC

1257. —— —— New York, R. Martin, 1849.
64 p. 11 pl.   NN

1258. —— —— New York, Martin Johnson, 1855.
45 p. 11 pl.   PPM,MWA

Thompson, Edward G.
See Woodward, George Evertson

1259. Thompson, Robert Ellis, 1844–1924
The development of the house . . . Philadelphia, Wharton school of finance, University of Pennsylvania, 1885.
25 p.   MB,MWA,PU
In: University of Pennsylvania Publications.

1260. [Thomson, John W   ]
Cast iron buildings; their construction and advantages, by James Bogardus, C. E., architect in iron. Iron building, corner of Center and Duane Sts., New York, J. W. Harrison, printer, 1856.
16 p. 6 pl.   MH,MSaE,NN,NNC-A,NNCoo
On verso of title page: "I am indebted for this pamphlet to my friend, Mr. John W. Thomson, A. M. I mention this not in apology for the manner in which my name is introduced, but in justice to him as the author. I endorse every word of its contents. James Bogardus."
Frequently listed under Bogardus.
This is the first authoritative description of the developed use of castiron structure introduced by Bogardus, and hence a document of prime historical importance.

1261. Tiffany, Charles Comfort, 1829–1907
Expression in church architecture . . . New York, T. Whittaker, 1875.
25 p.   CtY,MB

1262. Todd, Sereno Edwards, 1820–1898
Todd's Country homes and how to save money . . . Hartford, Hartford Publishing company, New York, J. D. Denison, 1870.

Todd, Sereno Edwards
    656 p. illus., 13 pl., incl. front.   CtHWatk,DLC,MH,MWA,NPV
    ". . . directions for choosing a home, erecting every description of houses
    and outbuildings . . ."

1263. Tower, F   B
    Illustrations of the Croton aqueduct . . . New York and London, Wiley
    and Putnam, 1843.
    viii, 152 p. 22 pl.   NNMM

1264. Town, Ithiel, 1784–1844
    A description of Ithiel Town's improvement in the construction of wood
    and iron bridges: intended as a general system of bridgemaking . . . New
    Haven, Printed by S. Converse, 1821.
    10 p. 3 pl.   CtY,ICJ,MB,NN,NNC,NHi

1265. —— —— New Haven, T. G. Woodward and co., printers, 1825.
    2 p.   NN
    Title varies slightly.

1266. —— —— New York, The author, 1831.
    3 p.   NN,NNC

1267. —— —— New York, The author, 1839.
    12 p.   CtY,MB,MH,NN

1268. *Tredgold, Thomas, 1788–1829
    Elementary principles of carpentry . . . 1st American from 2d London ed.
    Philadelphia, E. L. Carey and A. Hart, 1837.
    280 p. illus., 22 pl., tables.   CtY,MWA,MdBP,MoS,NN,NNC-A,
                                                 NHi,NNMM
    First appeared London, 1820.

1269. —— —— 2d American from 2d London ed. corr. and considerably enl.
    Philadelphia, Jasper Harding, 1847.
    247 p. 22 pl., 22 diagrs.   ICA-B,MdBP
    As this is a technical and not an architectural work the post-Civil War
    editions are not listed here. Of these the 4th, 1883, the 7th, 1890, and
    the 8th, 1892, were Spon editions, printed in England, and hence not,
    properly speaking, American imprints.
    See also Hosking, William

Tryon, Thomas
    See Brunner, Arnold William

1270. Tuckerman, Arthur Lyman, 1861–1892
    The five orders of architecture, according to . . . Vignola . . . New York,
    William T. Comstock, 1891.
    12 p. 84 pl.   ICA-B,MoS,MnU,NN,NNC-A,NNMM,PP

1271. —— A selection of works of architecture and sculpture . . . of the renaissance in
    Italy . . . New York, William T. Comstock, 1891.
    2 p. l. 90 pl.   DLC,MoS,NN,NNC-A,NNMM

1272. —— A short history of architecture . . . New York, Charles Scribner's sons, 1887.
    168 p. 24 pl.   CtY,DLC,InI,MB,MBAt,MiOC,MnU,NjP,NN,
                                       NNC-A,OCl,OClMA,OO,PP,PPFrankl,RIBA

1273. —— —— New York, Charles Scribner's sons, 1893.
    168 p. 24 pl.   PP

1274. Tuckerman, Henry Theodore, 1813–1871
A memorial of Horatio Greenough . . . New York, G. P. Putnam & Co., 1853.
245 p.   DLC,IU,MB,MBAt,MH,MWA,MnU,MoS,NN,NNC,NNMM,
NHi,NPV,PPFrankl,PPL,PU
This includes Greenough's important critical articles on architecture
("Structure and organization," "Criticism in search of beauty," etc.)
reprinted from Greenough's *Travels, observations and experience*, 1852,
q.v. Tuckerman's *Homes of American authors*, which he edited with F.
Saunders in 1853, is not relevant here.

1275. [Turner, A   A]
Villas on the Hudson. A collection of photo-lithographs of thirty-one coun-
try residences . . . New York, D. Appleton & co., Philadelphia, George S.
Appleton, 1860.
3 p. l. 31 col. pl., 21 plans.   DLC,MB,MH,NjP,NN,NNC-A,
NNMM,NHi,PP
Frequently considered anonymous.

1276. Tuthill, Louisa Caroline (Huggins), 1798–1879
History of architecture from the earliest times; its present condition in Europe
and the United States . . . Philadelphia, Lindsay and Blakiston, 1848.
426 p. front., illus., 34 pl.   CtY,DLC,MB,MH,MSaE,MWA,MoS,NN,
NNC-A,NNMM,NHi,OClWHi,OU,PP,PU

1277. Tuthill, William Burnet, 1855–1929
The city residence, its design and construction . . . New York, William T.
Comstock, 1890.
183 p. illus.   DLC,IU,MB,NN,NNC-A,NNCoo,PP

1278. —— Environment in architecture . . .[New York, Edwin W. Dayton, printer,
n.d.].
38 p.   NNCoo
Cover title. A paper read before the Gamma chapter of the Phi Beta Kappa
Society, April 25th, 1893.

1279. —— Interiors and interior details . . . New York, William T. Comstock, 1882.
5 p. l. 52 pl.   DLC,MB,MH,MWA,MoS,NjP,OCi,
OCl,OO,PP

1280. —— The suburban cottage . . . New York, William T. Comstock, 1885.
101 p. illus.   OCi,OCl,PPFrankl
The preface states: "This work was recently published in the form of a
series of articles in *Building*."

1281. —— —— 2d ed. New York, William T. Comstock, 1891.
101 p. illus.   DLC,MB,MnU,NNC-A
Tuthill's *Practical lessons in architectural drawing* [c1881] ran at least
to an 8th edition of 1892.

1282. U. S. Architect of the Capitol
Annual report . . . Washington, Government printing office, 18–
v.–   DLC,MWA(1864,68,87–),NNC-A(1861–),PP
Title varies; report year irregular. The reports are found in different
places for different years.
See DLC cards for details
See also Bulfinch, Charles
See also Meigs, Montgomery Cunningham
See also Walter, Thomas Ustick

U. S. Architect of the Pension buildings.
See Meigs, Montgomery Cunningham

1283. U. S. Supervising architect of the Treasury department.
Annual report . . . Washington, Government printing office, 18–
v.–   DLC,ICJ,IU(1875,88),MB,MH(1868–),MiOC(1877–81),MnU
(1874/75,79/80,84/85,88/89,89/90),NcD(1884,89–92),NN(1867–),
NNC-A(1861–63,86–90),NPV (1877–),PP,PU(1877–)
Title varies; report year irregular.
See also Civis, *pseud.*
See also Thayer, Rufus H.
See also Walter, Thomas Ustick
See also Young, Ammi Burnham

1284. Upham, Jabez Baxter, 1820–1902
Acoustic architecture or, the construction of buildings with reference to
sound and the best musical effect . . . New Haven, Printed by B. L. Hamlan,
printer to Yale College, 1853.
43 p.   MB,MBAt,MH,MdBP,NNC-A
Reprinted from *American journal of science and arts*, 1853, 2d series,
vols. 15, 16.

1285. Upjohn, Richard, 1802–1878
. . . Upjohn's Rural architecture. Designs, working drawings and specifica-
tions for a wooden church and other rural structures . . . New York, George
P. Putnam, 1852.
4 p. 23 pl.   DLC,IU,MB,NN,NNC-A,PU-F
At head of title: General Congregational convention.
Offered for sale by Fowlers and Wells for $5.00 in 1855.
See also Woodward, George Evertson, 1829–1905.

1286. Upjohn, Richard Mitchell, 1828–1903
. . . The state capitol, Hartford, Conn. . . . Boston, Ticknor & co., 1886.
22 pl.   CtHWatk,ICA-B,IU,MH,NNC-A(imp.),OU
Monographs of American architecture, II.

1287. Valk, Lawrence B
Church architecture. General description of some of the most prominent
buildings recently erected in iron, brick and stock together with full explanation of the new form of plan for churches invented by . . . New York,
Holt brothers, printers, 1873.
16 p. [5] plans, [2] pl.   MCE

1288. Van Brunt, Henry, 1832–1903
Greek lines and other architectural essays . . . Boston and New York, Hough-
ton Mifflin & company, 1893.
274 p. illus., 8 pl.   CU,CtY,DLC,ICA-B,ICJ,IU,MB,MBAt,MH,
MdBE,MnU,MoS,NjP,NNC-A,OCl,PP,RIBA
See also Viollet-le-Duc, Eugène-Emmanuel
See also Ware, William Robert

1289. Van Fleet, James Alvin
Old and new Mackinac . . . Ann Arbor, Mich., Courier steam printing house,
1870.
176 p. illus.   DLC

1290. —— —— Cincinnati, Western Methodist book concern, 1874.
173 p. illus.   DLC

1291. —— —— Grand Rapids, "The Lever" book and job office.
173 p. illus., 7 pl., incl. front.   DLC

1292. —— Summer resorts of the Mackinaw region . . . [Detroit] Lever print, 1882.
49 p. illus.   DLC

1293. Vanosdel, John M
   The carpenter's own book. Baltimore, John W. Woods, 1834.
   Pt. 1. 22 p. pl.   NNC-A
   Apparently only the first part was issued.

1294. Van Rensselaer, Marianna (Griswold), 1851–1934
   English cathedrals . . . Illustrated with one hundred and fifty four drawings
   by Joseph Pennell, also with plans and diagrams . . . New York, The Century co., 1892.
      395 p. incl. front., illus.   CU,CtY,DLC,ICA-B,InI,MBAt,MH,MdBE,
                           MnU,MoS,NNC-A,NNMM,NPV,OCi,OCl,PP,PU
   The material originally appeared in the *Century magazine* in the years
   1887–1890.
   There was a London edition also in 1892.

1295. —— —— New York, The Century co., 1892.
      2 v. illus.   ICA-B,NcD,NN,NPV
   Edition limited to 250 copies.

1296. —— —— 2d ed. New York, The Century co., 1893.
      396 p. incl. front., illus.   MH,OO

1297. —— —— New York, The Century co., 1893.
      483 p. incl. front., illus., pl.   CtY,DLC,MB,MH,OCl,PP
   With title: Handbook of English cathedrals.

1298. —— Henry Hobson Richardson and his works . . . Boston and New York,
   Houghton, Mifflin and company, 1888.
      152 p. port., illus., [36] pl.   CtY,DLC,ICA-B,ICJ,IU,MBAt,MH,
                           MdBE,NcD,NN,NNC-A,OCi,OClMA,OO,PBm,PU-F,RIBA

1299. *Varin, Pierre Amedèe, 1818–1883, and Varin, Eugène Napoleon
   Picturesque architecture of Switzerland . . . Boston, James R. Osgood and
   company, 1875.
      10, 4 p. 48 pl.   DLC,ICA-B,IU,MB,OCi,PPL
   First appeared Paris, 1861.

1300. Varney, Almon Clothier, 1849–
   Our homes and their adornments; or, How to build, furnish and adorn a
   home . . . Detroit, Mich., J. C. Chilton & co., 1882.
      496 p. front., illus., [12] pl.   MiGr,MoS
   Col. advertising plate of tile also.

1301. —— —— Detroit, Mich., J. C. Chilton & co., 1883.
      498 p. front., illus., [12] pl.   DLC,NNCoo,NNMM (imp.)

1302. —— —— Detroit, Mich., J. C. Chilton & co., 1884.
      498 p. front., illus., [12] pl.   DLC

1303. —— —— Detroit, Mich., Windsor, Ont., J. C. Chilton publishing co.
   [c1885].
      486 p. front., illus., [12] pl.   DLC

1304. Vaux, Calvert, 1824–1895
   Villas and cottages. A series of designs prepared for execution in the United
   States . . . New York, Harper & brothers, 1857.
      318 p. front., illus., 32 pl.   CU,DLC,IU,MBAt,MH,MSaE,MWA,
                           MoS,NcD,NNCoo,NNMM,NHi,NPV,OO,PP,Vi

1305. —— —— [2d ed.] New York, Harper & brothers, 1864.
      348 p. front., illus., pl.   CU,CtHWatk,CtY,DLC,ICA-B,InI,MB,
                           MH,MnU,NN,NNC-A,NPV,OCl,OU
   With a "Preface to the second edition."

Vaux, Calvert
1306. Villas and cottages . . . New York, Harper & brothers, 1867.
348 p. front., illus., 39 pl.   DLC,IU,MB,MH,NN,NNC-A,NNCoo,
OCl,OO,PPL,PPM,ViU

1307. —— —— New York, Harper & brothers, 1869.
348 p. front., illus., 39 pl.   MB,OO,PP,ScC

1308. —— —— New York, Harper & brothers, 1872.
348 p. front., illus., 39 pl.   NPV

1309. —— —— New York, Harper & brothers, 1874.
348 p. front., illus., 39 designs (i.e., plates)   DLC,MB,PP
See also Olmsted, Vaux and company.

*Vignola, Giacomo Barozzi da, 1507–1573
See Tuckerman, Arthur Lyman.

1310. *Viollet-le-Duc, Eugene Emmanuel, 1814–1879
Annals of a fortress . . . Boston, James R. Osgood and company, 1876.
390 p. col. front., illus., incl. [11] col. pl.   CU,CtMW,CtY,MB,MBAt,
MH,MdBP,MnU,MoS,NjP,NNC-A,OCl,PP,PPPM
First appeared Paris [1872]. Translated by Benjamin Bucknall. First London edition, 1875.

1311. —— Discourses on architecture . . . Boston, James R. Osgood and company, 1875.
517 p. illus., 18 pl., incl. front. (part. fold.)
CtHWatk,CtMW,CtY,DLC,ICA-B,InI,MB,MBAt,MH,MiOC,
MnU,NcD,NNC, NNC-A,NNMM,OCi,OCl,OClMA,PPPM
First appeared Paris, 1858, with accompanying Atlas, Paris, 1863.
"Translated and with an introductory essay, by Henry Van Brunt."
First London edition, 1877, translated by Benjamin Bucknall.
Binding marked Part I.

1312. —— —— Vol. II . . . Boston, James R. Osgood and co., 1881.
438 p. illus., pl., xix–xxxvi (incl. front., part fold., part col.)
CtMW,ICA-B,MB,NNC-A,NcD,PPL
With title: Lectures on architecture. First appeared Paris, 1872.
Translated by Benjamin Bucknall. First London edition, 1881.
Binding title Discourses on architecture . . . Part II.

1313. —— The habitations of man in all ages . . . Boston, James R. Osgood and company, 1872.
394 p. col. front., illus., 8 pl.   MB,MBAt,MSaE,OCi
First appeared Paris, n.d. Translated by Benjamin Bucknall.

1314. —— —— 2d ed. Boston, James R. Osgood and company, 1876.
394 p. col. front., illus., 8 pl.   CU,CtY,DLC,ICJ,MB,MH,MnU,
MoS,NcD,NjP,NNC-A,OCl,OClMA,PPPM,WaU

1315. —— The story of a house . . . Boston, James R. Osgood and company, 1874.
284 p. illus., XV pl., incl. front.   CU,CtY,DLC,ICA-B,IU,InI,MBAt,
MH,MSaE,MiOC,MnU,MoS,NcD,
NNC-A,NPV,OCl,OClMA,PP,PPPM,Vi
First appeared Paris, n.d. Translated by George M. Towle. London edition this same year, translated by Benjamin Bucknall.

Villas on the Hudson
See Turner, A   A

1316. *Vogüe, Charles Jean Melchior, Marquis de, 1829–   , and others.
Byzantine architecture and ornament . . . Boston & New York, Geo. H. Polley & co. [c1890].
1 p. l. 52 pl.   DLC,ICA-B,MSaE,MoS,OCi,PP,PU

1317. Wallis, Frank Edwin, 1862–1929
    Old colonial architecture and furniture . . . Boston, Geo. H. Polley & co.
    [ᶜ1887].
        4 p. l. 60 pl.   CtY,DLC,ICA-B,InI,IU,MB,MBAt,
                                        MH,NNC-A,NNMM,OCi,OCl,PP
    Wallis' *American architecture, decoration and furniture of the 18th century* is ᶜ1896.

1318. Walter, Thomas Ustick, 1804–1887
    A guide to workers in metal and stone . . . Philadelphia, Carey and Hart, 1846.
        4 v. illus.   CU(v.1,2,4),DLC,NNC-A,PP
    Sometimes listed under John Jay Smith, who was joint author. A book for craftsmen rather than for architects and builders.

1319. —— . . . Estimate—Congressional library . . . [Washington, 1853].
        3 p.   DLC,PP
    32d. Cong., 2d. Sess. House Ex. doc. 18.

1320. —— Letter to the committee of the U. S. Senate on public buildings, in reference to an enlargement of the Capitol . . . [Washington] Towers, printer
    [1850].
        7 p.   DLC
    Cover title.

1321. —— Report on the new Treasury buildings and Patent office at Washington . . .
    Philadelphia, Printed by L. R. Bailey, 1838.
        18 p.   DLC,NN

1322. —— Report of the architect of the Girard college for orphans, to the building committee. Also, report of the building committee of the Girard college for orphans, to the select and common councils of Philadelphia [Philadelphia, 1834–50].
        14 pamphlets.
        NNC-A(1 only),PHi,PP(2:1837,1840),RIBA(4:1834,1836,1837,1838)
        A series of similar reports with slightly varying titles (the latest two, for example, of 1848 and 1850, being called *A description of the Girard college for orphans, contained in a final report of the building committee.*) The printers vary: that of the earliest is not given; the 2d and 3d were printed by Thomas W. Ustick; the 4th and 5th by L. R. Bailey, both of Philadelphia; the 1848 and 1850 items were "stereotyped by R. P. Moggridge" and "printed for John Saunders," respectively. One pamphlet numbered 12 by the PHi was printed at Harrisburg by Samuel D. Patterson in 1837. The NNC-A holding is the pamphlet numbered 5 at the PHi. The 1848 pamphlet includes one plate.

1323. —— Report of the architect of the United States Capitol extension and the new dome . . . Washington, Government printing office, 1864.
        10 p.   CSmH,DLC,PP
    Similar reports are to be found listed in the U. S. Government Documents Catalogue, but apparently they were not issued as separate items.

1324. —— [Statement by Thomas U. Walter, architect, explaining designs submitted by him for a building for the Library of congress. Philadelphia, 1873.]
        6 p.   DLC
    No title page. The pamphlet begins: To the honorable, the commission; and is signed: Thomas U. Walter, architect. Philadelphia, October 25, 1873.

1325. —— Two hundred designs for cottages and villas, etc., etc., original and selected . . . Philadelphia, Carey and Hart, 1846.
        4 v. 120 pl.   CtY,NHi,PPL,OO
    John Jay Smith was joint author.

Walter, Thomas Ustick
1326. Two hundred designs for cottages and villas . . . 2d ed. impr. Philadelphia, Carey and Hart, 1847.
    4 p. 30 pl.   DLC,MB,NNC-A

1327. Ware, William Robert, 1832–1915
    Columbia college in the city of New York, report of professor W. R. Ware and F. L. Olmsted on the occupation of the new site ₍New York, 1893₎.
    16 p.   NNC-A

1328. —— . . . Greek ornament . . . Boston, S. Tilton, 1878.
    24 p. 12 col. pl.   DLC,MB,NNC-A,PPD
    Tilton's handbooks of decorative form, no. 1.

1329. —— The instruction in architecture at the School of Mines. . . . 1888.
    pp. 28–43.   CtY,MH,NNC-A,PP,RIBA
    A paper read before the Alumni association of Columbia college, June 12, 1888. From *School of Mines quarterly*, Nov. 1888, vol. x, no. 1.

1330. —— An outline of a course of architectural instruction . . . Boston, J. Wilson and sons, 1866.
    36 p.   ICN,IU,MB,MBAt,MH,MSaE,NN, PPAmP,RIBA
    "Printed for private distribution."

1331. —— . . . The memorial hall, Harvard university . . . Boston, Ticknor & co., 1887.
    Cover title, 14 pl.   CtHWatk,ICA-B,MBAt,MH,NNC-A(imp.),OO
    Monographs of American architectural, IV.
    By the firm of Ware and Van Brunt.

1332. Ware, William Rotch, 1848–1917
    Architectural odds and ends . . . ₍Boston, Boston Heliotype printing co., ᶜ1892–94₎.
    Nos. I, II, III, 40, 40, 40 pl.   CU(No. I only),ICA-B(No. I only),
                                MB,MBAt,MH(inc.),NNMM(No. I, II only)
    Contains: No. I, Renaissance fireplaces, 1892; No. II, Monumental staircases, 1894; No. III, Minor fountains, 1894; each with separate title page. No. I gives: American architect and building news company, Boston, as publisher.

1333. —— Examples of building construction . . . Boston, L. Prang and company, 1876.
    4 p. l. 48 pl. (part col.)   DLC

1334. —— —— Boston, L. Prang and company, 1887.
    4 p. l. 48 pl. (part col.)   RIBA
    The plates are dated 1880!

1335. —— Picturesque sketches: comprising architectural sculpture, statues, monuments, tombs, fountains, capitals, ironwork, details of ornaments, &c. Boston, James R. Osgood & company, 1885.
    2 p. l. 26 pl.   DLC,MB,MH,NNCoo,NNMM,PU
    Ware was not the author, but is known to have been the editor.

1336. Waring, George Edwin, 1833–1898
    The sanitary condition of city and country dwelling houses . . . New York, D. Van Nostrand, 1877.
    145 p. illus.   CtMW,DLC,IU,MB,MH,MWA,MnU,
                                        NNC,NHi,PPFrankl
    On cover: Van Nostrand's science series no. 31.

1337. Waters, Clara (Erskine) Clement, 1834–1916
    Artists of the nineteenth century . . . Boston, Houghton, Osgood and company, 1879.
    2 v.   CtMW,CtY,DLC,InI,MB,MBAt,MWA,
                                  MdBP,MoS,NjP,PPPM,OCi,OO,PP
    Lawrence Hutton, 1843–1904, was joint author.

Waters, Clara (Erskine) Clement
1338. Artists of the nineteenth century . . . Boston, Houghton, Mifflin and company, 1880.
2 v.   ICA-R,NNMM

1339. —— —— 3d ed. rec. Boston, James R. Osgood and company, 1885.
2 v. in 1   DLC,MBAt,MH,NjP,NNC-A,PP
With a new 1884 copyright.

1340. —— —— 4th ed. rev. Boston, Ticknor and company, n.d.
2 v. in 1   ICA-R
With the same 1884 copyright.

1341. —— —— 5th ed. rev. Boston, Houghton, Mifflin and company, 1889.
2 v. in 1   NN,NNMM,PP

1342. —— —— 6th ed. Boston, Houghton, Mifflin and company, 1893.
2 v. in 1   PP
There were several editions after 1895.

1343. —— A history of art for beginners and students: painting, sculpture, architecture . . . New York, F. A. Stokes, 1887.
3 pts. in 1 v. illus.   DLC

1344. —— An outline history of architecture for beginners and students . . . New York, White, Stokes & Allen, 1886.
206 p. incl. front., illus.   DLC,MB,OCi,PPL-R,MnU

1345. —— —— 2d ed. New York, Frederick A. Stokes and brother, 1889.
206 p. incl. front., illus.   MPly,PPWa

1346. —— —— 4th ed. New York, Frederick A. Stokes co., 1893.
206 p. incl. front., illus.   CU,MB
No copies of the presumptive 3d edition have been located.

1347. —— —— 5th ed. New York, Frederick A. Stokes co., n.d.
206 p. incl. front., illus.   MdBE
Possibly later than 1894 though still carrying the 1884 copyright.

1348. —— Painters, sculptors, architects, engravers and their work . . . New York, Hurd & Houghton, 1874.
600 p. front., illus.   CSmH,CtY,DLC,MB,MBAt,MWA,NN,OO,PP

1349. —— —— 2d ed. New York, Hurd & Houghton, 1874.
600 p. front., illus.   MH

1350. —— —— 2d ed. New York, Hurd & Houghton, 1875.
600 p. front., illus.   IU,MH,NNC,PP

1351. —— —— 3d ed. New York, Hurd & Houghton, 1876.
661 p. 86 pl.   MB,NN,ViU

1352. —— —— 4th ed. New York, Hurd & Houghton, 1877.
661 p. 86 pl.   MH,NPV

1353. —— —— 5th ed. Boston, Houghton, Osgood and company, 1879.
681 p. incl. front., illus. 8 pl.   I,ViU

1354. —— —— 6th ed. Boston, Houghton, Osgood, and company, 1879.
681 p. incl. front., illus., 8 pl.   ICA-R

1355. —— —— 7th ed. Boston, James R. Osgood and company, 1881.
681 p. incl. front., illus., 16 pl.   DLC,ICA-R,MH,MWA,NNC,
                                                     NNMM,NjP,NNC,PBA
With a new 1881 copyright.

112

Waters, Clara (Erskine) Clement
1356. Painters, sculptors, architects . . . 7th ed. Boston, James R. Osgood and company, 1882.
      681 p. incl. front., illus., 16 pl.   CtY

1357. —— —— 8th ed. Boston, James R. Osgood and company, 1884.
      681 p. incl. front., illus., 16 pl.   MH,NNMM,OClMA,PP

1358. —— —— 9th ed. Boston, Ticknor and company, n.d.
      681 p. incl. front., illus., 16 pl.   ICA-R
      Still with the 1881 copyright.

1360. —— —— 11th ed. Boston, Houghton, Mifflin and company, 1890.
      681 p. incl. front., illus., 16 pl.   CU
      No copies of the presumptive 10th edition have been located.

1361. —— —— 12th ed. Boston, Houghton, Mifflin & co., 1892.
      681 p. incl. front., illus., 16 pl.   PP
      Still with the 1881 copyright.

1362. —— —— 13th ed. Boston, Houghton, Mifflin & co., 1893.
      681 p. incl. front., illus., 16 pl.   ICA-R
      There was a later issue of the 13th edition in 1895.

1363. Weissenborn, Gustavus
      American engineering; illustrated by large and detailed engravings embracing branches of mechanical art . . . engines . . . mills, iron buildings, bridges, etc. of the newest and approved construction. New York, G. Weissenborn's engineering office, 1861.
      2 v. 52 pl.   DLC,MWA,MoS(v. 2 only),NN,NNCoo,OCi(v. 2 only)
      The Atlas volume of plates carries no date on the title page, but Pt. I No. II is dated 1855. It seems probable the parts of the Atlas began to be issued separately some years before the work as a whole was published.

1364. —— —— New York, American industrial publishing company, n.d.
      2 v. 52 pl.   CtY,NN
      Possibly earlier than the preceding issue.

1365. Westcott, Thompson, 1820–1888
      The historic mansions and buildings of Philadelphia . . . Philadelphia, Porter and Coates [1877].
      528 p. incl. front., illus., [7] pl.   CtY,DLC,MB,MBAt,MH,MWA,
                        MnU,NNC-A,NNMM,NHi,OCl,PP,PPFr,PU
      Westcott brought out other guide books and descriptive literature on Philadelphia about this time, as well as a Continental portfolio in connection with the Exposition of 1876.

1366. Wheatley, Richard, 1838–1917
      Cathedrals and abbeys of Great Britain and Ireland . . . New York, Harper & brothers, 1890.
      272 p. incl. illus., [44] pl. (31 double)   CSmH,DLC,ICA-B,InI,MoS,
                                    NNC-A,OCl,PPL
      Wheatley's other works, such as: *London past and present*, are even more completely guide books than this.

1367. Wheeler, Gervase
      Homes for the people in suburb and country; the villa, the mansion and the cottage, adapted to the American climate and wants. With examples showing how to alter and remodel old buildings. In a series of one hundred original designs . . . New York, Charles Scribner, 1855.
      443 p. front., illus., 10 pl.   CtY,DLC,MB,MH,MSaE,MWA,
                                   MdBP,NHi,NjR,OO

Wheeler, Gervase
The preface states that a complete edition of this work was destroyed by fire in 1854.

1368. —— —— 3d thousand. New York, Charles Scribner, 1855.
443 p. front., illus., 10 pl. DLC,ICA-B,NNC

1369. —— —— 4th thousand. New York, Charles Scribner, 1857.
443 p. front., illus., 10 pl. J.P.C.

1370. —— —— 5th thousand. New York, Charles Scribner, 1858.
443 p. front., illus., 10 pl. NN,NNC-A

1371. —— —— 6th thousand, rev. ed. New York, Geo. E. Woodward, 1868.
441 p. front., illus., 10 pl. IU,MH,PPM
With a new 1867 copyright.

1372. —— —— rev. ed. New York, American news co., n.d.
441 p. front., illus., 10 pl. OO
This issue carries the 1867 copyright like the issue above, but is presumably later.

1373. —— Rural homes: or, Sketches of houses suited to American country life, with original plans, designs, &c. . . . New York, Charles Scribner, 1851.
298 p. front., illus., 9 pl. CU,MB,MH,MWA,MdBP,NHi,NN,PP,PPM
The preface mentions "Mr. Ruskin's great maxim 'Until *common sense* finds its way into architecture, *there can be but little hope for it.*' "

1374. —— —— New York, Charles Scribner, 1852.
298 p. front., illus., 9 pl. CU,ICJ,NNMM,OO

1375. —— —— Auburn, Alden, Beardsley & co., Rochester, Wanzer, Beardsley & co., 1853.
298 p. front., illus., 9 pl. DLC,MBAt,MH,MiOC,NjP,NPV,PP

1376. —— —— New Orleans, Burnett & Bostwick, 1854.
298 p. front., illus., 9 pl. MSaE

1377. —— —— Detroit, Kerr & Doughty, 1854.
298 p. front., illus., 9 pl. ICA-B

1378. —— —— Auburn and Rochester, Alden and Beardsley, 1855.
298 p. front., illus., 9 pl. CtY,MH,MLy,MWA,MnU,MoS,NNC-A
Offered for sale by Fowlers and Wells for $1.25 in 1855.

1379. —— —— rev. ed. New York, Charles Scribner, 1868.
298 p. front., illus., 9 pl. MB
With a new 1867 copyright.

1380. —— —— rev. ed. New York, Geo. E. Woodward, 1868.
298 p. front., illus., 9 pl. DLC,MWA,OCl

1381. —— —— New York, Geo. E. Woodward, n.d.
298 p. front., illus., 9 pl. MH,MWA
Still with the 1867 copyright.

Wheeler, William Arthur
See Fuller, Albert W.

1382. Wheildon, William Willder, 1805–1892
The Maverick bridge . . . Charlestown, Press of the Bunker Hill Aurora, 1869.
40 p. DLC,MH,NNC,NNE,NHi
See also Young, Ammi Burnham

114

Wheildon, William Willder
1383. Memoir of Solomon Willard, architect . . . [Boston, Bunker Hill] Monument
association, 1865.
272 p. 2 pl., incl. front. 5 diagrs.   DLC,IU,MH,MWA,MdBP,NjP,NN,
NNC-A,NHi,PP

1384. Whibley, Charles
Cathedrals of England and Wales . . . New York, E. P. Dutton and company, 1888.
60 p. illus., 16 col. pl., incl. front.   DLC,PP

1385. White, Alfred Treadway, 1846–1921
Improved dwellings for the laboring classes, the need, and the way to meet
it on strict commercial principles, in New York, Brooklyn and other cities
. . . New York, 1877.
27 p. pl.   NNC-A

1386. —— —— New York, G. P. Putnam's sons, 1879.
45 p. front., 1 plan   IU,MH,PU
Title varies slightly.

1387. —— Improved dwellings for the working classes, 1879. Better homes for working men, 1885. Riverside buildings, 1891.
5 p. l. front., 45 p. 1 plan, 20 p. 3 p. l. 12 p. illus., 4 pl.   CtHWatk,
ICJ,MBAt
This half title and a prefatory note by White dated: Oct. 15, 1891,
Brooklyn, precede a reissue of the pamphlet above, with which are bound
two others. One of these has the title: Better homes for working men,
prepared for the Twelfth national congress of charities, held at Washington, June, 1885; the other: Riverside buildings of the Improved dwellings co. Brooklyn, 1890, has illustrated front and back covers, illustrated
title page and plans in the text, as well as four plates, including three of
plans, bound after the text.

1388. Whitefield, Edwin
The homes of our forefathers; being a collection of the oldest and most interesting buildings in Maine, New Hampshire and Vermont . . . Reading,
Mass., The author, 1886.
3 p. l. 36 col. pl.   DLC,MB,MBAt,MH,MSaE,MWA,Nh,NHi,OCi

1389. —— The homes of our forefathers; . . . in Massachusetts . . . Boston, A. Williams
and company, 1879.
3 p. l. 22 col. pl.   DLC,MB,MH,MWA,NHi,OCi

1391. —— —— 3d ed. Boston, A. Williams and company, 1880.
3 p. l. 32 col. pl.   CtHWatk,CtY,DLC,MBAt,MH,MSaE,
MWA,NjP,NNMM,NHi,OCi
The MWA has two variant copies of this 3d edition, one with 35 leaves,
the other with 36. No copy of the presumptive 2d edition has been located.

1392. —— —— New ed. Boston, 1892.
2 p. l. 39 l. 39 mounted col. pl.   InI,MWA,NNC-A

1393. —— —— new ed. Dedham, Mass., The author, 1892.
2 p. l. 39 l. 39 mounted col. pl.   DLC,MBAt,MH

1394. —— The homes of our forefathers in Rhode Island and Connecticut . . . Boston,
A. Williams & co., 1882.
[6] p. 33 pl.   MB,NNMM,NHi

1395. —— —— Boston, Whitefield & Crocker, 1882.
[5] p. 33 pl.   CtMW,DLC,CtY,MB,MH,MWA
Title varies.
It is uncertain which of these issues is the earlier.

Whitefield, Edwin
1396. The homes of our forefathers in Boston, old England and Boston, New England
. . . Boston, The author, 1889.
2 p. l. 138 p. col. pl.　　　　CtMW,CtY,MB,MBAt,MH,MWA,NHi

1397. —— —— enl. ed. Boston, The author, 1889.
[6] p. 138 p. col. pl.　　　　　　　　　　　　　　　MB

1398. —— —— Boston, Damrell & Upham, c1889.
2 pts. in v. 1 84 p. 38 col. pl.　　　　　　　MWA,NNMM
Pt. 2 is published by the author.

1399. Whittemore, Henry, 1833–　　, comp.
Homes on the Hudson; historical, descriptive . . . illustrated by Bierstadt.
New York, Artotype publishing co., n.d.
1 p. l. 43 pl.　　　　　　　　　　　　　MB,NN
First issued in the eighties.

1400. *Wickes, Charles
Illustrations of the spires and towers of the mediaeval churches of England
. . . Boston, Ticknor and company, 1889.
3 v. 72 pl.　　　　　CtY,ICA-B,MdBE,NNC-A,PU-F
Probably appeared London, 1858–59.

1401. Wicks, William S
Log cabins. How to build and furnish them . . . New York, Forest and
Stream publishing co., 1889.
44 p. illus., 18 pl.　　　　DLC,ICJ,MBAt,MH,MdBE,NNC-A,PP

1402. Wight, Peter Bonnet, 1858–
National academy of design. Photographs of the new building, with an introductory essay and description . . . New York, S. P. Avery, 1866.
10 p. 8 mount. pl.　　　　CtY,MH,NNC-A,NNMM,NHi,RIBA

1403. —— Remarks on fireproof construction . . . New York [American institute of
architects] Committee on library and publications, 1869.
8 p. illus.　　　　　　　　　　　MBAt,NNC-A,RIBA

1404. *Wightwick, George, 1815–1852
Hints to young architects calculated to facilitate their practical operations
. . . with additional notes and hints to persons about building in this country.
By A. J. Downing. 1st Amer. ed. New York & London, Wiley and Putnam,
1847.
157 p. illus.　　　　　　　CtY,ICA-B,IU,MB,MH,MSaE,MWA,
　　　　　　　　　　　　　NHi,NNC-A,NNMM,NPV,PPFrankl
First appeared London, 1846.

1405. —— —— 2d Amer. ed. New York, John Wiley, 1851.
157 p. illus.　　　　　　　MB,MH,MSaE,MnU,PPFrankl

1406. —— —— 3d Amer. ed. New York, John Wiley, 1859.
50, 157 p. illus.　　　CU,DLC,MB,MdBP,MH,NNC-A,PP,PPFrankl
With title: Hints to persons about building in the country. By A. J.
Downing, and Hints to young architects . . . By Geo. Wightwick . . .
with additional notes by A. J. Downing, evidently reorganized to capitalize Downing's popularity, but still with the original 1847 copyright.

1407. —— —— 3d ed. Amer. ed. New York, John Wiley & son, 1872.
50, 157 p. illus.　　　　　　　　　　　MH,PPFrankl

1408. Wilde, Edward Seymour
The New York city hall . . . [New York, 1893].
pp. 865–872 illus.　　　　　　　MB,NNC-A,RIBA,Vi
Reprinted from the Century magazine, April, 1884.

116

1409. Willard, Solomon
Plans and sections of the obelisk on Bunker's hill . . . [Boston, printed by
Samuel N. Dickinson, 1843].
31 p. 14 pl. (1 fold.)   DLC,ICN,MH,MWA,MiD,NNC-A,
NNMM,NHi,PHi,RP,Vi
See also Wheildon, William Willder

1410. Williamson, Thomas H
An elementary course of architecture and civil engineering . . . Lexington,
Va., printed by Samuel Gillock, 1850.
151 p.   Vi

1411. Wills, Frank, 1827–
Ancient English ecclesiastical architecture and its principles applied to the
wants of the church of the present day . . . New York, Stamford and Swords,
1850.
120 p. front., 19 pl. (1 fold.)   DLC,MBAt,MdBP,NNC-A,
NNMM,NHi,PPL

1412. Wilson, J
The mechanics' and builders' price book. Showing in detail the price of
wood, brick and stone work, painting and glazing, &c., to which is added
a dictionary of mechanical terms. Also a treatise on architecture . . . New
York, D. Appleton & co., 1859.
179 p. illus.   MB
Most other price books of this order have been omitted, but this has plans.

1413. Windrim, James H
Specifications for the erection of the building of the Agricultural department, International exhibition, Fairmount Park . . . Philadelphia, 1875.
7 p. (interleaved)   PHi

1414. Withers, Frederick Clarke
Church architecture; plans, elevations, and views of twenty-one churches
and two schoolhouses, photo-lithographed from original drawings, with numerous illustrations showing details of construction; church fittings, etc.
. . . New York, A. J. Bicknell & co., 1873.
xxi, [47] p. illus., 51 pl.   CtHWatk,CtY,DLC,IU,MB,MH,MWA,
MoS,NN,NNC-A,OCi,OO

1415. Woodward, Calvin Milton, 1837–
A history of the St. Louis bridge . . . St. Louis, G. I. Jones and company, 1881.
391 p. front., illus., 46 pl.   DLC,I,ICJ,IU,MB,MH,MWA,
MnU,NjP,NHi,NNC,PP,Vi

1416. Woodward, George Evertson, 1829–1905, *comp.*
Rural church architecture . . . by Upjohn, Renwick, Wheeler, Wells, Austin,
Stone, Backus, Reeve, and Eveleth . . . New York, Geo. E. Woodward, n.d.
45 pl.   MB
The form of the imprint implies a date between 1868 and 1875.

1417. —— —— new and rev. ed. New York, Geo. E. Woodward & co., 1876.
[39] p. 48 pl.   DLC,MB,NNC-A

1418. —— Woodward's Architecture, landscape gardening and rural art. No. I—1867
. . . New York, G. E. & F. W. Woodward, 1867.
120 p. illus.   CU,DLC,ICA-B,IU,MB,MH,MWA,NNC-A,OCl
Francis W. Woodward was joint compiler.

1419. —— —— New York, Geo. E. Woodward, 1868.
132 p. illus.   CtMW,CtY,DLC,IU,MH,MoS,NHi,PPM
The second part of the item above, with title: *Woodward's Architecture
and rural art. No. II—1868.* No mention of Francis W. Woodward.

117

Woodward, George Evertson
1420. Woodward's Architecture . . . New York, Geo. E. Woodward, 1869.
        144 p. illus.   CtMW,MH,NNCoo
        A new issue of the 1867 item, with title: *Woodward's Architecture and
        rural art. No. I—1867*. No mention of Francis W. Woodward.

1421. —— —— New York, Geo. E. Woodward, n.d.
        144 p. illus.   NNCoo

1422. —— Woodward's Architecture with hints and notes on building, and a priced
        catalogue of all books on architecture, engineering, mechanics, science, . . .
        New York, Geo. E. Woodward, 1870.
        4 pts.   MB

1423. —— Woodward's Cottages and farm houses . . . New York, G. E. & F. W.
        Woodward [1867].
        144 p. illus.   IU,MBAt,MH,MiGr,NNC-A

1424. —— —— New York, Geo. E. Woodward & co.; Orange Judd & company,
        n.d.
        144 p. illus.   MnU,OO,OU
        Still with the original 1867 copyright.

1425. —— Woodward's Country homes . . . New York, Geo. E. & F. W. Woodward,
        1865.
        166 p. illus.   CtY,MB,MBAt,MBHo,MSaE,NN,NNC-A,PP

1426. —— —— 4th and 5th thousand. New York, Geo. E. & F. W. Woodward,
        1866.
        166 p. illus.   CU,MB,MWA,MoS,NNC-A,NNCoo,PPM

1427. —— —— 8th ed. rev. & enl. New York, Geo. E. & F. W. Woodward,
        1866.
        188 p. illus.   MH,MWA

1428. —— —— New York, Geo. E. Woodward, 1868.
        188 p. illus.   IU

1429. —— —— New York, Geo. E. Woodward, 1869.
        188 p. illus.   MH,MSaE

1430. —— —— New York, Geo. E. Woodward, 1870.
        188 p. illus.   ICA-B,MH

1431. —— —— New York, Geo. E. Woodward, n.d.
        188 p. illus.   CtMW,NNC-A,NNCoo
        With the 1865 copyright.

1432. —— —— New York, Orange Judd & company, n.d.
        188 p. illus.   OO
        Still with the original 1865 copyright.

1433. —— Woodward's Graperies and horticultural buildings . . . New York, G. E.
        & F. W. Woodward, 1865.
        139 p. illus.   CtY,DLC,IU,MB,MBHo,MH,MWA,NNC-A,OCl,PPM

1434. —— —— New York, G. E. & F. W. Woodward, 1867.
        139 p. illus.   CU,DA,IU,NN,OU

1435. —— Woodward's National architect; containing 1000 original designs, plans
        and details, to working scale, for the practical construction of dwelling
        houses for the country, suburb and village . . . New York, Geo. E. Wood-
        ward, c1868.
        [x], 48 p. 100 pl.   NNCoo
        Edward G. Thompson was joint author.
        Added lithographic title page.

Woodward, George Evertson
1436. Woodward's National architect . . . New York, Geo. E. Woodward [ᶜ1869].
    [x] 48 p. 100 pl.   CtHWatk,CtY,ICA-B,InI,MB,MH,MSaE,
                             MWA,MnU,NNCoo,NPV,OCl,OO,PP,PPFrankl

1437. —— —— New York, Geo. E. Woodward [ᶜ1869].
    28 p. l. 100 pl.   NN,NNC-A
    It is not clear which of these issues is the earlier.

1438. —— —— New York, Geo. E. Woodward [1873–77].
    2 v. illus.   DLC,MH(v. 2 only)
    Vol. 2 is by Woodward alone and published by the American News co.,
    New York.

1439. —— —— New York, Geo. E. Woodward, 1874–77.
    2 v. illus.   NNMM

1440. —— Woodward's Suburban and country homes . . . Geo. E. Woodward; Orange
    Judd and co. [ᶜ1873].
    132, 10 p. illus.   MII,NN

1441. —— —— New York, American News co. n.d.
    132, 10 p. illus.   IU,MB,OCi
    With the 1873 copyright.

1442. Woolett, William M
    Old homes made new: being a collection of plans, exterior and interior views,
    illustrating the alteration and remodelling of several suburban residences.
    With explanatory text . . . New York, Λ. J. Bicknell & co. [1878].
    20 p. 22 pl.   CtY,InI,MB,MWA,NHi,NNMM,OCi,OCl,PPM
    Woolett is described as "Fellow of the American Institute of Architects."

1443. —— —— New York, Bicknell and Comstock, 1879.
    20 p. 22 pl.   MB

1444. —— Villas and cottages, or homes for all. Plans elevations and views of twelve
    villas and ten cottages, being a collection of dwellings suited to various in-
    dividual wants and adapted to different locations . . . New York, A. J. Bick-
    nell & co., 1876.
    [4] p. 40 pl.   CtY,MB,MSaE,OCi,OCl
    Advertising material at rear.

1445. Worthen, William Ezra, 1819–1897, ed.
    Appleton's cyclopedia of drawing, designed as a text-book for the mechanic,
    architect, engineer . . . geometrical, mechanical, architectural, . . . drawing,
    perspective and isometry. New York, D. Appleton & co., 1857.
    410 p. illus., 94 pl.   ICA-B,IU,MH,MdBP,NN,NNCoo,OCl,PP

1446. —— —— New York, D. Appleton & co., 1862.
    410 p. illus., 94 pl.   MiOC

1447. —— —— New York, D. Appleton & co., 1866.
    410 p. illus., 94 pl.   IU

1448. —— —— new and enl. ed. New York, D. Appleton & co., 1869.
    469 p. illus., 120 pl. (part double, part col.)   NNC,OCl
    Appleton published other works of this order in the seventies and eighties,
    here omitted.

1449. Wright, Frank Ayes, 1854–   , ed.
    Architectural studies . . . [Parts 1–10] New York, William T. Comstock,
    1885–[ᶜ1890].
    2 v. in 10 pts., 60, 60 pl.   DLC,MB(imp.),MH,MoS,NNC-A(v. 2
                          only),PP(v. 1 only),OO(Pt. 10 only)

Wright, Frank Ayes
   The outer title page in vol. 1 reads: Architectural studies. Part I. Twelve designs for low-cost houses shown on a large scale, with very full details, including prize designs from "Building competition," with which are given specifications, bills of materials and estimates of cost. This part will be followed by others, containing "Store fronts," "Barn plans," "City dwellings," and other architectural subjects, each complete in itself. New York, William T. Comstock, 1885. Copyright by Wm. T. Comstock. An inner title page reads: Architectural studies, Vol. I. Low cost houses. Store fronts and interior details. Stables. Sea side and Southern houses. Out-buildings. F. A. Wright, architect, editor. New York, William T. Comstock, 1886. The title page of Vol. II reads: Architectural Studies. Volume II $500 to $2,500 houses.—Interior woodwork of houses of moderate cost.—Store fittings—City houses—Chapels and churches. New York, William T. Comstock, n.d.
   Contents of the separate parts: 1. Low-cost houses. 2. Store fronts and interior details. 3. Stables. 4. Sea side and Southern buildings. 5. Outbuildings. 6. Houses costing $500 to $2,500. 7. Interior woodwork of houses of moderate cost. 8. Store fittings. 9. City houses. 10. Chapels and churches.
   The parts have separate title pages and that of Part 10 carries the copyright date 1890.
   As Wright's name as editor appears only on the inner title page of Vol. 1, the parts when held separately and even whole volumes or the whole work are usually entered under the name of Comstock only. Wright also published a work on *Architectural perspective*, ^c1885, of which there were several issues before 1895.

1450. Wylie, Walker Gill, 1848–
   Hospitals their history, organization and construction. Boylston prize essay of Harvard university for 1876 . . . New York, D. Appleton & co., 1876.
      240 p. illus., 2 fold pl.   DLC

1451. —— New York, D. Appleton & co., 1877.
      240 p. illus., 2 fold pl.   DLC,DSG,ICJ,MnU,MoS,NN,NNC-A,PBm

1452. Wyman, Morrill, 1812–
   A practical treatise on ventilation . . . Boston, James Munroe and co., London, Chapman, brothers, 1846.
      419 p. illus.   NNC-A

1453. Young, Ammi Burnham, 1799–1874
   An architectural description of the new court house in the city of Cambridge, Mass., built in 1848 . . . Charleston, W. W. Wheildon, printer, 1849.
      11 p.   H.R.H.

1454. —— New Custom house, Boston . . . Boston, 1840.
      Broadside, 13⅛" x 9⅝"
                                                                MB
      Plans and sections.

1455. —— General description and specifications of the alterations and repairs required to be made in the present Custom house in the city of New York . . . New York, J. Clarke, printer, 1862.
      16 p.   DLC

1456. —— Plans of public buildings in course of construction under the direction of the secretary of the Treasury, including the specifications thereof . . . [Washington] 1855–56.
      Oblong folio. pl.
      Specifications in 2 v.   MH(Nos. 1–13,15–19,25–38),MWA(Nos. 3–38), NNC-A(Nos. 1,2,5–8,10–15,19,26–32,36),RIBA(2 v.)

Young, Ammi Burnham.
Engraved cover title with each number.
Usually entered under: U. S. Treasury department.
It is not clear how many numbers were issued in all. Most numbers include
from 9 to 14 plates. See also separate *Specifications*, below.

1457. —— —— [Philadelphia, A. Kollner, lithographer, 1856–59].
Oblong folio. 12 nos. in a portfolio.   MH
Apparently this is a "New Series"; the smaller number of parts correspond-
ing to the decline of building after 1857, and properly an official government publication like the preceding item.

1458. —— Specifications for the Custom House and post office at Bath, Maine. . . .
Washington. Gideon and co., printers, 1853.
16 p.   NNC-A

1459. —— Specifications for the Custom house and post office at Waldeboro, Maine
. . . Washington, Gideon and co., printers, 1853.
15 p.   NNC-A

1460. —— Specifications for the Custom house, Post office and United States Court
rooms, &c., Wilmington, Del. . . . Washington, Gideon and co., printers, 1853.
14 p.   NNC-A
These specifications are presumably a part of those in the 2 v. which some
holders report with the *Plans of public buildings*, above.

Young, Thomas, 1773–1829
See Hoskings, Thomas

1461. Zucker, Alfred, 1871–
Architectural sketches photographed from designs for buildings and from buildings erected . . . New York, Chicago, St. Louis, National chemigraph co.,
I. Haas, selling agents, 1894.
39 pl.   OCi

SUBJECT INDEX

Roebling, John Augustus, 85
Strickland, William, 102
Town, Ithiel, 105
Weissenborn, Gustavus, 113
Wheildon, William Willder, 114
Woodward, Calvin Milton, 117

BUILDERS' GUIDES
See also CARPENTRY
Benjamin, Asher, 9
Bicknell, Amos Jackson, 14
Biddle, Owen, 16
Brown, William, 19
Bullock, John, 21
Hammond, J   H, 46
Haviland, John, 49
Hills, Chester, 50
Langley, Batty, 59
Nicholson, Peter, 69
Norman, John, 71
Norman, William, 71
Pain, William, 74
Shaw, Edward, 94
Sloan, Samuel, 98
Swan, Abraham, 103
Vanosdel, John M, 108

BUILDING CODES AND REGULATIONS, see LAWS AND REGULATIONS

BUILDING METHODS AND MATERIALS
See also CARPENTRY; CONSTRUCTION; FOUNDATIONS; IRON; MASONRY; PISE; STEEL; TILE
Cleveland educational bureau, 25
Derby, Nelson L, 30

BYZANTINE
Dehli, Arne, 30
Voguë, Charles Jean Melchior, Marquis de, 109

CARPENTRY
See also BUILDERS' GUIDES; CONSTRUCTION
Bell, William E, 8
Benjamin, Asher, 9
Gould, Lucius D, 44
Hale, Benjamin, 45
Hosking, William, 52
Nicholson, Peter, 69
Pain, William, 74
Riddell, John, 83
Silloway, Thomas William, 97
Sylvester, William Allen, 103
Tredgold, Thomas, 105
Vanosdel, John M, 108

CATALOGUES, see EXHIBITIONS—C A T A-LOGUES

CHURCHES
See also BUILDERS' GUIDES; COLONIAL; DESCRIPTION—U.S. 19TH CENTURY; GOTHIC AND GOTHIC REVIVAL; INDIVIDUAL BUILDINGS AND PROJECTS; ROMANESQUE AND ROMANESQUE REVIVAL
B   , W, 4
Bacon, Leonard, 5
Bicknell, Amos Jackson, 14
Board of church erection, 18
Bowler, George, 19
Congregational churches in the U.S., 27
Dexter, Henry Martyn, 30
Disosway, Gabriel Poillon, 31
Dwyer, Charles P, 35
Everts, William Wallace, 38
Gardner, Eugene Clarence, 42
Hart, Joseph Coleman, 47
Historic churches of America . . ., 50
Holly, Henry Hudson, 51
Kennion, John W, 57
Leahy, William Augustine, 60
Otis, Calvin N, 73
Parker, Francis Jewett, 77
Patterson, W   M, 77
Pierce & Dockstader, 78
A plea for the use . . ., 78
Randall, Gurdon P, 80
Ripley, M   M, 83
Scott, Sir George Gilbert, and others, 93
Shinn, George Wolfe, 95
Sholl, Charles, 96
Sloan, Samuel, 98
Tiffany, Charles Comfort, 104
Upjohn, Richard, 107
Valk, Lawrence B, 107
Wills, Frank, 117
Withers, Frederick Clarke, 117
Woodward, George Evertson, 117
Wright, Frank Ayes, 119

CODES, see LAWS AND REGULATIONS

COLONIAL
See also INDIVIDUAL BUILDINGS AND PROJECTS
Bacon, Leonard, 5
Boston. City Council, 18
Chamberlain, Nathan Henry, 24
Chandler, Joseph Everett, 24
Corner, James M, 27
Dexter, Henry Martyn, 30
Disosway, Gabriel Poillon, 31
Drake, Samuel Adams, 34
Dunlap, William, 35
Foote, Henry Wilder, 40
Goforth, William Davenport, 44
Historic churches of America . . ., 50

125

U.S. Supervising architect, 107
Walter, Thomas Ustick, 110
Young, Ammi Burnham, 120

GREEK AND ROMAN
See also BUILDERS' GUIDES; HOUSE PAT-
TERN BOOKS
Adams, William Henry Davenport, 1
Howe, Hezekiah, 52
Norton, Charles Eliot, 72
Paine, Timothy Otis, 75
Smith, Thomas Roger, 100
Van Brunt, Henry, 107

GREEK REVIVAL, see BUILDERS' GUIDES;
DESCRIPTION—U.S. 1 9 T H CENTURY;
HOUSE PATTERN BOOKS; INDIVIDUAL
BUILDINGS AND PROJECTS

GREENHOUSES
Leuchars, Robert B, 61
Woodward, George Evertson, 117

GUIDE BOOKS, see COLONIAL; DESCRIP-
TION—U.S. 19TH CENTURY; INDIVIDU-
AL BUILDINGS AND PROJECTS

HANDBOOKS, MANUALS, ETC.
See also BUILDERS' GUIDES; CARPENTRY;
CONSTRUCTION; IRON; MASONRY;
STEEL; TEXTBOOKS
Brunton, Robert, 20
Burr, William Hubert, 22
An easy method . . ., 36
Kelt, Thomas, 56
Knapen, D   M, 58
Nicholson, Peter, 69
Overman, Frederick, 73
Smeaton, A   C, 99
Van Rensselaer, Marianna (Griswold), 108

HEATING
Lupton, Nathaniel Thomas, 63

HISTORY AND CRITICISM—GENERAL
See also BYZANTINE; COLONIAL; CRITI-
CISM; GOTHIC AND GOTHIC REVIV-
AL; GREEK AND ROMAN; MAYAN
AND AZTEC; ORIENTAL; RENAIS-
SANCE; ROMANESQUE AND ROMAN-
ESQUE REVIVAL; SWISS CHALETS
Fallet, Celine, 38
Farrar, Charles Samuel, 39
Hamlin, Alfred Dwight Foster, 46
Heck, Johann Georg, 49
International correspondence schools, 53
Lafever, Minard, 58
Lefèvre, André-Paul-Emile, 60
Lossing, Benson J, 63
Ludlow, Miss, 63
Memes, John Smythe, 65
Nevill, Ralph Henry, 69

Otis, Calvin N, 73
Ripley, M   M, 83
Rosengarten, A, 85
Ruskin, John, 85
Schweinfurth, Julius Adolph, 93
Spooner, Shearjashub, 101
Thompson, Robert Ellis, 104
Tuckerman, Arthur Lyman, 105
Tuthill, Louisa Caroline (Huggins), 106
Viollet-le-Duc, Eugene Emmanuel, 109
Waters, Clara (Erskine) Clement, 111

HOSPITALS
Lee, Charles Alfred, 60
Mills, Robert, 65
Wylie, Walker Gill, 120

HOUSE PATTERN BOOKS
Allen, Frank P, 1
Allen, Lewis Falley, 2
Arnot, David Henry, 3
Atwood, Daniel Topping, 3
Baker, Z, 5
Barber & company, 5
Benjamin, Asher, 9
Bicknell, Amos Jackson, 14
Biddle, Owen, 16
Brown, William, 19
Brunner, Arnold William, 20
Buck, C   C, 21
Bullock, John, 21
Burn, Robert Scott, 22
Carpenter, James H, 23
Chase, C. Thurston, 24
Clark, Alfred C, 25
Cleaveland, Henry William, 25
Comstock, William Thompkins, 26
Croff, Gilbert Bostwick, 28
Cummings, Marcus Fayette, 28
Cutter, Manly N, 29
Davis, Alexander Jackson, 29
Downing, Andrew Jackson, 31
Dwyer, Charles P, 35
Elliott, Charles Wyllys, 37
Examples of architecture . . ., 38
Field, M, 40
Fowler, Orson Squire, 40
Fuller, Albert W, 42
Gardner, Eugene Clarence, 42
Garnsey, George O, 43
Gibson, Louis Henry, 44
Hall, John, 46
Hammond, J   H, 46
Harvey, T. W., lumber company, 47
Haviland, John, 49
Hills, Chester, 50
Hobbs, Isaac H., and son, 51
Holly, Henry Hudson, 51
Homes in city and country, 51

Hopkins, David S, 51
Hussey, Elisha Charles, 53
Illsley, Charles E, 53
Jacques, Daniel Harrison, 53
Johnson, William K, 55
King, David W, 57
Kirby, Henry P, 57
Lafever, Minard, 58
Lakey, Charles D, 59
Lang, William Bailey, 59
Leffel, James, and company, 60
Leicht, Alfred F, 61
Leland, E   H, 61
Lent, Franklin Townsend, 61
Levy, Albert, 61
Loring, Sanford E, 62
Loudon, John Claudius, 63
National architects' union, 68
National building plan association,
    69
Norman, William, 71
Page, Harvey L, 74
Pain, William, 74
Palliser, Palliser & co., 75
Pfeiffer, Carl, 77
Pierce & Dockstader, 78
Ranlett, William H, 80
Reed, Samuel Burrage, 81
Richardson, Charles James, 82
Riddell, John, 83
Ritch, John W, 84
Shaw, Edward, 94
Shoppell, Robert W, 96
Sidney, J   C, 97
Skillings, David Nelson, and Flint,
    D B, 97
Sloan, Samuel, 98
Smith, Frank L, 100
Smith, George T, and Robinson, Charles
    Morrison, 100
Smith, Oliver P, 100
Stevens, John Calvin, and Cobb, Albert
    Winslow, 102
Swan, Abraham, 103
Tabor, Clarence H, 104
Thomas, T   , jr, 104
Todd, Sereno Edwards, 104
Tuthill, William Burnet, 106
Upjohn, Richard, 107
Varney, Almon Clothier, 108
Vaux, Calvert, 108
Walter, Thomas Ustick, 110
Wheeler, Gervase, 113
Wicks, William S, 116
Woodward, George Evertson, 117
Woolett, William M, 119
Wright, Frank Ayes, 119

HOUSING
King, David H, 57
Loring, Sanford E, 62
Potter, Edward Tuckerman, 78
White, Alfred Treadway, 115

INDIVIDUAL BUILDINGS AND PROJECTS
Baltimore, City Hall, see Forrester, Allen
    E, 40
Boston
    Customs House, see Young, Ammi
        Burnham, 120
    King's Chapel, see Foote, Henry Wilder,
        40
    Old State House, see Boston. City Coun-
        cil, 18
    Tremont House, see Eliot, William Ha-
        vard, 37
    Trinity Church, see Richardson, Henry
        Hobson, 83
Burlington, Vt., Billing's library, see Rich-
    ardson, Henry Hobson, 83
Cambridge
    Austin Hall, see Richardson, Henry
        Hobson, 83
    Courthouse, see Young, Ammi Burnham,
        120
    Memorial Hall, see Ware, William
        Robert, 111
Charlestown, Mass., Bunker hill monu-
    ment, see Willard, Solomon, 117
Charlottesville, Va., University of Virginia,
    see Adams, Herbert Baxter, 1
Chicago, Grand opera festival auditorium,
    see Pratt, S, 79
Croton, N.Y., Aqueduct, see Tower, F
    B, 105
Hammond, George, Mill-built house,
    46
Hartford
    Armsmear, see Barnard, Henry, 5
    State capitol, see Upjohn, Richard Mit-
        chell, 107
Mt. Vernon, Va., Washington's tomb, see
    Strickland, William, 102
New York
    Central park gateways, see Hunt, Rich-
        ard Morris, 53
    City hall, see Wilde, Edward Seymour,
        116
    Columbia college, see Ware, William
        Robert, 111
    Crystal palace, see Carstensen, Georg Jo-
        hann Bernhard, 23
    Customs house, see Young, Ammi Burn-
        ham, 120
    Halls of justice, see Haviland, John,
        49

127

Henry Parish house, *see* Hatfield, Robert Griffith, 48
Houses on 138th and 139th streets, *see* King, David H, 57
National academy of design, *see* Wight, Peter Bonnet, 116
St. John the divine, *see* Description of drawings . . ., 30
W. H. Vanderbilt house, *see* Shinn, Earl, 95
Newport, R.I., Redwood Library, *see* King, David, 57
North Easton, Mass., Ames buildings, *see* Richardson, Henry Hobson, 82
Philadelphia
Eastern penitentiary, *see* Haviland, John, 49
Girard College, *see* Walter, Thomas Ustick, 110
Independence Hall, *see* Scattergood, David, 93
Philadelphia savings fund society building, *see* Sloan, Samuel, 99
Public buildings in Penn square, *see* Philadelphia. Commissioners . . ., 77
Public ledger building, *see* Childs, George William, 24
Pittsburgh, Allegheny county courthouse, *see* Richardson, Henry Hobson, 83
Price, Bruce, Country house by, 79
Roxbury, Mass., Highland cottages, *see* Lang, William Bailey, 59
Saratoga Springs, The Pompeia, *see* Smith, Franklin Webster, 100
Schenectady, First reformed church, *see* Potter, Edward Tuckerman, 79
Tennessee, State prison, *see* Smith, William C, 101
Washington
Library of congress, *see* Poole, William Frederick, 78; Walter, Thomas Ustick, 110
National gallery, *see* Smith, Franklin Webster, 100
Pension bureau, *see* Meigs, Montgomery Cunningham, 64
Smithsonian institution, *see* Arnot, David Henry, 3; Owen, Robert Dale, 74
U.S. Capitol, *see* Bulfinch, Charles, 21; Latrobe, John Hazlehurst Boneval, 60; Mills, Robert, 65; U.S. Architect . . ., 106; Walter, Thomas Ustick, 110
Water works, *see* Mills, Robert, 65

INTERIORS
See also BUILDERS' GUIDES; DETAILS
Brunner, Arnold William, 20

Eastlake, Charles Locke, 36
Edis, Robert William, 36
Elliott, Charles Wyllys, 37
Examples of architecture . . ., 38
Falke, Jacob von, 38
Gardner, Eugene Clarence, 42
Guillaume, L, 45
Haweis, Mary Eliza (Joy), 49
Little, Arthur, 62
Loudon, John Claudius, 63
Morris, William, 67
Polley, George Henry, 78
Shoppell, Robert W, 96
Tuthill, William Burnet, 106
Varney, Almon Clothier, 108

IRON
See also BRIDGES
Birkmire, William Harvey, 17
Campin, Francis, 23
Dubois, Augustus Jay, 34
Fairbairn, Sir William, 38
French, Benjamin Franklin, 41
Fryer, William John, 41
Hatfield, Robert Griffith, 47
Henrici, Olaus Magnus Friedrich Erdmann, 50
Kent, William Winthrop, 57
Mosely, Thomas W   H, 68
Randall, Gurdon P, 80
Ruskin, John, 85
Thomson, John W, 104
Town, Ithiel, 105
Weissenborn, Gustavus, 113
Wight, Peter Bonnet, 116

LANDSCAPE GARDENING
Downing, Andrew Jackson, 31
The house and its surroundings, 52
Hunt, Richard Morris, 53
Martin, George A, 64
Olmsted, Vaux and company, 73
Ranlett, William H, 80
Scott, Frank J, 93
Sidney, J   C, 97
Smith, Charles H   J, 99
Ware, William Robert, 111
Woodward, George Evertson, 117

LAWS AND REGULATIONS
Boston. City Council, 18
Clark, Theodore Minot, 25
Fryer, William John, 41
Lloyd, Augustus Parlett, 62

LECTURES, *see* ADDRESSES, ESSAYS, AND LECTURES

LIBRARIES
Poole, William Frederick, 78
Smithmeyer, John L, 101

128

Walter, Thomas Ustick, 110